Life with Sudden Death

Library of Congress Cataloging-in-Publication Data

Downing, Michael, 1958-
Life with sudden death : a memoir / Michael Downing.
p. cm.
ISBN-13: 978-1-58243-522-0
ISBN-10: 1-58243-522-7
1. Downing, Michael, 1958—Childhood and youth. 2. Downing,
Michael, 1958—Family. 3. Downing, Michael, 1958—Health.
4. Authors, American—20th century—Biography. 5. Sudden
death—United States—Case studies. 6. Genetic
disorders—United States—Case studies. 7. Defibrillators—United
States—Case studies. I. Title.

PS3554.O9346Z46 2009
813'.54—dc22

2009025605

Cover and interior design by Gopa & Ted2, Inc.
Printed in the United States of America

COUNTERPOINT
2117 Fourth Street
Suite D
Berkeley, CA 94710

www.counterpointpress.com

Distributed by Publishers Group West

10 9 8 7 6 5 4 3 2 1

life with sudden death

a tale of moral hazard and medical misadventure

Michael Downing

COUNTERPOINT · BERKELEY

for Peter Bryant

The peculiar striations that define someone's personality are too numerous to know, no matter how close the observer. A person we think we know can suddenly become someone else when previously hidden strands of his character are called to the fore by circumstance.

—Elliot Perlman, *Seven Types of Ambiguity*

Contents

Elementary School

1. Occupational Hazards

Sister Rose was young for a nun. She had blue eyes and sometimes cried in class, so I was not surprised years later when I heard she'd left the convent. Her blond hair often caused her problems by sticking out around her ears, and there was a lot of whispering during recess about her not being holy enough to shave her head like a total nun. I think she might have been a rookie when I had her. She often had to go out into the hall to adjust her veil, and instead of lying, she'd tell us all exactly what she'd been up to out there. This was a mistake. It let us know we could leave class to get a drink of water or pee whenever we felt like it.

During the first week of school, I noticed that Sister Rose didn't know half the things my kindergarten teacher had known. For instance, she tried to force us to take naps while sitting in our chairs with our heads resting on our wooden desks. By the second week, some kids just ignored her and went back to the cloakroom and curled up on their jackets for half an hour. Also, she never prepared snacks, and when we complained about it, she told us that snacks weren't the teacher's responsibility. This didn't inspire confidence.

Our lessons never went as well as she hoped they would. Reading groups were a perfect example. First of all, when she divided us all up, she pretended to think really hard before choosing a bird name for each group. Notre Dame was a Catholic school, so most kids had plenty of older brothers and sisters. We knew what was coming. You just hoped you didn't get labeled as a chickadee or some other puny bird. Second, Sister Rose pretended the sparrows were just as good as anybody else, as if first-graders had never heard of the American bald eagle. Third and worst of all, after we got into our groups, instead of patrolling the aisles with a ruler or some other weapon, Sister Rose usually sat on her desk at the front of the classroom, smiling and swinging her legs. She looked like a swimming instructor who forgot to take off her shoes. Nobody was afraid of her.

Birds will be birds. A blue jay would overhear a stupid mistake in another group and crack a joke, and one of the girl chickadees would start bawling halfway through her out-loud sentence. Sister Rose would call her up to the front of the classroom and make her stand there until she stopped crying. Then one of the robins would start chirping and flapping his wings like a scared baby chick, and he'd be called up to the front, along with a couple of the other boys who thought he was so funny. As a result, Sister Rose was constantly sharing the stage with the most entertaining kids in first grade.

I liked Sister Rose for her unmanageable hair and her blue eyes and because she allowed a few of us to work ahead when she was having discipline problems. Still, I had my doubts. I complained about her to my best friend, Joey T., early in the school year.

Joey T. lived across the street from me in a duplex that his family owned. They needed the rent because their father worked for General Electric, which forced men to get up early and leave the house before their kids ate breakfast. My family was proud of GE's patriotic past, like when the Nazis hand-wrote a secret list of bomb targets in America and made Pittsfield number two. We were right after Washington and Boston, which were in a perfect tie for first place because of the White House and Boston's Irish Catholic population, including most of my parents' relatives. Still, we couldn't forgive GE for taking people who just wanted a decent life for their families and turning them into working men who couldn't afford half the stuff I took for granted, which explained Joey T.'s getting his haircuts on the front porch without the advice of a barber.

Joey T. had bowl-cut silvery blond hair, and because he was half Polish, he was a big kid. Older boys and teachers used to put pressure on him by telling him he was a natural-born football player, but he always shrugged it off like they had him mixed up with somebody else—namely, his older brother Chucky. Chucky T. was already a sports star. He was the exactly the same age as my brother Gerard, who was sixth oldest out of the nine Downings but the smartest kid ever to come down the pike, by his own admission. As a result of being compared unfavorably to our famous brothers, Joey T. and I never got into competitions. For instance, I could freely admit his mother was a better baker than my mother based on sampling her drop cookies, both with and without the chocolate frosting. We stayed friends, even though Joey T. usually was not allowed to work ahead because he was apt to devote an hour of class time to unbending a paper clip and getting it stuck in some unusual place, like the zipper of his pants or his gums. He'd made the trip to the front of the class more than once, but he told me hadn't noticed anything wrong with Sister Rose while he was up there.

I knew if I complained to my brother Joe, who was in third grade already, he'd probably tell me to offer it up. He'd be serious. Joe and I shared a bedroom, so I eventually complained to him anyway.

To my delight, Joe said I was in a serious situation. He said Mom would tell me to offer it up, "so leave her out of the loop." He advised me to write a report stating everything Sister Rose was doing wrong and then leave it on her desk. When he thought about it some more, he said I should write the exact same report again and mail it to the principal of the school because I wasn't a good enough writer yet to use carbon copying paper in public. This made me mad, so I reminded him he was famous for his bad penmanship. Joe hated being criticized for things that weren't his fault. He reminded me that the second-grade teacher had made him write something on the blackboard a thousand times and ruined his right hand forever. He also said, I know the Nazi death grip. I can cut off your blood supply.

I said, If I had brass knuckles on, I could punch you and go through your skull.

I'd have a steel helmet, then, he said, and a Bowie knife, which is designed to spill your guts and make it feel like nothing, or maybe a paper cut, before you bleed to death.

About half of our many fights were hypothetical. Joe was a history buff and won most of them.

It was soon after Joe threatened to eviscerate me that Sister Rose made all the first-graders stand up and say aloud what their fathers did for a living. We had to do it by last names, alphabetically, she said. After a dramatic pause, Sister Rose added, "but starting with the letter Z." The backwards rule caught us off guard, which we liked. This was the sort of teacher story you could take home to dinner. Sister Rose was starting to get the hang of it.

I only remember two of the jobs—that is, if Joey T.'s father was a welder at General Electric, and Barbara Jean's father repaired televisions and radios. I wasn't paying strict attention. I was nervous. When we got near the Ds, I wasn't even sure whether I should stand up or just stay seated, but Sister Rose nodded and smiled, so I stood up.

Jobs were about the least important thing anyone did in my family. You had to have one until you figured out your vocation, but then you could quit it. The worst mistake you could make was taking a year-round office job with regular hours, which interfered with family obligations, especially in the summer, when the rest of us liked to spend a couple of hours in the morning discussing politics until my mother announced the peonies needed weeding, and the fifty-odd windows with triple-track storms and screens had to be washed, and someone had to collect in the neighborhood for the American Cancer Society.

I know that the job quiz in first grade happened in the autumn of 1964, around the first anniversary of the assassination of President Kennedy. I know that his vicious murder had been the most significant event in the lives of my eight brothers and sisters that year. My mother didn't allow any Republicans to teach us, so I bet my kindergarten teacher had set up a TV and forced my class to watch the president's funeral. I don't remember. Unlike normal Americans of my age, I don't even remember where I was when I heard about the assassination.

A couple of years later, in third grade, Mrs. Shaw assigned us to interview people we knew and ask them private questions, like how they were affected by the assassination of John F. Kennedy. I asked my mother. Mrs. Shaw was a lay teacher who'd already forced us to write our autobiographies, so my mother was used to her taking such an unusual interest in our personal business. This time, though, Mrs. Shaw was showing bad timing. One of the girls in my third-grade class had recently died by being thrown out of the back of a truck, and for third-graders enough was enough.

My mother ended up giving me some great quotes for my assassination story, but she started out by talking off the record about the girl who'd died. I'd been at the funeral with my class, and I'd reported on the unfriendliness of the girl's parents to us. They'd acted like we weren't there. My mother told me I couldn't blame them. After Daddy died, she said, I didn't feel anything for a long time.

My father died in 1961. After that, when something terrible happened to somebody else, my mother explained, she could make herself say all the right things at the wake and funeral, but she couldn't feel them. She said she didn't really feel anything for two or three years. When I asked what it felt like not to feel anything, she said either it was like everything went black or everything went blank. I wasn't taking notes on this part, and I often tried to remember which word I'd heard, but eventually I figured out that either one would fit in and make a complete sentence.

I didn't totally black out the Kennedy tragedy. I do remember being shown a newspaper picture of the president's kids and feeling something like a paper cut in my guts when I noticed the little boy. I'd seen some old black-and-white photographs of my mother and the nine Downing kids lined up at public events to honor my father, and I knew exactly what it felt like to be the only one forced to wear short pants in public.

When I announced to my classmates and Sister Rose that instead of having a job my father was dead, some kid said, Already?

I sat down.

Barbara Jean said, Maybe his mother has a job.

It was the first time Barbara Jean had ever spoken out of turn. It made me brave enough to stand up again. But I didn't have anything to add. My mother was unemployed. She did her chores every day, but none of us paid her. Plus, a couple of the older kids were in college, so my mother's job was easier than ever, with only seven school lunches to make while we ate breakfast, and less laundry, too.

Michael's father is with the angels in heaven, Sister Rose said, and Mrs. Downing is a saint.

I'd heard this before, but I had nothing to back it up.

Sister Rose told the class the Downings said the Rosary every single night, including weekends. Obviously, she'd been doing her homework. And she added, "as a family," just in case some kid was thinking about mentioning an old aunt or a grandmother who owned some rosary beads. Sister Rose also hinted there was a lot more where that came from, and then she suggested that the other kids go home and ask their mothers and fathers if they could say the Rosary as a family.

This was the final blow to the significance of jobs and the sort of people who had them. I mean, Sister Rose didn't tell us to go home and ask our parents to teach us to weld or how to repair our own TVs.

I'm sure I sat down and the next kid with a D name stood up. I ignored him. I probably worked ahead in my phonics book. Even the chickadees and sparrows knew the game was over unless your father was an archangel, or the president of the United States.

To show my gratitude to Sister Rose, I let it be known that she was now my favorite teacher. I was good at the important subjects in school, like any Downing, but it helped to be able to coast on my family's prayerful reputation when it came to math so I could get into a good college and major in the liberal arts. This was the most effective way of not turning higher education into a career mill. Your next-best choice was the social sciences. Whenever one of their friends decided to major in nursing or business administration, my brothers and sisters would lead a dinner discussion to identify the most boring or sickening aspects of the job that poor person would be stuck with after graduation.

Everything went according to plan until I actually applied to colleges. I hit a snag with the personal essays they required. I had used up my best material—the surprise death of my father when I was three—filling out the financial-aid forms. To protest, I complained bitterly about being forced to do assignments before they even let me in the door.

During one particularly heated outburst from me about the indignity of having to tell a bunch of strangers about the person who had influenced me the most in my life, my mother said, For God's sake, and started fishing around in the deepest drawer of the desk we called Daddy's desk. She pulled out my autobiography. You can write a little essay about yourself, she said. You wrote your whole life story in third grade.

It was three pages long, not counting the red construction-paper covers or the flowering-vine border I'd drawn around the title, "The Story of My Life (8 Years)." I shoved it aside on the dining room table.

Read it, my mother said.

I read it. I figured this humiliation was fair punishment for my griping, and it was. Along with a lot of thanks to Jesus and Mary for their help along the way, I'd made up eight acts of kindness or generosity and attributed one to each of my brothers and sisters and included their dates of birth in parentheses. Those pages also contained more hard facts about my father's career than I could claim to know as a senior in high school. And at the bottom of page three, I'd crammed in a P.S. about my godfather, an uncle who was the captain of an icebreaker. In the printed edition of my life, he did well, though I barely knew him. When on land, he lived in California with no kids of his own, just a wife who dyed her hair blond. I only remember one of his visits. He wore his white Navy uniform and hat in the house and promised to take me on a voyage to see polar bears, and then he never turned up again.

My mother said, Notice anything?

I listed the document's literary demerits.

Anything else?

I hoped we weren't going to discuss the cover art.

She nodded. She said, There's not a single mention of me. She cracked a smile. She added, Not a word about what a great job I did. You'd think you never had a mother.

I'm sure I tried to explain away my oversight, but I don't remember what I said.

My mother assured me she was not insulted. I believed her. We sat for a while in a familiar, companionable silence, just looking at each other. It must mean something, though, she said, letting her smile fade. She was drawing a blank.

2. *Other People's Parties*

By second grade, I considered an invitation to a birthday party an impo-sition. After my father died, cleaning the house and fixing up the yard took up most of my family's time on Saturdays, and a lot of kids in my class chose to pretend they were born on Saturdays, as a way of attract-ing bigger crowds to their birthday parties. The worst ones began with hand-delivered envelopes you couldn't open because the kid had finally found a use for all the Easter Seals his parents had bought from him during our annual sales event.

Sister Jeanne Arthur did not allow mail delivery during class time because too many kids ended up with hurt feelings. You'd find the party invitation in your desk after lunch with an RSVP demand, usu-ally in capital letters or underlined. If the kid was unpopular or not well known in class, he'd spend the rest of the day distracting you with notes asking if you'd received the invitation yet. The only way to pro-tect yourself was to raise your hand and ask Sister Jeanne Arthur to remind you what the punishment was for passing notes.

Sister Jeanne Arthur was popular and strict. She was bigger than anybody else at Notre Dame grammar school, and she used size to her advantage when necessary. She never hit second-graders full-force, but she'd just as soon punch a sixth-grader as look at him, and if anyone brought a radio or a weapon into school, Sister Jeanne Arthur was the one they sent in to steal it from him by force.

Sister Jeanne Arthur had rules for just about everything, including gifts for the teacher. Gifts didn't work as bribes on her, but they were a good way for second-graders to practice the Golden Rule. She let us know she was pretty well provided with rosary beads and holy cards, and she had to share any cash she got with a houseful of other nuns. Unless it was a lot, money wasn't going to do her much good. She knew children often had a hard time picking out the right gifts, so she saved us the trouble by asking for potato chips, and she hinted that the State Line brand was especially worthy of our attention.

My mother admired Sister Jeanne Arthur for knowing exactly what she wanted. She also admired this trait in total strangers at the super-market who "moved along at a decent clip" instead of blocking the aisles while making up their minds. My mother always knew exactly which item any person with a brain in her head should buy.

If you were ever confused about a choice, all you had to do was exam-ine your conscience. This worked for all the Downings we knew, except me. I was about three when this became apparent, and the story was retold a million times. Unfortunately, my father was still alive when this happened, so it was probably one of the few things about me that stuck in his mind for eternity.

I had to be punished by my mother because I wouldn't stop asking to try on the boxing gloves my father had bought Gerard for his tenth birthday. I was sent to the laundry room to examine my conscience. This was not my first trip to the isolation booth, but my mother had never closed the door between me and the kitchen before. I admit I was probably sobbing and ruining the party atmosphere.

Things went wrong immediately. I got distracted by the idea of turn-ing the laundry room into my private bedroom. In part, I blame the bleachy darkness, which made me think of nighttime and clean sheets. When I lay down on my back on the cool linoleum between the laundry machines and the built-in cabinets, I fit perfectly, with room to spare for growth spurts. I folded my hands behind my head, bent my knees, and crossed my legs. Directly above me, I noticed, the ceiling light had already been outfitted with a pull-chain. If I added a shoelace, I'd be able to operate it as a nightlight. If I drummed up a decent pillow, the world would be my oyster.

A knock at the door brought me to my feet. Somebody, not my mother, said, Are you done examining your conscience?

I remember almost nothing of what happened next. It's just a story told about me. I don't even remember my father being in the kitchen, so if I ran into him when I was released, I hope I was polite. I doubt it, though, because I do know I was panicky. I also remember that Gerard's new inflatable boxing bag had been attached to the door of the built-in broom closet in the kitchen, and it was hanging there like the shiniest apple on the forbidden Tree of Knowledge. And I remember one other detail. I remember clearly that I did not know the meaning of the word *conscience*. Still, it was nobody's fault but my own that I had wasted my prison time on another of my many home-makeover fantasies.

Either my mother or my father asked me if I was sorry for causing a ruckus. (The sources vary on this point.) Everyone agrees that I said I was sorry, acing that test. But my mother expected our A's to come with plusses, so she tossed me a bonus question: What do you want to say to your brother for interrupting his birthday party?

I screamed, I want boxing gloves.

I won a return trip to the isolation booth. The story leaves me stranded there, cut off from the family, wanting things I should not want.

After my father died, instead of missing him or the status and money that accrued to us during the last years of his life, most of my family just stopped wanting the things we didn't have—hence their attitude about strangers at our parties. It was not economic or space constraints that dictated our policy. It was our good fortune not to need outsiders to gin up a celebration.

Anybody can turn necessity into a virtue. My family could perform moral alchemy, turning anything that was not available to us into a vice. I never mastered this skill. I constantly craved what other people had, but I also craved the heady feeling of being a Downing—being morally superior to people who craved that stuff. I wanted it all. I wanted to live above reproach with a heated in-ground pool in the backyard.

By second grade, I knew it was not okay to want all the right things and all the wrong things. Managing my irreconcilable longings was going to require some fancy footwork. The world was famously a minefield of sinful pleasures for normal Catholics, but our family cata-logue of shameful indulgences went way beyond color television sets and jewelry. It included pets, family vacations, and grandparents.

The H. family up the street had a live grandmother, and they kept her in the other side of their duplex house. As I understood this arrange-ment, they'd installed her as a built-in babysitter. I never had any live grandparents, so it was lucky I came from a family that didn't need the kind of help they could offer. Nana spoke to us only through the win-dow screens, like a prisoner, to tell us when we were about to trample her flowers, and she often showed signs of weakness. She had white hair and wore cardigan sweaters over her shoulders in the middle of summer. I knew it was morally unacceptable to make your grand-mother live in like a slave, and I constantly inquired about her well-being. Did she ever have guests? Was there heat on her side? I was relieved when Cathleen H. sneaked me in one day to prove Nana had her own bathroom and kitchen. All along, I'd pictured her with just a pail and a toaster.

My brother Joe was not impressed when I reported the results of my investigation to him. I bet they lose a ton of rent on Nana, was all he said. I repeated this to my mother rather proudly, giving Joe no credit. She said, With five children and her nerves, Mrs. H. is smart to keep her mother nearby.

My mother could always find a way to compliment people who weren't related to us on their bad habits.

I had a lot of friends in second grade because I didn't criticize them to their faces and I was preternaturally gifted when it came to ana-grams. One Friday, Sister Jeanne Arthur dictated a simple sentence and instructed us to jumble up the letters over the weekend and then see how many new words we could make. She told us this was going to be a weekly contest to improve our vocabulary.

On Monday, most kids came in with ten or fifteen new words, a lot of them written with crayons on construction paper, as if they didn't know the difference between language arts and visual arts. It didn't surprise anyone when Barbara Jean held up her Palmer-method cursive list and flipped it around dramatically to show that she'd needed the second side to fit in her thirty-something words. She'd already won the first big spelling bee of the year, and she was getting pretty famous for her study habits.

I had not used both sides of the paper, so I worried that I'd broken a rule and would be disqualified. I had used seven pages of my brother Joe's best lined paper and four of my mother's staples for my words, about 140 of them, from which I had purged plurals, possessives, and proper nouns based on accusations of loafing made by my brother Gerard against me.

Sister Jeanne didn't play favorites based on brains. She congratulated us all, and instructed us to walk up in orderly rows to place our results on her desk. We'd spent the first couple weeks of second grade practicing this assembly-line delivery system, which involved a full classroom circuit on the way back to your desk. When I got up to the front, she opened the bottom drawer of her desk and handed me a bag of State Line potato chips, but she wasn't smiling. You know what this means, Michael, she said, shifting into her all-business baritone. I did not, and neither did the other kids, who automatically froze in place, which left everyone at somebody else's assigned place. I'd shut down the second grade. I was the wrench in the works. Sister Jeanne said, No weekend homework for the class this Friday. The place erupted in cheers and victory dancing. Before anybody got hurt or accidentally peed, Sister Jeanne loudly instructed me to offer a handful of chips only to those kids sitting quietly at their proper desks.

As usual, I got exactly what I wanted and exactly what I didn't want. I liked winning, but for a prize I would have preferred a new assignment with some tougher letter combinations. I didn't really need more popularity or party invitations. I needed something to do at home when the older kids were playing Scrabble or shouting out the answers as my mother filled in the blanks in the Jumble puzzle in the daily newspaper.

Word games were a chance for my family to enjoy the brains God gave us, but you couldn't expect the older Downings to participate in Chutes and Ladders or Parcheesi. And forget party games. Party games were a sign of desperation. After the cake was cut at home, you did the dishes and then went outside and played if you didn't have anything original to say about Vatican II or the Democrats' chances in the upcoming elections. Pin the Tail on the Donkey and Musical Chairs were associated with small families that lacked children and had to rely on noisemakers and store-bought crepe-paper decorations to create cheap imitations of family events. I liked having a reason based on moral superiority not to play games in other people's houses. I wasn't crazy about being blindfolded or dizzy in front of strangers, and by second grade, because of painful accidents, the mothers of a lot of children had started throwing parties where they substituted Scotch Tape for pins on the donkey tails, and everybody was looking for an excuse not to play.

By second grade, even my First Communion was an imposition. The parish let Catholic-school kids cut a lot of the preparation classes, but they forced even us to memorize the Ten Commandments. When I brought them up, my family didn't show much interest in the Commandments. They were just grateful they were there so the Jews had something from the Bible to guide them. After a while, I stopped trying to interest people in my First Communion. Most of the other eight kids in the family had received the Holy Sacrament years ago when it was a more sacred event in St. Charles parish, where we lived before my father died. Plus, my First Communion was scheduled for May, and I was born in May, so every time I brought it up I was competing against myself for attention.

And then Father F. turned up. I never knew where Father F. came from, but he was always on his way to Haiti, a hot country specializing in witch doctors. Father F. was a missionary. No matter how hot he got in Haiti, he never took off his black cassock and white collar, and he wore rosary beads around his waist, instead of a normal belt. The crucifix was usually all that was protecting him from the latest tropical jinx or curse. He was a small man. There was something appealingly wrong with his face—maybe his skin was pockmarked, maybe one side didn't line up properly with the other. You could see he had suffered. This wildly inflated his romance quotient for me.

Father F.'s last visit that I recall coincided with my sister Marie's birthday. Marie was four years older than I was, two years older than Joe, and about ten times more spoiled than either of us because she was the youngest girl in the family and always willing to cry for sympathy. Visiting missionaries were a bigger deal than birthdays in our house, so Father F.'s just happening to turn up at the right moment to make Marie's party memorable seemed suspicious to Joe and me. Joe was in fourth grade by then. He'd long since figured out that most of the benefits of being Downing kids had been used up or worn out by our seven older brothers and sisters. For instance, Joe had seen home movies from before we were born starring a rented pony and dozens of party-hatted guests eating fistfuls of chocolate cake. Joe and I weren't allowed to invite extras, and the supply of ponies and pointed hats had completely dried up. And after my father died in 1961, no matter how old you were, you got the same birthday cake. My sisters Elaine and Mary Ann must have made two or three hundred of those pink-frosted white cakes with seeded raspberry jam between the layers. I can still hear my mother saying, Can one of you girls whip up a one-egg cake for tonight?

Somebody, somewhere along the line, must've preferred a dense cake.

Father F. was good with kids because he didn't mind frightening them. This made him my favorite priest. Usually we ate in the dining room when we had priests in the house, but Father F. was an old friend of the family, so we ate in the kitchen around the oval maple table. Father F. told stories about "the dark side of Haiti," but he made it clear he wasn't talking about the color of people's skin. Like us, he couldn't care less about your color as long as you were a Catholic who voted for anybody named Kennedy. His worst enemies were the witch doctors, who could paralyze people with the Evil Eye.

If Father F. visited your house in Haiti, anything could happen. Once, when he was young, he stayed overnight on a big farm operated by recently baptized Catholics who wanted to give him the profits from their sugarcane crop to build a church. All night, the witch doctors hooted in the fields like crazy owls. In the morning, the sugarcane was nothing but crispy black stems. They could burn down your house without ever lighting a match, Father F. said. We didn't have dimmer switches in those days, but something made the pendant light over the kitchen table flicker and fade.

My mother asked Father F. what the Catholics did to survive. He said, You fight fire with fire. Everyone else nodded solemnly as if they knew what this meant. Before I could ask for clarification, somebody turned out the light and the one-egg cake was carried in from the dining room by candlelight, and we sang for Marie.

The older kids had long ago perfected their rendition of "Happy Birthday," and they did just fine without the two oldest, Roberta and Jack, who were absent because Jack had gotten married the year before and Roberta was annoyed Jack had beat her to the punch, so she was not wasting any more date nights on birthday parties or priests. Roberta was the oldest Downing kid, and she'd fallen in love plenty of times but always managed to meet somebody else she liked better than the guy who'd just given her a diamond ring. She was known for giving us all fits. She was also known as the prettiest one in the family because of her dark wavy hair, pale skin, dark eyes, and lipstick, all of which the actress Loretta Young copied but not successfully. Of all the sisters in the photographs above the piano, Roberta was the only one who dared to wear a strapless gown. Joe pointed this out to me, but he said it was sinful to bring it up in polite conversation. This was another mystery for me to contemplate while we said the Rosary nightly in the living room—that, and why Roberta had recently announced she wanted to marry a fat guy.

Elaine sang the melody. Mary Ann added an alto harmony. Next came Peg, who was the middle child but a natural soprano who'd eventually end up an octave above everyone else. Gerard usually did an Al Jolson imitation. Joe and I were expected to be able to stay on tune, which was impossible since all the on-tune parts were taken. Marie stood up on her chair. She didn't need the extra height to blow out her candles, but she was wearing a new dress and showing it off for Father F. This was the sort of behavior that would win Joe and me a trip to the laundry room to examine our consciences. Everybody tolerated it from Marie because she'd lost her father. Joe was considered too young to have really lost much of a father. I was even younger, and when I'd had my chance to start a relationship with him, I'd made it pretty clear that my father's legendary charisma was lost on me.

This was proven by one of the few stories from my father's life in which I figured. He comes home from work, is mobbed by eight kids, and finally notices that I am playing on the floor near the stove. He's amused and confounded by my lack of interest in him. I think you brainwash him when I am at work, he says to my mother in his good-natured way, but everybody knows he really doesn't mind losing one out of nine times.

This story was a source of great pride to me. It allied me singularly with my mother. It also implied I had miraculously foreseen the tragic future and saved myself a terrible loss. And it tallied perfectly with my one visual memory of my father.

My father was available to me in a fifteen-second sequence I had committed to memory. It is morning in our big, square kitchen. The windows are silvered with the sun, and the fake-brick linoleum floor is warm, as if I am walking on the real-brick hearth in the living room while a fire is crackling. I am two feet tall, and I walk into the kitchen wearing footed pajamas with rubber soles. My parents are seated at either end of the oval maple table. My mother is drinking orange juice. It must be a Sunday: There are place mats beneath the eleven breakfast settings. I walk straight to my father, who balances his no-filter Camel in a clear glass ashtray, picks me up, turns my face to his, kisses me on the lips, and settles me down on his lap. His torso is broad and soft. Beneath the pleasing scent of the toasty cigarette smoke, I smell coffee. I put both of my hands on the edge of the table. Everything that is happening is deeply familiar to the three of us. We've been through this routine many times. We are all still waking up, but we're happy. My father helpfully shoves his chair back a few inches from the table. He doesn't say anything. I hop down, walk around the table, past the warm radiator covered with pairs of mittens smelling like winter, and climb into my mother's lap, where I intend to spend some time with her, watching my big, dark-haired father enjoy a few minutes without the other kids.

It's all I ever had of him, priceless footage, the only original, singular claim I ever had to knowing him, feeling him, smelling him, measuring and negotiating the distance between him and me. Without it, I was not a real Downing but a spectator, a witness to what happened to a family.

Father F. caught Marie's attention just before she blew out her birthday candles. He said her name, and he smiled, and then he told her she'd forgotten how to blow out the candles. She nodded. Somebody turned on the pendant light, and Marie tried mightily to blow it out. It was hilarious and scary.

Father F. said, That isn't a candle, Marie, and Marie nodded again and started trying to blow out her fingers. Then she stared at the candles for a while. She looked delighted and confused.

I sat up, trying to divert Father F.'s attention to me, but my sister Peg was laughing the loudest. Father F. smiled and said, Peg? You know what else is funny, Peggo? You forgot how to cut the cake, so cut the cake. Peg banged the silver cake server on the table a couple of times, and then she picked up her empty dessert plate to examine the bottom of it, as if her slice of cake should be there. He told somebody else to serve the cake, and then told the older kids it was too bad they'd forgotten how to eat it. A couple of them tried to push it through their cheeks and necks. This went on for about an hour. He sent some people to the hall closet to forget how to put on their coats, and he made a couple of my sisters believe their feet were so heavy that they couldn't move. He could make them cry and laugh and wander around and bump into each other like blind people just by paying close attention to them for a couple of seconds and saying their names.

I'll never forget how he said their names. He spoke them as soft and confident questions, as if he knew they believed they were lost but he knew they were not. Gerard? Marie? Peg? I'd never heard a man speak so tenderly to children. It was definitely a good weapon to use against the witch doctors.

Out of respect, Father F. did not mesmerize my mother. He did not mesmerize Joe out of respect for the miracle cure my mother arranged after he was born with an incurable disease. He wouldn't mesmerize me, he said, because he didn't know me well enough, which I took as an insult. I really didn't mind not being forced to smash cake into my own face, but I desperately wanted him to speak my name as a question only he could answer. He never did.

Like so many memories made in that stucco house on Howard Street, Father F.'s last visit ended with Joe and me in our bedroom above the kitchen, listening for a while as the party continued beneath us. We didn't try to hear what tricks were being performed in the kitchen without us. We drowned out the laughter by regaling each other with accounts of what we had been allowed to see, convincing each other that we were lucky just to have witnessed such amazing goings-on.

Joe and I taunted each other constantly and cruelly about being born sick and being born too late to remember our own father. But we didn't use it against each other that night. We didn't even make each other admit we hadn't been worth mesmerizing.

Years later, in that same bedroom, I will confess to Joe that I have only one real memory of our father. Joe will ask me to tell it to him. I will. But even before I get to the coffee and cigarettes—my favorite details, as they supplied me with the material for conjuring my father later in life—Joe will ask me to stop the story and start again, "from the top." As I rewind the well-worn tape, Joe will say it seems suspicious that the floor was warm enough for me to feel it through my footed pajamas. He will remind me that they probably had slip-proof rubber safety soles. I will stop the tape and examine one frame—my feet, the fake-brick pattern, sunlight, a table leg, one of my father's feet in a black sock. Joe will say Daddy usually wore shoes in the house. I will worry over that sock. Maybe his foot was slippered? Did he own black loafers? Joe will tell me not to worry about the shoe. That shoe is the least of your worries, he will say. Michael?

At that point, I will pretend to be asleep, but Joe will say my name forty or fifty times—his version of Chinese water torture—until I say, What?

For your information, he will say—Joe-code for *it pleases me to inform you*—that brick linoleum was installed about five years after Daddy died.

In May 1966, exactly one day before my eighth birthday, Jack's wife suddenly had a baby, the first Downing grandchild. She wiped out my party, and my First Communion was now competing with a baptism. I was eight and Joe was ten, and we'd heard a rumor that Jack and Jerry and the baby were moving back to Pittsfield so Jack could look for a job. While everybody was trying to embarrass Joe and me by telling us we had to start acting like uncles, all we could think about was our erratic oldest brother being back in town. We couldn't discuss it in public, but we stayed up late in private, planning our defenses. We certainly weren't going to sleep well anymore. I compared the situation to a flood in a Fizzy factory. Joe said Nagasaki, which sounded worse.

When the parish priest issued me a full-length clip-on white tie to wear, I got excited about First Communion again. My family was used to seeing me only in bow ties. Right at that moment, though, my sister Roberta started appearing around the house at odd moments in a wedding dress, demanding everybody's attention. She was quitting her teaching job at a local junior high and getting married in June to Dick. He was a nice guy with a giant beer belly who used to be a bus driver in Springfield, Massachusetts, but was hoping to land a job at Bickford's Pancake House. Joe and I were not allowed to crack the obvious fat jokes. My mother just said, He's the man your sister is determined to marry. She treated Dick very well, allowing him to sleep on the sofa in the den when he visited, which might've looked bad morally but was actually Christian charity because Dick couldn't afford to stay at a decent motel. Plus, there was another rumor flying around about his mother being alcoholic.

Although we all ate oatmeal on Mondays, Wednesdays, and Fridays, and poached eggs on toast on Tuesdays and Thursdays, and cold cereal on Saturdays, and bacon and eggs on Sundays, Dick was allowed to order eggs any day of the week. This impressed me as my mother's way of showing him a good example for his career at the pancake house, but not a particularly good way of teaching him the discipline he and Roberta lacked. I think Dick's breakfast privileges started after my mother accidentally totaled his car.

My mother had been in a rush to get to morning Mass. She was going by herself, probably to persuade a saint to intervene in Roberta's wedding plans. The driveway was rimmed with four-foot banks of shoveled snow. It ran about seventy-five feet downhill from the garage to the street. This was a dicey drive in reverse, but midway you could back into the carport—where Joe forced you to play half-court basketball in the summer—and then drive straight down the rest of the way. When my mother backed the green Pontiac Bonneville three-seater station wagon out of the garage and into the carport, she heard something unusual. She got out to look and didn't see anything but the snowbanks, which was odd, because Dick's VW Beetle had been parked there when she left the house. It took her a while, but she finally spotted it. She'd banged Dick's Beetle right up over the snowbank, where it had sunk clear out of sight into the drifts in the backyard. She'd tried to wake up Dick, she claimed, but he was snoring, so she figured she'd tell him when she got back. Dick woke up while she was gone and noticed his Beetle wasn't in the carport. He didn't panic and call the police like a normal person. He just waited around. This confirmed his reputation for being an easygoing guy and his reputation for lacking initiative.

Meanwhile, changing your mind had caught on like wildfire with the older kids. My sister Elaine was ditching her last year of college in Vermont so she could go work with recently baptized Catholics on an Oklahoma Indian reservation. Jack had flunked out of college before he got married. Joe tried to launch investigations into all this dropping out, but nobody would discuss it out loud because it didn't make sense of our being smart and valuing a college education. Elaine was not punished, probably because she didn't ever admit she was dropping out in front of us. Elaine's punishment was the way we learned to compliment her for being kind and for having good sewing skills.

At the same time, my sister Mary Ann was attending Berkshire Community College instead of a four-year college, even though she'd had all A's in high school and had been told to apply to Smith College by a guidance counselor who obviously hadn't heard about Catholic four-year colleges. Mary Ann was my favorite sister. Her being at home was good luck for me, but it was not okay to be happy about it in public. She was on punishment because she'd changed her mind about going into the convent in the middle of her senior year of high school, after her name had already been sewn on tags attached to her towels and bedsheets and black dresses. She was grounded, which my mother liked to call "campused" to emphasize where Mary Ann wasn't. This included not dating and not even attending funerals for members of her friends' families. And Mary Ann was allowed to be only a part-time student. The rest of the time, she had to work counting the collections in the rectory, and then catch up by taking summer-school courses. I took it on faith that this somehow proved how highly my family valued a college education.

In First Communion classes, they moved on to drilling us in how to walk in pairs up the aisle without concern for our partner's appearance. Some nuns we didn't know who were experts in perfect unison were brought in to run these sessions for the priests. A lot of our practice time was taken up by girls' questions about their veils and how to handle them, until a public school boy said too loudly that the veils would make it so you didn't have to worry if you were paired up with a real goon.

Public school kids could always dish it out, but they could never take it, and nobody knew this better than the nuns. One of them asked him to stand up and say his name out loud. She asked him if his parents were planning to attend his First Communion.

He said yes, and his little sister. And all four of his grandparents were expected, he said. I started to feel a little sorry for him. He thought he could talk his way out of it. But then he started bragging, adding in godparents from out of town, too. That's when I lost sympathy for him. All the good godparents for my family had been used up by the time I was baptized, so I got the uncle and the bleached-blond aunt who lived in California in a troubled marriage. As a result, I wasn't expecting any great gifts. I was just praying they didn't get divorced.

For punishment, the nun said, the wiseacre was not going to have a partner for his march up the aisle on the day of his First Holy Communion.

For a minute, the kid thought he could handle the punishment.

It was entirely a matter of his own free will, the nun said, whether to tell his out-of-town godparents in advance or just let them make the trip to St. Teresa's parish and be surprised to see he was the only boy in the class not worthy of a partner. "Who'll be the goon then, mister?"

The kid started to cry, completely proving her point.

I was always confident that when it came to the actual day of my First Communion, my family would act in a way that would make other kids envious. If they felt like it, a couple of my brothers could arrange to be altar boys for the event, and some of my sisters could sing in the choir, and the rest would still fill up one of the front benches. The only thing I was really worried about was First Confession.

I tried to bring it up at dinner one Friday night, but my mother had fried smelts, which we loved because tartar sauce was a mayonnaise by-product and no other seafood item supported such a disproportionate ratio of tartar sauce to fish. No one wanted to talk. After the Rosary, I stopped outside Marie's bedroom to see if she'd be willing to give me some tips. She opened her door just enough to accommodate her ear. She was experimenting with a wedding hairdo by wearing somebody else's curlers, but I ignored them to stay on her good side. I said I was worried. A lot of my friends were practicing pretty hard for First Confession. She said to make up a bunch of sins of omission, and then she closed the door. I knocked for a while and finally yelled, Like what? Through the oak door, she said, Like failing to remember to thank Mom for cooking your meals. And then she turned on the hairdryer to drown me out.

I checked this with Joe. He told me it would be a sin, and I wouldn't be pure enough to take Holy Communion at Roberta's wedding. We were in our bedroom. He shut the door and made me get down on my knees and show him how I examined my conscience.

Joe said my method was all wrong, starting with bad posture. He turned out the desk light and turned on the closet light, and in that dimness he demonstrated his technique. It put mine to shame. His eyes were closed tight enough to cause wrinkles, and he held his hands like somebody getting ready to karate-chop a brick in half. At first, he seemed to be staring straight down into the fires of hell. I noticed how he started to move his lips after a while, and then he slowly raised his head bit by bit, but not so far that he'd be accused of trying to talk to God directly.

It helped that he was amazingly skinny and always pulled his pants up under his ribs so he could cinch his belt on the very last hole. It made him look like a starving hobo whom anybody would forgive.

I didn't tell him, but I decided to memorize a list of sins of omission. In the heat of the moment of my First Confession, though, I changed my mind. As soon as I closed the curtain in the confessional, I wished I'd practiced better posture. The darkness really threw me off my game. I blew my first line, claiming it had been "one week since my last confession," and Father H. said, Start again, Michael.

A lot of kids hated the idea that the priest might know who you were, but I took it as an advantage. He wouldn't be expecting any big sins from a Downing. On my second attempt, I got through the opening without any problems and told Father H. I had been tempted to lie and almost had, but I hadn't.

He said, Who tempted you?

I didn't know he had the right to ask questions, so I panicked. I knew Marie would never forgive me if I used her real name, so I said, An older kid I know from school.

Father H. said, How did he tempt you?

I said I couldn't remember, but I reminded him that I hadn't lied, trying to change the subject.

He said, How well do you know this boy?

I said, It's a girl, which was a huge mistake. I'd opened up a whole new area for investigation.

Father H. said, Why were you talking to her at all, then?

Now all I could see was Marie in curlers, chasing me with a hairbrush. I said, She's a crossing guard. Our only crossing guard was Sister Jeanne Arthur. To get myself back on track, I forced myself to imagine Sister Jeanne Arthur wearing an orange shoulder strap. It worked. I whispered, And I said unkind things about my brother Joe to his face. I used his name for realism.

Father H. said, How many times?

I closed my eyes. This was a lot like Pin the Tail on the Donkey.

I said, Three. At least three.

He forgave me.

If this had happened at home, my mother would have been holding the telephone receiver in one hand and handing me the telephone book with the other so I could look up the girl crossing guard's home number.

For my penance, Father H. gave me one Our Father, three Hail Marys, and one Glory Be. This was basically a belated birthday gift. These prayers were exactly what we said at home every night just to warm up for the Apostle's Creed, five decades of the Rosary, a long praise prayer that began *Hail, Holy Queen* and a longer prayer "for Daddy" via the Sacred Heart, followed by the litany of the names of the nine Downing children, plus one uncle, my godfather, the one who had the troubled marriage that made it impossible for him to concentrate on my birthday every year.

I had to wait more than ten years for a godparent to do anything about my birthday. I was turning nineteen, and I had made two true-blue friends during my first year of college, though I really didn't know it until they showed their colors on the event of my first birthday away from home. One was Perry, one of my two assigned roommates in a two-bedroom suite in Harvard Yard. The other was Liz, a sophisticated, generous, sardonic smoker who'd arrived with sophomore standing in English and lived two flights above us. Her affection was singularly heartening to me, and it was occasionally undercut by an inexplicable diffidence—just my style.

Perry was a six-foot-tall Japanese American football player from Southern California who intended to major in economics. We had almost nothing in common and no mutual friends. We didn't even share a bedroom, though we both disliked our other roommate, with whom I shared a bunk bed. Perry never offered to trade off and give me a break from the other guy. This solidified my admiration for him. He knew what he wanted. If I'd got the single bedroom, I'd have traded with Perry halfway through the year and ended up resenting Perry as much as I did the other guy.

My birthday fell on a Sunday in May that year, and late on Saturday afternoon Perry announced that his godmother, Aunt Mary, had sent him a check to take me out to dinner. His aunt had previously flown us both to Washington, D.C., to celebrate his birthday, and she'd funded a number of other outings during which I had acquired a profound fondness for roasted duck. When I balked at the idea of a birthday celebration, Perry said we were eating at the Hampshire House overlooking the Public Garden. When he made the reservation, he said, he had checked—we needed ties, and they served duck.

When we sat down in the leather club chairs and took in the room and the view, I relaxed for the first time in months. I felt I'd finally got in to Harvard. We ordered mixed drinks—if nothing else, in my first year of college I learned that most people didn't take their gin straight, as I had whenever I nicked a couple of shots from the dusty bottle in the pantry in Pittsfield. Instead of a toast, Perry said he had a confession to make. Way too quickly, I said, Whatever it is, I forgive you. He was a Lutheran, and I hoped he would take my word as a Catholic that he didn't have to ruin a perfectly good friendship by telling me the truth about anything.

I have to tell you this, Michael. Right about now, a bunch of people are standing around in Liz's room, probably with the lights out. They're waiting for me to get you up there with some excuse about an English paper Liz is writing on Thomas Hardy.

I was genuinely surprised Liz liked me well enough to throw me a party. I was even more surprised Perry knew me well enough to whisk me away from the event. I said, I hate surprises.

I was elated.

3. False Pride

In third grade, a lot of my baby teeth fell out. It didn't worry me. My mother said that none of the Downings held on to their baby teeth for long, and I was pleased not to be a kid in one of those other families that did hold on to things too long.

I knew there was no tooth fairy. Sometime during my stint in kindergarten, I'd spit up my first loose tooth while I was gargling with Listerine from my brother Gerard's private stash. I didn't ask Gerard about the tooth fairy. Gerard reminded people of my father, which translated into high hopes for his future, so he wasn't expected to waste his time with his youngest brothers. Joe and I made him pay for ignoring us in mouthwash, cologne, and aerosol deodorants.

I had asked Joe about the fairy. The tooth fairy is against our faith, he'd said. Joe was deeply religious. So is Santa Claus, Joe added, and P. S., keep it all to yourself.

Joe was taller than I was and he had darker hair, and his only apparent disadvantage was a wicked cowlick he occasionally tried to master with a combo of the sprays and pomades he could dig up in Gerard's bedroom. He was wearing his maroon cotton long-sleeve jersey with the fake black dickey. It must have been a Saturday. I was wearing my mustard-colored long-sleeve jersey with the fake black dickey. These were bought-new jerseys, and Joe and I knew they were more sophisticated than the striped things our friends wore. Out of modesty, we rarely kept them on when we left the house.

I liked the way we looked in those almost-matching jerseys. I knew Downing boys weren't supposed to care about style, but I didn't much like the way we looked in the wide-wale corduroys and cable-knit sweaters that came in plastic bags from the family of the man who owned the local newspaper, one of many prominent civic leaders who had been my father's best friend. Whenever Joe and I put on some not-new clothes and stood in front of the full-length mahogany mirror in the upstairs hall, we could see that our knees and elbows weren't where the previous owner's joints had been. My mother would say they fit "like a glove." She'd say this out of one side of her mouth. She'd be on her knees, a threaded sewing needle pressed between her lips, and she'd be tugging on a sleeve or cuff.

If I was in kindergarten, my mother must have been forty six, maybe forty seven. Joe and I weren't pitiless, but we didn't pity our mother any more than we pitied ourselves. I think we knew that anybody fortunate enough to be a member of our family was above pity. This was a matter of some pride, which was okay. As far as I understood the policy, pride was an indoor virtue that became a problem outside the family, like my favorite jersey. Pity was reserved for the poor and needy and other people who weren't related to us.

We didn't even pity my father, who was only forty-four when he died in 1961. And it would be almost two decades before I got a sense of how needy we all had been. My parents never had any savings. In 1960, they had put down $1,000 on a $20,000 stucco house about two miles across town from the small three-and-a-half bedroom house in which they had lived since 1947. There were eleven of us before my father died; the new house had six bedrooms. My father's life insurance policy paid out $50,000. When a couple of his best friends sat down with my newly widowed mother, they added up the annual Social Security payments she would receive and the estimated interest on the life insurance. Until I graduated from college, her annual income was between $6,000 and $7,000. She gave 10 percent to charity every year, as did all of her children from their part-time jobs.

We never spoke of these details, even amongst ourselves. We were the children of a widow, and the Church and its Missions received more than their share of our mites. We knew the parable. But to admit we saw any parallel to our own lives would have been false pride. Instead, we behaved like aristocrats who knew better than to squander their fortunes on new bikes with banana seats or restaurant food. We accepted the hand-me-down clothes and free Oriental carpets and tickets to Tanglewood and part-time jobs with flexible hours in the spirit in which they were given. As tribute to the temple of my dead father. This was the same spirit in which we swallowed the peculiar hash that was served up for dinner in the homes of friends and in prosaic homilies by the parish priests. We recognized that it was the very best other people could do.

Joe had advised me to wrap my first lost tooth in toilet paper and try selling it to one of our older sisters. Much of what Joe did and almost all of what he said puzzled me, but I respected his advice because I was in kindergarten and he was in second grade. Plus, he had managed to accumulate a vast, secret collection of smelly chestnuts, which were sprouting roots in all three drawers of an oak desk we allegedly shared in our twin-bedded bedroom.

I took the tooth to my sister Marie, who was always allowed to have friends over because she was sandwiched in the family between Joe and me on one side and Gerard on the other, and she claimed half her secrets could be shared only with girls. Marie never liked to be interrupted, but she did like to be asked for her opinion. Mom has to pay you a quarter for every single tooth, she said after chasing me out of her bedroom, where she was putting makeup on a girl named Rose, who was wearing a white dress decorated with a big pink picture of a rose. Marie was wearing a red-and-white muumuu purchased by one of our older sisters, which was supposed to be an outdoor dress but was worn only as a housecoat by a Downing. We'd had a couple of informative dinner table discussions about muumuus. The upshot was, muumuus were Hawaiian and we weren't.

I knew we weren't allowed to stick old teeth under pillows and pretend not to know how they got there, so I knocked to get Marie's attention again. She spoke to me through a two-inch opening in her bedroom door. She often did this. For years, I imagined this was how members of the Supreme Court handed down their decisions. Give me your tooth, and I'll give it to Mom, she said, sticking her hand out into the hall.

She must have seen the toilet paper I'd packed around it, because her hand disappeared and she hissed, Sterilize it. I knew this would require bleach, but my mother kept the Clorox in the laundry room, and she was constantly running in and out of there all day with baskets of clothes, which made it very hard when you wanted to do something private with bleach or ammonia.

I tracked down Joe in the garage, where he often spent time alone after he'd been forced out of the house to play with kids in the neighborhood. I asked him a general question about sterilizing procedures people used before bleach was invented. He suggested a bonfire. Since he'd joined the Boy Scouts, Joe was constantly angling to get me to start a forest fire he could put out. But I knew if I hung around long enough, he'd come up with something else just to get me to leave him alone. He finally told me Gerard's cologne would work. He was right. A long soak in half a bottle of Excalibur decanted into the bathroom glass did the trick. And I also discovered that hydrogen peroxide got rid of the smell of cologne in a drinking glass. This was after I'd figured out how to dribble the hydrogen peroxide I'd snagged from my sister Mary Ann's private stash of hair-care products into the inconveniently tiny hole at the top of the Excalibur bottle to replenish Gerard's supply.

Marie accepted the tooth without comment. She was often a lot of things I didn't appreciate, but she wasn't a thief. The payment turned up under my pillow the next morning.

Over the next two years, I got refunds on at least a dozen baby teeth. Then, during the spring of 1967, I swallowed two teeth while eating a bologna-and-cheese sandwich at my desk in the third-grade classroom of Notre Dame grammar school. We hadn't had a lunchroom for a couple of months because of a flood, but we'd been allowed to turn around and face our neighbors while we ate. I motioned to my best friend, Joey T., whose desk was four rows away, but he couldn't understand what had happened, so I had to pass him a note.

On the way home, we stopped just one block from school on a rise in First Street, which was actually a bridge over a stretch of railroad track. We hung our heads over the concrete railing to see if there were any bad kids playing down there who might get their arms chopped off by a passing train. We'd heard it had happened. We couldn't prove it, but we knew for sure that in second grade one bad kid had told Sister Jeanne Arthur he'd by mistake dropped his penmanship homework off the bridge. She didn't believe him, and neither did I. Whenever I brought it up, though, Joey T. always said he could believe it. This particular day, when I brought it up I added some of the worst stuff from the bad kid's résumé—his parents were divorced, his mother yelled; plus, I'd once watched him set some of his own hair on fire—but Joey still said he could believe a homework paper could just fly away.

Standing on the bridge, looking for potential amputees, I asked Joey if you got paid for teeth you swallowed. He'd know. He'd swallowed a metal bottle cap, a nickel, and a lot of our marbles.

Joey said, You mean, *prove it*?

I nodded.

Joey had a sister exactly the same age as my sister Marie, and they both said *prove it* every time either one of us said just about anything. He told me if I had any problems proving I'd swallowed two teeth, I could always check to see when it came out in my B.M. I didn't know what he was talking about. He was pleased to know something I didn't know, and after he explained the abbreviation, he asked me what I called my bowel movements. I was embarrassed and a little scared that we were talking about them at all. I was going to tell him how in my family you never even touched toilet paper if somebody else had touched it, but I didn't want to insult his family's bad hygiene. I just let him know that my family never discussed anything that happened in bathrooms. At first, he didn't believe me, but after a while, Joey said, You better find out what you call it before it's too late. He went on to explain how much work had gone into his recovery of the nickel he'd swallowed. It had taken a couple of days. It was worth it, he said, because it was a buffalo head.

This somehow reminded him that he had swiped a bunch of Sweet Tarts from his sister's bedroom for us to eat, so he dropped his green book bag and fished around in it, and then he dumped everything on the sidewalk. He had some old spelling tests and a lot of pencils and his dog Cindy's leash in his bag, but he didn't have any candy, and I noticed he didn't have his geography book, which meant he was not going to live up to his potential again on the test. He did find the note I'd written him. He read it to himself and smiled. He didn't make a big deal out of proving his point or anything. He just placed my note on the concrete railing and flicked it like a carom until it slid off and floated down to the gravel between the tracks. About halfway home, he remembered he'd eaten the Sweet Tarts secretly during art period.

It was not until I was eating dinner that I remembered eating my two teeth during lunch. Our kitchen table was always crowded, but even I eventually got a chance to speak. My mother often had to make a special plea for people to listen to me, which sometimes added to the pressure, but I appreciated it anyway. I made my announcement, and immediately one of my sisters said, I swallowed three teeth today, and then another one said she'd swallowed four teeth, and my brother Gerard asked my mother how much he'd get for swallowing one of his ears, and then they were told to change the subject. Even Joe wouldn't look at me, even after I drank from his milk, which almost always got his attention.

It occurred to me that maybe I hadn't swallowed two teeth. I didn't know what "prone to" meant, but I knew I was prone to exaggerating. I was first prone to it when I tried to wiggle out of wearing some donated woolen clothes because they gave me a rash, and I was prone to it again when I explained to my mother why I had been kept after school one day by Mrs. Shaw. Mrs. Shaw had asked me to remain in my seat after dismissal, and she'd sat down at the desk beside mine and said someday she'd be voting for me for president of the United States. That was it. She said she hadn't wanted to embarrass me in front of the other kids. And before I stood up, she said, You should be proud of yourself.

I wasn't stupid. I didn't repeat the "be proud" part at home. I did drop the news of my presidential timber.

My mother said, Why would Mrs. Shaw say that to you? She said it quickly, in her flat, adult voice, and I instantly knew that she was taking this way too seriously. As if I'd declared my candidacy and started to raise funds already, she said, Are you sure you'd like the job of president? She pulled the plug on the mangle—a sort of freestanding pasta press that she used to iron all of our bedsheets once a week. Mangling made her head sweat, and it didn't often bring out the best in her personality. She explained that being president was not all spelling bees and multiplication tables, at which I excelled, she admitted. It was obvious she was not jumping on Mrs. Shaw's bandwagon. After she recited the president's daily duties, she said, Don't you think someone like your brother Gerard would make a better president?

Mrs. Shaw was my first lay teacher, so it made sense that we were both prone to exaggerating.

After dinner, we all knelt down in the parlor on the thick red Oriental carpet donated by a local rug-store owner, another of my father's best friends. We said the Rosary facing a painting of Jesus over the fireplace. He was ripping his own bloody Sacred Heart out of his chest. It was shining and tattooed with a cross. Above the piano, my father smiled a benign black-and-white smile from his perch above the color high-school graduation photos of the older kids. When I'd entered first grade, my brother Joe had pointed out that nobody else would be at home by the time a picture of me made it onto that wall.

By the time we had finished the Rosary, I completely doubted I was missing any teeth, so I persuaded Joe to check my mouth. He made me sit on the toilet in the half-bath under the stairs, and he used a flashlight and a clean Popsicle stick. He said it was pretty clear that I'd lost one tooth, and then he added, "at most." That stung. He was already famous for having some of the worst teeth in the family, and I told him so. We started wrestling then. My mother came in and told me she wanted to speak to me in the kitchen. She must've spotted Joe's dentistry kit, because she mentioned that it was time for another visit to Dr. F.

I hadn't yet learned to fear the dentist. I did know it was my right as a third-grader to walk from school to his North Street office without supervision, which my mother confirmed. She told me again she wanted to see me in the kitchen.

I liked Dr. F., and I knew that his credentials were impeccable. He had all the latest equipment. He had eight kids, and they were in our parish. And after my father died, Dr. F. never charged any of the Downings for his professional services, which was something we let him do to demonstrate Christian charity. He was the best dentist in Berkshire County and better than the dentists in Boston. If his name came up at dinner at our house, you'd discover that a seat in Dr. F.'s office was more coveted than box seats at Tanglewood. When any of my brothers and sisters had a dental emergency at camp or college, the previous work done by Dr. F. was admired and even envied by his peers.

My father had dedicated the last years of his short life to promoting tourism and industrial development in the Berkshires. After he died, my siblings and my mother and I carried on his work amongst ourselves, selling to each other claims of singularity and excellence. When I met people who chose other dentists—and in a town of 50,000, some did—I didn't criticize them, for the same reason we didn't criticize Protestants.

In the kitchen, all evidence of dinner had been wiped up and put away. My mother was seated at the oval table with her back to the stainless steel sink. She asked me how many teeth I had swallowed.

I knew I'd lost two teeth. I knew she didn't believe me. I knew there'd be trouble if I changed my mind right in front of her. I said, Two. It had become a preposterous lie.

Sometimes my mother seemed to be making an effort not to look disappointed, and I felt bad because she already had too much work to do. She had dark curly hair and dark eyes. I could tell she was pressing her tongue against the back of her front teeth. She had a lot of ways of showing you she was not showing you her emotions.

I said, You can ask Joey T., and told her I'd even written him a note about it.

She said she didn't have to ask Joey T. or read any notes.

Well, you can, I said, though I knew that note was long gone, like the bad boy's penmanship homework that supposedly went over the bridge. Instead of developing a new sympathy for the bad boy, I took this as an opportunity to deepen my hate for him. If he hadn't lied about his homework to Sister Jeanne Arthur—a story I'd naturally retold at dinner more than once—I'd have stood a decent chance of selling my mother the story of my own truly lost note.

I didn't say anything else. My mother didn't say anything else. She handed me two quarters. I ended up giving one of them to the Missions, a contribution Mrs. Shaw recorded under the *Boys* column on the blackboard and Joey T. later recorded as a waste of five perfectly good packs of Sweet Tarts. I never tried to collect on another tooth.

I did walk down North Street alone about a week later. The five or six blocks from my school on Melville Street to Dr. F.'s office constituted half of Pittsfield's commercial downtown. Only a few of the storefronts meant anything to me. I really didn't do a lot of shopping, except to buy cigarettes for Roberta. She was eighteen years older than I was, and besides reminding each other that she was at her senior prom when I was born, we didn't have much to talk about. Luckily, she loved to smoke. After she graduated from college and started teaching at a junior high in Pittsfield, Roberta was too busy to buy her own cigarettes, so she took to writing notes to shopkeepers within biking distance of our home. She'd give me the notes with a dollar for two packs of extra-long filter tips. She always said *Keep the change* in a way that made you notice her lipstick, which mostly ended up on her cigarette butts. This was the sort of behavior that got Roberta identified with my father's older sisters, whom we learned to love and judge harshly for their wild ways.

Most of my older brothers and sisters worked part-time during the school year in department stores and jewelry shops on North Street owned by men who had known and loved my father. When we did have to buy anything, we always went to a store owned by a friend of the family. This was just good manners, because they usually wanted to offer us discounts. England Brothers department store was our hometown Macy's, and though the England brothers never came to our home, even my sister who worked in their wrapping department was on a first-name basis with them. I'd never been introduced to Ben or Dan England, and I suppose I resented the exclusion and thus decided I liked shopping at Besse-Clarke better. There, men you were supposed to recognize as famous former high-school athletes sold us our school uniforms and gym clothes every August.

Besse-Clarke was almost directly across the street from The Bridge, a notorious hangout. It was exactly two blocks west of the identical bridge on which Joey T. and I stood every day after school. On North Street, the concrete rail seemed to be there to keep drunks from falling off The Bridge to the railroad tracks below. Typically, at least four or five guys were leaning on that wall with brown bags of beer purchased at the nearby Pipe and Tobacco shop, which sold dirty magazines, rolling papers, Narragansett and Schlitz singles to the regulars, and pipe cleaners to boys like Joey and me when we were feeling brave enough to lie and say we needed them for a school project.

I could've avoided The Bridge by crossing one more block on the Besse-Clarke side, but the denizens of The Bridge were magnetic. I often tried to catch the gaze of one of them to see what he'd make of me. As a very young child, I'd cooked up a recurring nightmare featuring those scary guys, and by third grade I'd turned it into a wild fantasy that one of the booziest guys might lunge toward me, grab me by my blue school tie, and dangle me over the tracks and demand something from me. I'd have given them whatever they wanted. They were the nearest thing to pirates Pittsfield had to offer, and most of them were decades ahead of the fashion curve with their shaved pates and stubbly unshaved cheeks and chins.

It was not okay to admire them, of course. They were uneducated dropouts. They were there to teach us the value of a college education, but my mother was something of a Zen master when it came to imparting such moral lessons. She didn't criticize the bums, and she wouldn't tolerate any bad remarks about them. Instead, after we'd been tape-measured for a new uniform of polyester blue slacks and short-sleeved white shirts at Besse-Clarke, she'd point to The Bridge and say, They started out just like you.

I was of no interest to the malingerers, but something about my gums really caught Dr. F.'s fancy that day. I was pleased. I'd tried to impress him with my two-teeth-in-one-lunch story when I climbed into the chair, but he just harrumphed and said I should know better. He was a big man with wiry steel-gray hair on his head and arms, and whenever I didn't open wide enough, he'd just insert his thumb and forefinger into my mouth and crack open my jaw another few inches. He'd taught me to raise my hand whenever he did something that hurt, but the first and only time I'd used the distress signal he had very politely asked me to try to keep my hand out of his face while he was working.

He took a lot of X-rays that day, and he reminded his assistant they were not cheap, which I understood as a reprimand about her rolling her eyes whenever he handed her another slide from my mouth, as if she had better things to do. Then he announced he was going to drill a cavity even though it was in a baby tooth.

I'd heard a lot about the drill, and it was often screaming in my brother Joe's mouth while I read the women's magazines in the waiting room, but I honestly believed Dr. F. would never turn it on me. He'd already packed me with cotton and hung a hose from my lower lip, so he probably didn't hear my offer to just swallow the infected tooth. He said I had a molar growing under my jawbone. He was a man of few words, so I was not expecting anything else by way of explanation. Then he said, Sideways, and he sounded disgusted. You're going to need an operation someday, he said. He also made it clear he wanted no part of the surgery. He intended to patch up the temporary molar and leave the whole mess to someone else.

If you can't move your lips or your tongue, you really can't pronounce the letters *n* and *v*, so I said, "hohocay" about twenty times until he nodded and said, Novocain? I'd never had it, and neither had Joe, but we knew kids who got it from their second-rate dentists when they had a loose tooth. I also had to pee, but nothing bugged Dr. F. more than pee breaks, so I figured I'd settle for the Novocain pill.

He took a step away from me and said, Do you really want your mother to have to pay an extra seven dollars for Novocain? For a baby tooth? He also produced a huge, chrome hypodermic needle with pistol grips, implying that the Novocain was a bitter pill.

I took a pee break, and he wasn't pleased.

Initially, I was humiliated. No one had ever come so close to accusing me of being unable to afford something in the normal range of things a kid might need. Then I was a little indignant. After all the good press he'd gotten around my house, how could he possibly make me pay for something he already had in stock? Then it got worse. I realized that either Dr. F. was lying about charging my mother for the shot, or my mother was prone to exaggerating about his generosity. Were we so poor that we couldn't afford Novocain and bought-new corduroys? Or had we actually paid for that Oriental carpet in our living room? Just how popular had my father been?

Dr. F. repacked my mouth. He decided I didn't want the Novocain. He was right. I was ashamed I'd asked for it. While he drilled, I held on to the arms of the chair and practiced my multiplication tables. Thirteen baby teeth times twenty-five cents plus the two disputed swallowed teeth times twenty-five cents made three dollars and seventy-five cents. My total take from the tooth fairy wasn't enough for one shot of Novocain, and that was before the Missions got their cut.

By the time I was eighteen, I had graduated from basic dentistry to the care of an orthodontist, but instead of tackling the sideways molar, he'd diagnosed an alignment problem and tried to sell me braces at regular retail rates. My mother bargained him down to a retainer, and after a few visits it was obvious that he was not equal to the task of correcting my underbite. My mother was not surprised, as I'd inherited that from her side of the family. I was sent back to Dr. F., who threw up his hands and sent me to an oral surgeon, a friend of his who had full charge-account privileges with the insurance companies. He knocked me out with anesthesia and extracted my sideways molar. While he was in there, he did some shopping for his friend and plucked an incisor that had always bugged Dr. F.

When I graduated from high school, I was missing a couple of teeth and I had an acceptance letter from Harvard—the same ticket out of town my brother Joe had cashed in two years earlier, despite my mother's profound objections to his choice of a secular college, and lectures from our brothers and sisters about the academic superiority of the Catholic colleges they'd attended. Near the end of that summer, my mother asked me to go for a ride with her. She was the least offhand person I knew at the time, so I figured she had something on her mind that would be easier to say if we weren't looking at each other directly.

We drove in silence from our house to Park Square and right past Dr. F.'s office, and then my mother pulled a U-turn in the new station wagon and parked in front of Besse-Clarke. And still neither of us said anything. We were almost equals by then in our ability not to express a normal human response to things like sudden U-turns or scalding hot water in the dishpan or an imminent leave-taking. I was not unimpressed by my mother's correct estimation of the turning radius of the Oldsmobile, but I kept my tongue against the back of my teeth instead of smiling. She turned her face away from mine and stared at The Bridge. I figured I knew what she was going to say.

She didn't say anything. My mother surprised me by leading me into a pet store. We'd had one dog, and he'd died not long after my father. We'd never replaced either of them. I pitied people who kept pets, as I pitied people who planted showy, ornamental flower gardens. They were squandering time and money doing exactly what we weren't doing: They were trying to patch up the holes in their hearts. Joe, on the other hand, tried for years to get permission to keep just about every kind of rodent that wouldn't kill you if it got loose, but he never prevailed.

My mother said hello to the bald, mustachioed man behind the counter. He was wearing a green smock, as if maybe he also worked part-time as Dr. F.'s dental hygienist. My mother tapped on a few of the cages and smiled sadly when the tiny cats and dogs scurried through the wood shavings to lick her finger. There were a lot of birds that didn't belong in the Berkshires complaining in cages in the back of the store. I pretended I might buy a painted ceramic dog-food bowl. None of us said anything until my mother said, "Thank you very much," and led me back to the car.

There were two guys seated on the sidewalk across the street, their backs against the wall of The Bridge, rolling joints. My mother said I could drive, which always pleased me and her, I think, though you couldn't have proved it. Just before The Bridge dropped out of my rear-view mirror, my mother said, That man I said hello to in the pet store? He graduated from Harvard.

4. Negative Capability

When my brother Joe was in sixth grade, he started wearing ankle weights. He said they were designed to improve your basketball skills. We were both on the St. Teresa's team in the Catholic Youth Center's parish league. I sat on the bench and Joe played, and our team usually lost. I was in fourth grade. This was the year St. Mary's parish started using their second string by the middle of the first half in games against us. Kids my age were able to hold a lead against kids Joe's age. Our coach, Mr. C., said it was bad sportsmanship. Joe said St. Mary's was just breaking our spirits, and he admired them for it.

Joe didn't think Mr. C. had the right killer instincts and blamed him for a lot of our losses. He also blamed a couple on the coach's son David, who was Joe's age and just as skinny but had the liability of often losing his glasses and seeing a blur at important moments, like when shooting and passing. David was Joe's friend and our best scorer, but sport bands didn't work on his head, for some reason. Joe said if he had a head with a problem like that, he'd use Red Cross adhesive tape, which held firm to eyeglasses but could be removed without ripping your hair out. I'm sure he suggested this to Coach C. Joe was known for making helpful suggestions in the locker room after we lost games. He also started wearing his ankle weights to bed while he listened to staticky broadcasts of Weber State college basketball games on a Rocky Mountain radio station he could pick up after the local Berkshire stations went off the air.

Joe was devoted to basketball. He practiced his layups and bank shots for an hour every day, using the backboard and hoop posted above our tarred-over carport. He wore terrycloth sweatbands on his head and both wrists. For his birthday, he asked for tube socks and extra lead bars for his ankle weights. Whenever he was waiting for me at the barbershop or Dr. F.'s, he'd snag all the free trial-subscription offers for basketball magazines. He used them methodically, so he appeared to be a regular subscriber and became eligible for all the superstar posters they gave away free to paying customers.

Joe figured out how to mount the posters of Wilt Chamberlain and John Havlicek with masking tape on flattened cardboard boxes he collected from the A&P, and he suspended them from the wooden ceiling molding with string all around his half of our bedroom. We weren't allowed to nail into the wall, except for crucifixes over our beds and a small foot-square mirror for combing our hair in the mornings, which was always off-kilter, like the parts in our hair, because we stuffed the blessed palms from Palm Sunday behind the mirror. Joe's ability to invent a poster gallery without breaking any rules or wall plaster caught everyone off guard. At dinner, we discussed how this was a prime example of Joe's bad habit of doing things according to the letter of the law.

My mother must have complained privately to one of the older kids, because somebody taped up four felt banners on my side of the bedroom—two greenish ones from the Ice Capades and two red ones from the Ice Follies from years before I was born. I really didn't know if the banners were supposed to be revenge against Joe, home decor, or just proof that the older kids had attended big-ticket sporting events in person when our father was alive. Joe said ice shows weren't real sports, which annoyed me because I had no other memorabilia. After a bitter argument, I threatened to tell my mother his posters were giving me trouble sleeping. Then Joe said maybe he would consider the Capades a semipro sports event, but definitely not the Follies.

In sixth grade, Joe was still constantly acting surprised that our seven older brothers and sisters were no more interested in his basketball career than they were in our piano lessons or paper route. He used to ask me if I'd noticed that neither of our brothers ever wanted to play one-on-one or coach you in calisthenics. Usually he would ask while he was flat on his back and sweating. I was supposed to be timing his leg raises, but I would lose count and he'd get frustrated and warn me that I was showing signs of lacking the discipline to be a sports star. He'd be lying on his back with his ankle-weighted legs in the air. Despite all we'd heard about our brother Jack—he was practically world famous in our family for being a natural athlete—Joe would darkly add, Name one Downing who ever got a varsity letter.

I'd say Jack, in any sport he tried. And maybe Peg, I'd guess, in basketball and softball and swimming. I knew Joe wouldn't count a girl, but she was my next-best bet because she was four inches taller than Gerard, and stronger and faster. She also had much better natural aim with balls and rocks. I would add Gerard, in debating.

Usually Joe's legs would be shaking in midair by then, and he'd be panting when he'd say, That's why they all have letter sweaters and hero jackets, I suppose.

That *I suppose* was cynical, according to my mother, and I didn't like it from Joe any more than she did, so I'd estimate his legs had been in the air for only 24 seconds, or something way below his record. Even though he knew I was lying, he'd keep going until his head started to vibrate. I'd spend the rest of the day scouring everybody's closets and bureau drawers for evidence of athletic prowess to prove Joe wrong, until a housecoat with snaps or a pair of particularly complicated slingback shoes with buckles caught my eye.

Unlike Joe, I was not eager to have my older brothers coach me. When I was eight, a new kid named Danny moved onto our street and tried to make friends with me. I was interested in him because he was new, and he was my size, and he kept his Red Sox jacket zippered up to his chin, even if you invited him indoors, because he'd always sneaked out of the house wearing his pajama tops instead of a proper shirt. Also, he owned a jump rope, which I coveted. In my house, only the girls got those.

One day, Danny and I got into a fight about something—my father was dead and his father was in Arizona, and figuring out who was worse off occasioned a lot of fights. Neither Danny nor I had ever landed a blow. We both twirled our arms like propellers and threatened to move closer, and then we'd get tired and call it even. But this time, Gerard, who was too old to be playing with us, came out of the house and sat on one of the swings in the backyard and watched our fight. He called us both sissies and yelled, Stop slapping the air. Make a fist.

I did, and Danny stopped whirring and said, I dare you, and he put his hands on his hips and bent toward me. Maybe he doubledared me.

Gerard said, Punch him.

I punched Danny in the head, and he fell down crying. I felt like crying, too, but Gerard said, He took a dive, which I didn't understand, so I ran away. My hand hurt, but I wouldn't look at it. I had a terrible feeling that part of Danny's skull and some of his hair was stuck to my knuckles. That night, I worried that Danny would call the cops or my mother, but he didn't. He came over the next day with his jacket zippered up and said, I'm sorry.

I wanted to tell him that I liked his jacket, but I was too ashamed to say anything.

Danny said, I'm not a sissy, though.

I said, Neither am I.

And after that we couldn't figure out how to be friends. Danny and his mother moved away a few months later. I never had another fistfight. Nobody ever punched me in the head. I did learn how to tie old window cords together to make a jump rope, and my brother Gerard said it was okay as long as I told everybody I was training to become a boxer.

Joe was never accused of being a sissy. The problem with Joe was that he wanted to become good at things. This went against the idea that members of our family could "wing it" in most situations that other people had to prepare for. We used our God-given talents for winging it and devoted practice time to getting better at saving our souls.

Our daily prayer routine was rigorous—morning prayers by yourself on your knees beside your bed; grace before meals; Mass on Sundays, sometimes followed by nighttime Benediction services; Mass on holy

days, brothers' and sisters' birthdays, every morning in Lent, all during the month of May to honor Mary, every First Friday of the Month
to beef up your plenary indulgence account, and First Saturdays as
well—though I suspected early on that this was my mother's personal
innovation, sort of like the coach who makes you do *fingertip* push-
ups; ejaculations like "Jesus Save Me" or "Blessed be Mary, Mother of
God" for a couple of minutes, at least, on the way to and from school
every day, and when you were bored and not allowed to work ahead
in class; a sign of the cross and another ejaculation or two whenever
you heard an ambulance or fire-truck siren; the Rosary after dinner "as
a family"; night prayers by your bed, occasionally with a monitor at
your door to make sure you weren't skipping essential beseechments
and litanies; and once you were in bed, you received a final dousing
with Holy Water—Gatorade for sleeping spiritual athletes—from the
wall-mounted font in the upstairs hall. There was also a Holy Water
dispenser by the back door, in the kitchen, which Joe dipped into every
time he left the house.

This stuff was just normal. But practicing or training or even quitting
smoking for sports or musical instruments meant you were missing the
whole point of being one of the Downings. Joe was always in danger
of becoming a scrupulous fanatic with the wrong priorities, and one of
the best things the older kids could do for him was to try to get him to
lighten up with jokes about his training regimens.

Joe often tried to convince me that we were at a disadvantage because
our dead father was not able to teach us anything useful, but I mostly
liked things the way they were. Unlike Joe or our older brothers, and
like most of my sisters, I was a natural swimmer. Every summer, about
a week after swimming lessons ended at Pontoosuc Lake, I would enter
a few events in the Berkshire County Swimming Championships and
come in fifth or sixth. In fourth grade, these races were moved from the
lake to a new private outdoor pool, but I was still allowed to enter.

By then, my sister Elaine had finished her missionary work in Oklahoma. She was living at home and working as a laboratory technician
at St. Luke's Hospital. She wasn't a nurse, but she had natural talents
in the field, so she was allowed to take my blood at home one night.

Maybe I was sick and we were getting a discount on the blood work. More likely, my mother thought Elaine needed practice to keep her new job. I know that Joe was in his bed and told not to watch. He'd seen Elaine practicing with needles on oranges around the house, so he didn't think I had anything to worry about.

I asked if it would hurt.

Elaine said, You'll feel a pinprick.

My mother said, You won't feel anything.

Elaine adjusted the desk lamp so it spotlighted my veins and I couldn't see her face. She rubbed a cotton ball on my arm and said I should look at the Ice Capades banners. She had a soft voice that made you think she would not end up hurting you.

My mother said, When you're nervous, Elaine, you make the patient nervous.

She didn't have a nursing degree, either, but she was always very informed about professional standards.

Elaine said, He has big veins.

My mother said, He's a real Martin, which was her maiden name. I was pleased. The kids who were more like my father's relatives had practically no veins.

Elaine jabbed my arm.

I watched the needle draw out brown sludge, and I asked about the unusual color. I didn't want her to feel bad, but I thought she should know she'd probably tapped into the wrong system.

Elaine said, Blood isn't red.

I looked to my mother.

She said, That's enough. He's just a child.

This made me think it was just for practice.

I never found out what they did with my blood. After they were gone and the room was dark, Joe said, How'd it go?

Okay, I said.

He said, I suppose no one's ever heard of the school nurse around here.

I especially trusted Elaine because she was the best of the natural swimmers in my family. That summer, she and my mother surprised me by coming to watch me swim in the county championships. I took this as an apology. It was common knowledge that nobody in the family had to attend sporting events for Joe and me.

As usual, I had trained for the big meet by practicing my racing dives for a couple of days and asking some kids at the lake if they knew what time we had to be at the pool. In between my events, when other kids were eating dry Jell-O or taking cold showers, I cheered for kids I knew, especially Barbara Jean. Barbara Jean's grades and conduct marks were as good as mine from first grade through fourth at Notre Dame grammar school. She was also able to win almost every swimming race she entered. She wore a red-white-and-blue–striped tank suit, like Olympic swimmers, and by fourth grade, no one had beaten her in anything but breaststroke. It was just good luck that breaststroke was my best stroke, so swimming did not interfere with my crush on Barbara Jean.

There were usually between ten and thirty kids entered in every event, but they put all the kids they thought had a real chance in the last heat. I'd finished sixth or seventh in a couple of events before my mother and Elaine showed up, and then I had to swim the breaststroke. I dove in, and after the splashing died down and I'd taken a couple of strokes, I counted how many kids were ahead of me, which cost me a couple of seconds. But I had to keep my head above water for a while to make sure I'd counted everyone. My goal was not to let any more kids pass me. This was my idea of a competitive strategy.

When I finally finished counting, I looked to the end of my lane and saw my sister Elaine. She was small and compact, with short dark hair, and her eyes were almost almonds, making her pretty in a peaceful, Eskimo way. She was the quietest of all my sisters. When I saw her, though, Elaine was bent over at the waist, and she was holding her hair off her face with one hand and using her other hand to make a cup around her mouth. I'd never seen anything like it. I kept my head up for a couple of strokes just to hear what she was saying, and I realized she was screaming at me—Put your head down! Pull! Pull!

I did. I thought Elaine might get in trouble. I'd seen other kids' parents and older brothers doing this, and my family had explained it was a low-grade form of cheating. Pull harder, Elaine shouted, correctly guessing I wouldn't remember to keep it up. You're in fifth place, she yelled, which was really a surprise, unless I'd miscounted.

As I hit the turning wall, Elaine really let me have it. YOU HAVE TO PULL HARDER. MICHAEL! PULL ON EVERY STROKE. FASTER!

I'd never been so excited in my entire life. No one had ever cheered out loud for me. It was a big help. I passed one kid, and Elaine kept yelling, Pull! whenever I popped my head up for a breath of air. I pulled even with two other kids, and I felt my hands slam against the wall. I came in third or second. I don't remember.

I do remember that an embarrassingly handsome college guy wearing a white-and-green–striped bathing suit and a stopwatch and nothing else told me I was invited to join the county team for a championship meet in Springfield, Massachusetts. His name was Donny. Donny told me that the kid who'd won my event was turning thirteen in a couple of days, and he needed an eleven-year-old "who can really turn it on in the last lap." Donny had a perfectly even all-over tan. He was reading across columns on a stack of papers he had attached to a silver clipboard. I was watching how the sun gave his reddish brown hair highlights. Donny also thought I could drop my time with better starts and turns.

I was eager to sign on for the whole Donny program. It was the first swimming medal I'd ever won, and though I would go on to win more medals and a few trophies and a varsity letter, I knew right then that I was in danger of becoming a fanatic with the wrong priorities.

The story of my surprising performance was told often, to my delight, even though my medal was not the point. Elaine's performance was rated as much more surprising. She completely forgot where she was, my mother would say. It was a public embarrassment, but we laughed it off, knowing it would never happen again. I came to understand that it was perfectly okay to get caught up in the excitement of something pointless like a swimming race while it was going on. This was part of our natural competitiveness, which was fierce but fleeting. No one in the family attended my races after that. I learned to lie to other swimmers and myself about how much I practiced between meets so my victories could always be the result of my natural abilities and my losses could be chalked up to my well-rounded character and coming from a family with good priorities.

The next summer, Joe convinced my mother to let him go to the Catholic Youth Center's basketball camp for two weeks instead of the regular CYC day camp we'd attended for a couple of years. She sent me along, too, and I blamed Joe for robbing me of the pleasures of adding to my collection of plaster molds of the Holy Family's Flight into Egypt and squandering whole afternoons in the woods with boys from St. Mary's and St. Mark's parishes, who shared their cigarettes and clove gum if you agreed to pee with them on piles of pine needles and bark they set fire to when we were supposed to be capturing a flag. In truth, Joe had argued for keeping me in the regular day camp. He said I was a swimmer, and he was the basketball player. This distinction was lost on my mother.

Joe and David C. and a couple of other skinny sixth-graders with acne practiced lay-ups and passing plays while the shorter kids I liked complained about the Gatorade being warm and begged to go swimming. For a couple of days, the counselors tried to make us run laps in the sun for being lazy, but finally a fat kid threw up and aimed it onto the court, so they dismissed the rest of us most afternoons. All we had to do was take fifty foul shots every day.

It humiliated Joe that I'd sometimes shoot underhand, and he mentioned it every day when we were walking to catch the bus.

I said I was bored.

He said it was bad for his reputation.

I said I didn't complain about the crazy way he wagged his head when he swam the crawl.

He said how would I feel if he used the dog paddle during free swim?

I started shooting normal foul shots.

In the middle of the second week of basketball camp, an old man I'd never seen before read out ten names, including mine, and said we'd be taking even more foul shots every day. The counselors claimed he was a well-known coach. He had white hair and clip-on sunglasses, like a cop. I figured he was a public school principal they'd hired to work with the discipline problems. I tried explaining to him that I was a natural defense player who never needed to shoot the ball, and he said

I should ask at home for high-top sneakers. He was wearing brown loafers and white tube socks and plaid Bermuda shorts. No one in my family ever needed high-tops or nylon-mesh jerseys or even jock straps until we got to high school.

Out of the blue, the old man blew his whistle and announced that all the foul shots had been part of a contest, and we had the ten best records in camp, and the winner would "take home a trophy." There was only one other kid my age in the final ten, and I knew he had a real chance of winning. His name was Jimmy M., and his father ran the CYC. Jimmy was my size but looked tougher and was not as good a student. I told him I would root for him. He said he would root for himself first and for me second. This was normal for a public school kid, so I didn't take it as an insult.

Joe didn't mention anything about the contest, except to say he was glad he'd have more time to practice zone defenses. And he said he didn't spend much time at the line because he was able to pivot around the defense.

I was surprised to find out I was naturally good at foul shots. During the regular season on the indoor court at the CYC, Coach C. had noticed that a lot of my practice foul shots were hitting the net and sailing out into the vending machine area. He asked me if I thought I could try to hit the backboard once in a while, so team members wouldn't have to leave the gymnasium so often. Until then, I had thought it was illegal to use the backboard on purpose from the foul line.

Whenever I wasn't sure about rules, I didn't ask questions that would make strangers think they were being forced to do my dead father's work for him. Instead, I made up very strict rules that most human beings couldn't tolerate, and I figured they would keep me and my father's reputation safe.

It was relatively easy to hit the backboard compared with shooting the ball right through the hoop, and more often than not, the ball went in. This happened repeatedly during the second week of camp. By Thursday, there was a rumor that I was near the lead. Jimmy M. said he was ahead of me with one tall kid, and he privately showed me a scorecard he'd been keeping for all two weeks. It was written with different color inks for each of the contestants. It made me hope he'd win. He cared about basketball the way Joe did.

On Friday, the coach with the clip-ons announced a shoot-off between me and Jimmy. We had to take turns for a total of twenty shots, five at a time. Jimmy's father stood with the counselors and watched us. It was another time when having a dead father was an advantage, because there was nobody around to be disappointed or to give you some last-minute advice that cramped your style. Jimmy blessed himself before every shot. I considered this a disrespectful use of praying and just said silent ejaculations, not for me but for the souls in purgatory. I won the contest, and after we got our awards, I immediately told Jimmy it was not important. Jimmy was crying, but only from his eyes. He wasn't making any sounds. I told him he was way better at basketball than I was, and I didn't even care about foul shooting. At the time I said it, I was holding the trophy.

Joe told everyone at dinner about my triumph. He tried to make it sound more important than it was, though, so instead of dwelling on the specifics, we discussed how all of the Downings had great aim and could beat other people at horseshoes. I stuck the trophy in a box in my bedroom closet with my swimming medals.

After that, Joe attended all of my CYC basketball games, even when he was a freshman in high school. I was a starting guard for St. Teresa's by then, though the only points I ever contributed came at the foul line. Even when I had a clear shot, I'd usually look to pass to Jimmy M. or my best friend, Joey T., who was always happy to plow into all the kids standing around in the key and shoot over anyone who was left standing. Coach C. said I was a great team player. I just didn't want to be the one who missed.

Even when I was in seventh grade, Joe still occasionally tried to get me to practice leg lifts or to play one-on-one, but by then I was allowed to complain right in front of him about taking things too seriously. St. Teresa's won the CYC league championship that year. Julius Erving was playing for the University of Massachusetts, and he came and gave us our hero jackets and the team trophy, and he was supposed to give us a speech, too. Instead, his eyes rolled back into his head and he fainted and fell off the fake stage they'd set up in the CYC gym. The team was in the front row, so we were able to say we'd saved Julius Erving's professional basketball career by breaking his fall.

I knew about Julius Erving only from the posters Joe had hung up on his half of the bedroom. He kept them up until his sophomore year. He'd made the junior varsity team as a freshman in high school, and I went to two of his games at the Boys' Club. He got injured trying out the next year, and when it was clear he wasn't going to make the varsity team, he didn't ever play organized sports again. No one at home encouraged him to play a second year of junior varsity. No one asked why he'd stopped wearing ankle weights. He started to devote more and more of his time to politics and religious activities. Everyone thought it was normal for him to quit basketball.

Years later, Joe told me I was the only one in the family who ever saw him play high school ball. I remember being in the bleachers. The arena was really ten times bigger than the CYC, and the court was far away and shiny. I wanted Joe to do well, and I probably clapped when he did, but I'm sure I didn't stand up and yell his name. If you'd seen me, I would've looked like a normal fan, not a fanatic. What you couldn't have seen, though, was that I was also teaching Joe not to take a junior varsity basketball game so seriously.

5. Principles of Accounting

I ran into a serious financial problem in fifth grade. This was not the normal kind you had to expect at the end of every month if you were forced to have a paper route. With some people paying weekly and a bunch of others paying monthly, plus unpredictable tips, there was bound to be a lot of confusion when you had to walk up to the *Berkshire Eagle* headquarters and pay them what they claimed you owed.

The paper route was my brother Joe's brilliant idea. We got paid allowances every week, but Joe had noticed that we were always broke after spending a quarter for milk at school and putting the other quarter in the Sunday collection.

I had a couple of ways of making money that were better than a paper route, but one of the biggest causes of wrestling matches between Joe and me was his tendency to do exactly what we were ordered to do and his tendency to try to force me to go along with him, so I didn't suggest my best solution, which was shortchanging the Church. I used a nickel instead of a quarter most weeks in my Sunday envelope to spare me twenty cents for hot balls and cheese twirls. If I had told this to Joe, he probably would've said it was a matter for Confession. There'd be no use arguing with him. He could easily force me to confess things by threatening to tell the priest he was in a sticky position on account of knowing about my sinful ways and not being able to stop me.

Instead, I suggested that Joe could just ask for a bigger allowance. This seemed to me a doubly good idea because my best chance of ever getting a raise would be arguing with my mother about equal rights after she started paying Joe extra money. But Joe used this suggestion as a perfect opportunity to deliver his favorite lecture, the one about our responsibility for being sons of a mother who was a permanent widow with no job. I think this was the time he also accused me of being prone to bribery.

Joe never actually invited me to become his newspaper partner. I'm sure no family members discussed the topic with him, or he would have begged them to leave me out of it. He was shocked when my mother finally gave him permission to become a paperboy, and he was really shocked by her one condition: He had to split his paper route with me.

Joe was constantly surprised by this sort of stuff, which even I could see coming. Maybe my mother wanted Joe to be a good influence on me because I was prone to things like TV and slouchy posture as an altar boy. Maybe she just wanted time alone and she learned to use the stones Joe was always handing her to temporarily kill two birds. Or maybe she didn't like Joe's way of taking her impossible moral demands so seriously, and I was her way of getting back at him. All I know is that Joe had recently been forced to take me with him to join the Boy Scouts. After a couple of troop meetings at the parish hall, Joe's goal was to make Eagle Scout. My goal was to avoid the jamborees where you had to sleep in tents, eat food cooked by kids, and prove you could use a compass just to get permission to go find a private place to pee. Over the next few years, Joe wasted a lot of his time trying to teach me to treat my uniform with respect. I wasted a lot more of his time sabotaging his attempts to earn merit badges.

It took Joe a couple of months to convince my mother to let him become a paperboy. She didn't instantly go for ideas that weren't originally her idea. That gave me time to talk to some kids my age who had paperboys for brothers.

I didn't like what I heard.

First of all, you had to do it every afternoon around four o'clock, which cut into exactly the time when most kids had finished their homework and were allowed to go bike riding before supper. Plus, you couldn't quit during the summer, so forget sleepover camps. And every

Saturday, the *Berkshire Eagle* became a morning newspaper, ruining the one chance I had to control the TV.

A girl in my class named Lori was the first one to mention the special bag and how heavy it was. Lori was shy by reputation, but she was getting to be well known for being pretty because of her dirty-blond bangs and see-through blue eyes. She had barely ever talked to me before, not counting polite smiling when we happened to notice we were accidentally standing right next to each other.

Lori said, My brother has a paper route. You could try on his bag someday.

I really didn't know what she expected me to say back to her. I didn't want to tell her, but just about every kid I knew had been trying since first grade to invent ways to get Lori to kiss him.

After a while with neither of us saying anything, Lori mentioned I could come to her house after school if I felt like it. This was impossible to answer. I knew if I did go to her house, we'd end up making out like crazy.

I waited a week or so, and then I followed Lori most of the way home from a safe distance, using parked cars and convenient trees like a spy. A couple of times, I noticed Lori looking back, but she didn't wave or anything, so I didn't reveal my location to her. Finally, half a block from her house, she just dropped her book bag and started tying her shoes. This was already known as a famous trick for looking casual, but Lori could pull it off. I crossed the street so I could keep heading in her direction and then suddenly just happen to notice her squatting on the opposite corner.

I probably yelled something like, Hi, Lori. When I crossed back to her side, to take the pressure off, I added, It's me. Mike.

She said, I know your name. Like a lot of shy kids, Lori didn't always know how to keep up her end of the conversation.

I politely ignored her and asked her something about church. This was a topic we had in common, and she probably had noticed I was an altar boy, and her brother was an altar boy, and by putting two and two together, she could avoid forcing me to bring up her offer about trying out her brother's newspaper bag. Instead, she looked at her shoes. They were known as bucks, and in the sun I couldn't tell if hers were

white and black or white and navy blue, but they reminded me of shoes
you'd expect to see on a stylish nurse. Her laces were perfectly even
bows. Suddenly, she looked right at me with both of her eyes. I knew
where this was going.

But out of the blue, Lori said, Our families both know each other.

This was true, and it got truer the more I thought about it. Most of
my best adventures ended exactly this way, with me thinking about my
family. I mean, all along, I knew Lori's last name, and I knew she had
the same last name as her older brother and sisters, and I knew they all
had the same last name as the tall guy who was one of the Boy Scout
troop leaders, and I knew he was the father of the family I knew with
that last name, but until that moment I had not actually drawn the
lines connecting all of those dots. Fathers rarely figured in my imagination of other kids' lives. I knew most kids had fathers, and I'd even
met a couple of them, but they didn't make a big impression on me. I
definitely never imagined fathers as normal family members who could
stay over for meals and ask what grades their kids got in school and
other private business, like who they might've kissed. Plus, I remembered just then that Lori's father was half-bald, and there was always
something extra risky about talking to a man when you knew that he
knew that you could obviously see his bald head and neither of you
dared to mention it.

To escape, I used Lori's shyness to my advantage by just basically
walking in the general direction of my house instead of heading toward
hers. She didn't say anything. The last time I looked back at her, we
smiled in the same way we did whenever we bumped into each other at
school or church. It was like we were both bald and not admitting it.

I think this was the first time it occurred to me that it might be fun to
kiss total strangers. I suppose this moment figures in the peculiar weft
and warp that distinguished my later attempts to knit together intimacy and anonymity. I know I would have done a lot more to under-
mine Joe's paper-route proposal if I'd followed Lori into her house
and tried on her brother's regulation newspaper bag that day. The bag
we were given by the *Eagle* fit Joe just fine, and for the first couple of
months he refused to let me wear it. This was okay by me. I'd tried on
that bag in private and stuffed some of our old newspapers into it for

practice, and when I tried to walk anywhere, the bag kept cutting me off at the knees.

For the first few months, Joe forced me to take all the jobs of "junior partner." After we picked up our newspapers on a street corner two blocks from our house, Joe would force me to hold up the wire banded around the bundle while he snipped it with wire cutters. I was only allowed to use the cutters for practice on the already cut wire, and Joe was pretty critical of my technique. He claimed I left sharp edges on the wire that could penetrate a car tire if I ever left it lying around. I claimed that by leaving the wire cutters in the bag all the time, he was risking one of us getting a finger chopped off by mistake. Joe claimed they could sew anything back onto your body nowadays but the car-tire thing would involve jail time for public-safety reasons.

Before we left the corner of Appleton Avenue and East Housatonic Street every day, Joe always counted all the papers twice to make sure nobody had shorted us, and then he'd make me follow a few steps behind him "to learn the drill," like whether the customer demanded the paper be delivered to a mailbox. The nice ones let you just throw it anywhere as long as you tried to aim for the front porch. The worst people had mail slots, which were normally made to handle one or two letters a month. These customers considered it your job to fold the newspaper like it was one of those flags the Army gives out at funerals, and they'd let you know your tip depended on it. Joe had a special method for this, which started with slamming the paper across his thigh "to make the first crease really stick" and then concentrating on which way the headlines were pointing before he made the next fold. My method for the slot people was more like jamming it in there and shredding the front page a couple of times so they'd let you aim for the porch.

After a few months with me walking annoyingly close behind him and occasionally squashing down on the heel of his sneaker to trip him up, Joe started sending me ahead on the route to some of the less demanding customers. He'd give me three or four newspapers at a time—prefolded by him according to his rigorous standards, a process I had to "watch and learn" about two hundred times. I hated doing the paper route with Joe almost every day, but when I got good enough so he could skips days and I ended up doing it by myself, I discovered what it was like to really hate a paper route.

The bag never fit me. I had to wear the strap like a headband, so the sack part was a two-ton ponytail. Plus, I'd have my mother's voice in my head claiming that I was wrecking my spine for life. I had noticed I wasn't doing my hair any favors, either. Usually, if it was just me, it was raining before I even got there, and it was a long time before the *Eagle* figured out that plastic wrapping worked better than a sheet of brown paper as protection. I admit I wasn't great at folding newspapers even on dry days, but wet newspapers didn't take a crease. I'd be walking around the neighborhood with my head bent back, trying to make a front page out of a couple of fistfuls of papier-mâché, while half the customers would be standing in the little windows cut out beside their front doors like stained-glass saints, just daring me to not use the proper delivery method.

It was always on these days that somebody at the *Eagle* would short you by a paper or two. It was impossible to know you were running low until near the end if you constantly forgot to count the papers at the start, and because Joe had worked out the route to end at our house, it was too late by then. You couldn't stiff one of the next-door neighbors and expect to get away with it. Once in a while you could call the *Eagle* and successfully beg them to send over a couple of extras, but not every week. Instead, I'd have to go back and select one of the ancient women who was too nice to call up the house and hope she hadn't found her paper in the bushes yet. It was easy to misjudge people, though, and sometimes an old lady who was perfectly friendly and a decent tipper did get desperate enough to call and start making accusations. I soon learned that the only way to calm them down was by immediately offering to bring over my mother's only copy of the newspaper. There weren't a lot of old women who wanted to be known at church for taking my mother's newspaper away from her.

If Joe ever came up short during all the months he took our collection money to be counted at the *Eagle*, he never mentioned it to me. I don't remember ever being there with him, but I am sure he made me accompany him on at least a dozen training missions before trusting me to go it alone. Still, it never went as well as I hoped it would.

It didn't help that the woman who counted your money was known as a friend of the family. This meant she could damage your reputation by letting people know if you tried to shortchange her. Mrs. K. was always very friendly toward me, but she never took my word for it when I emptied out my green money sack.

The dollar bills, she'd count by hand. You could watch her and count along, and usually I was able to predict how many dollars she'd find. What made you sweat were the coins.

Mrs. K. would flick a switch and this whirring sound would start, like someone was grinding up a pound of Eight O'clock Coffee at the A&P. The automatic change-counting machine was definitely faster than Mrs. K., based on her time with the dollar bills, but the noise was nerve-wracking. Plus, her job didn't come with an office. This added to the pressure. The *Eagle* made Mrs. K. work behind a counter in one of the most popular hallways in the whole building, so old men with hats or ties on were constantly walking by, and they could stop whenever they felt like it. There was a good chance one of them had just written a newspaper story about one of my older brothers or sisters winning a debating contest or starring in the latest musical comedy at St. Joseph High School. Publicity like this was nobody's fault, but every time one of these stories got printed, my mother did have to spend a lot of time on the telephone apologizing to friends of hers who were *Eagle* readers with kids who didn't ever do anything newsworthy. She'd let you know that other families were probably getting pretty tired of reading about the Downings all the time. That's why the refrigerator door was only for taping up pictures of infant babies belonging to one of the married older kids, and for poems or jokes with good moral messages that appeared in one of my mother's favorite Catholic magazines. Taping up newspaper items about ourselves would have been rubbing it in when other mothers came to the house to discuss how to discipline children or to have my mother justify God's taking away their dead husbands while they were still young.

By fifth grade, my name had only turned up in public in a couple of lists of kids who won swimming races, and these were not worth a discussion at dinner. My family didn't object to the sports section. They considered it a decent way for the *Eagle* to make money off people who had the wrong priorities, like want ads and comic strips. Luckily, I'd never accidentally got my picture taken for the news sections of the newspaper, like my brother Gerard did when he was marching around Park Square supporting the Vietnam War with a bunch of guys from the American Legion. Gerard was in high school when this happened, so he didn't know the difference between patriotism and his pituitary gland, a part of the body that my mother explained had nothing to do with me. We had a good discussion at dinner about how Gerard was entitled to his wrong opinions, which went against the posters my sister Mary Ann had picked up in college about peace being good for you, but the point was that a photograph was part of your permanent record and it might come back to haunt Gerard if he ever wanted to become a patriotic draft dodger.

To prevent publicity whenever I was at the *Eagle*, I'd always do something polite, like holding open the swinging door so reporters wouldn't linger in the hallway where Mrs. K. was counting my collection money. All I could do was pray I wasn't off by more than a dollar, which was the total of nickels and dimes I usually brought along in a safety pocket.

Mrs. K. was not out to get you, but she was short. She always tried to look somewhere above my head, but we usually ended up staring right at each other when she called out my cash total and added, "Close!" or "Almost!"

There were plenty of problems with the newspaper business besides being expected to have the exact change every single month, but during the first year or so, Joe and I found a way to handle most of them without causing a family discussion. We were helped out by being the youngest of the nine kids, so nobody was apt to be interested in us during dinner unless I was suspected of carrying a peculiar odor or Joe was having an acne breakout and making it hard for people to enjoy their food—"people" being one of my sister Marie's favorite ways of referring to herself. As in, "Some people take care of their skin." Marie knew how to burn off her acne with a portable sun lamp in the bathroom, and she refused to let Joe or me watch. I don't know about Joe, but I blame Marie for a lot of the wicked sunburns I accidentally gave myself in that bathroom.

During the summer before I entered fifth grade, Joe got really discouraged about our monthly profits from the paper route because there basically weren't any. In August, he set up a meeting with me in the dining room to discuss the situation. This surprised me for at least three different reasons.

First of all, I never really considered the newspaper route a paying job. For me, it was another form of Catholic slavery. Whenever I collected my 50-cent allowance, my mother made it clear I wasn't being paid for mowing the lawn, taking out the garbage, shoveling our unnecessarily long sidewalk and driveway, cleaning the bathrooms, dry-mopping the bedrooms, or sweeping out the garage even though I didn't drive and wasn't allowed even to sit and enjoy the view of my handiwork from the driver's seat. My mother explained that being paid would make my work meaningless. On the other hand, money people gave you out of their own free will as an allowance, or tips and gifts, was your reward for coming from a good family.

Second of all, Joe and I did make money when we ended up splitting the tips at the end of every month. This wasn't fair, but it was typical of Joe to go fifty-fifty with me even though we both knew I lost us a lot of tips with my faulty delivery methods. Joe never let me forget my shortcomings, but he never tried to profit by them. I wanted Joe to like me more than I wanted to be treated fairly by him, but I never offered him any of my tip money. The point was, according to Joe, tips weren't profit. He claimed we were supposed to earn money on every paper we delivered, but we ended up so short all the time that we were spending some of our tips just to pay Mrs. K.

Joe was not accusing me of anything (surprise number three). He had brought along to our meeting both The Book and The Box. The Book was a four-by-six–inch green paperback ledger with the names of all the customers, followed by an origami arrangement of folded-down pages that somehow worked to reveal to Joe which ones paid weekly or monthly, when they had paid, when they were supposed to pay next, whether or not they'd tipped last time, and probably a few key actuarial statistics. I wouldn't know. I rarely was entrusted with the book, and except for making a check mark when somebody paid me—NOT AN X! HOW MANY TIMES DO I HAVE TO REMIND YOU ABOUT THE DIFFERENCE?—I wasn't permitted to write in the book, despite my obviously better penmanship skills.

Also, my mother had damaged my reputation for math during her last birthday party. I'd designed my usual gift by carefully printing a column of the normal stuff, like *Rosaries, Ejaculations, Masses (not counting Sundays because of the holy obligation taking away free will), Novenas, Litanies of the Saints*, and another column of underlines on which I wrote the total number of times I did the prayer items while thinking of her. This was how you made a spiritual bouquet, obviously, and it was well known that my mother wanted it and not the crazy powder and puff I tried to substitute the year before, which was the last time I took shopping advice from my best friend, Joey T. Even after I explained to him how some of the older kids had been allowed to smell it and dust their heads with the puff, Joey T. swore his mother would kill to have it as long as you could still read the Jean Naté label.

I know I attracted unnecessary attention to my spiritual bouquet by adding a drawing of colorful flowers between the two columns to explain the bouquet part, which was the sort of rookie mistake the older kids had outgrown. And I admit I might've miscounted my *Novenas*, partially because of often confusing them with *Ejaculations* even when I was in the middle of doing one of them. Even so, I was totally caught off guard when my mother started checking my math and grilling me during her party about my suspiciously big *Holy Saturdays* total. Gerard suggested I probably also double-counted in my *Masses* column. All I could do was pray somebody would cut the cake. Joe's spiritual bouquet was about ten times bigger than mine, but nobody dared to challenge his prayer habits or his record-keeping. That party definitely influenced Joe's attitude about letting me write in The Book.

The Box was a gray metal first-aid kit into which you had to dump out all the money—payments and tips—the minute you got home, not forgetting to check your jacket, your pants, your shirt pocket, and any other surprising places, like a cuff or a sock, where you were apt to lose spare change. The Box was kept in the laundry room, where we kept our boots and coats, and there were plenty of wrought-iron hooks screwed into the bead board so you could undress in private to your underpants without a problem if you suspected some money of getting down somewhere below the belt. The Box had been invented after my very first time collecting by myself from the weekly customers and then not remembering where I'd put the money. This turned into a very unpleasant Easter egg hunt, with Joe commanding me to empty out all my bureau drawers and shake down all the clothes from our closet that I might have had on while collecting. We came up with a lot of cash, but Joe said this still proved I had a disrespectful way of treating money. He didn't have any problem leaving my clothes in a disrespectful tangle.

In the dining room with Joe, The Book, and The Box, I was probably sweating from the start. Money was not my best topic, and Joe knew it. Using his voice to raise suspicions, Joe said he'd asked Mom about installing a lock on The Box. Often Joe didn't think I could handle subtlety, so he developed a lot of tricks, like raising an eyebrow and leaving it there on his forehead too long, or squinting his dark eyes at you like he was threatening to squeeze something out of you. I never told him so, but years later, these habits sometimes wrecked his best performances in musical comedies. Instead of making me more nervous, though, his lock idea seemed like a dream come true, especially if I wouldn't be allowed to handle the key. I was all for anything that took me out of the money game.

After a long silence, Joe said, Mom won't allow us to use a lock. Up went the eyebrow.

I don't remember Joe ever using the words *thief* or *stealing*. But he let me know that somebody who had access to the laundry room was robbing us blind.

In moments like this, you had no choice but to believe Joe. He was backed up by his reputation for being so prayerful that total strangers would come up to him after Mass to tell him he was going to grow up to be a priest. Plus, out of curiosity, he'd already read *The Rise and Fall of the Third Reich*, and he kept the huge, yellowed paperback on display in our bedroom, where I would have to pass it and notice the swastika on the cover and pray I didn't have another dream about German invaders.

My family had a robbery problem once before. I'd heard about it from some of the older kids who occasionally told stories to prove that Joe and I had it so easy that we were basically getting away with murder. The stars of these stories were always my mother and a wooden spoon. I was usually either a baby upstairs or not even alive yet. This time, my mother had discovered some money missing from her purse, and forced the five or six older kids into the living room for a line-up. They all knew who the thief was, but none of them would say Jack did it. My family was fiercely loyal as long as you were there when the discussion about you broke out. Everybody also knew that my mother knew the identity of the guilty party but she refused to be the one to say the name. (This is where the story got confusing if you were trying to turn it into a learning lesson and prevent repeats.) Anyway, that's when the wooden spoon got involved. Everybody got hit. A couple of weaklings cried. Nobody confessed.

After Joe discovered the latest robberies, I kept expecting another line-up. Fortunately, a few days later, Mayor Daley formed an army in Chicago and tried to assassinate half the Democrats who agreed with my sister Mary Ann about Vietnam. Nobody in my family ever admitted to watching television, but under these conditions, my mother considered it a public service for Downings to be "glued to the tube." I ended up siding with Mary Ann against the cops and the war, mostly because Mary Ann was the only person who asked for my opinion.

The next week, by pure coincidence, my sister Elaine got married to a guy we didn't know very well named Bill and caused a distraction. Bill had a lot going for him, including a tendency to drive sportier cars than normal people and a willingness to let Elaine talk at the kitchen table while he took you skiing, usually not at one of the local places but somewhere he knew about in Vermont, which would use up an entire day. Bill was also impatient and willing to pay for your lunch instead of waiting around for homemade bologna and cheese. This made it easier for me than for my mother to see why Elaine wanted to marry him.

I don't remember the wedding, but I'm sure it was a success. For her reception, like all of my sisters, Elaine chose the Stanley Club, which was just a few blocks from our house and right across the street from the funeral home where they'd had my father's wake. This was all part of the cycle of life for good Catholics, but it wasn't something you had to point out to wedding guests. Elaine was the third Downing married, but the first one to leave the country for her honeymoon, which also said a lot about Bill, good or bad, depending on who you were.

I'm sure Joe probably spent as much time as I did at the Stanley Club dancing with cousins and hanging around the bar, eating free maraschino cherries. This was the best way to force the bartender to get rid of you by mixing you up a Shirley Temple "on the house." Unlike me, though, Joe hadn't forgotten about the thief in our midst. He'd had to move The Box out of the laundry room to make space for all the baked goods we were piling up for the party at home after Elaine and Bill took off. He'd put it somewhere in our bedroom. I never saw it. We weren't allowed to go in there for several days. Neither of us was particularly happy about being kicked out of our bedroom so Bill's aunt could have it all to herself and save money on a motel, but Joe's anger was fueled by suspicion. When we came up short at the end of September, he tried to pin the theft on Bill's old aunt. I'm sure he made the accusation as politely as possible, like maybe she hadn't been expecting a cash bar. I wasn't present during any of these sessions, but Joe told me later that nobody was buying his theory.

I knew Joe expected me to aid in his ongoing investigation, but by then I was under a lot of pressure at school on account of our teacher. Sister Urban was alienating most of the kids. She'd started out the year wrong by being much, much older than expected and by using a name that immediately led to jokes about Urban Renewal. It wasn't the fault of the kids. We'd just finished having fourth grade with Sister Paul, who was young and played folk songs right in the middle of class when she felt like it. She was the first nun at Notre Dame grammar school to claim you could sing Peter, Paul, and Mary songs in church if you had the idea of God the Father being the hammer and the Holy Spirit being the bell and Jesus being the *Song! To! Sing! All over this land.*

Sister Urban taught all the fifth-grade subjects as forms of religion class, and she let it be known that she wasn't a big fan of the Folk Mass. It was hard to learn anything because Sister Urban had to spend so much class time on punishments, and hers were so unusual that they wiped out the little bits of geography or history you had tried to memorize. For instance, she once made a kid stick his hand in a flowerpot filled with nothing but soil and just stand there like an idiot for the rest of the day. After that, for about a week, she called the idiot Mr. So-and-So—not filling in the blank, just So-and-So, to emphasize how she wished she could just forget he was ever born.

My mother claimed that she considered Sister Urban and her punishments normal. According to her, this was proved by the fact that nobody ever died of a dirty hand. The worst she would say if I pressed her on something like So-and-So was, Those nuns are French Canadian. This is exactly what she said whenever we passed my schoolyard, which was a parking lot behind the convent, and we had to pretend there was nothing embarrassing, though we had both noticed the clothesline where the nuns had hung up their bras and girdles in public. She didn't mean "French Canadian" as an insult, but as in "versus normal Irish Catholics."

Admittedly, my mother was also distracted during my fifth-grade year. My sister Peg was living at home, and we were all praying she'd finally live up to her potential at Berkshire Community College. My brother Gerard was a senior in high school and seemed to think he could walk into any college in the country, even though his grade point average was dropping like a stone. And my sister Marie was a freshman in high school, which had already been discussed for years as a cause for concern because after my father died she developed a habit of flirting with men who came to the house, which wasn't her fault but could be considered embarrassing for my family if outside guests noticed that Marie was treating their visits as an opportunity to shop for another father.

Fortunately, in terms of our flirting concerns, on one of the first Friday nights she was allowed to go out with friends, Marie was in a car crash with Elaine T. (broken collarbone); a guy named Joe (not a scratch), who had made the varsity football team in his freshman year and was constantly voted by Elaine T. and my sister Marie as having the biggest thighs in America; and a driver (ended up with annoying bells ringing in his ears). Marie was in the hospital for about a week. My mother would say only, Her pelvis was crushed, without ever explaining *pelvis*.

My sister Mary Ann, who was threatening to get married before we'd even used up all the paper plates left over from Elaine's wedding, had graduated from college and was teaching at Pittsfield High School and living at home. She gave me an overview of the human skeleton and said something about how babies were born that neither of us wanted to pursue, and by then Marie was installed on the sofa in the den with a wheelchair and a lot of face time with Joe, the football player, which must've made Elaine T. wish she'd broken a more important bone.

Until her pelvis was crushed, Marie was known as a spoiled brat, a tease, and a crybaby, often all at once, which had been proved a couple of years before her car accident. One night in about seventh grade, Marie persuaded Gerard to help her skip school the next day instead of flunking a test she wasn't prepared for. They were plotting the whole thing in the kitchen. My mother was out, which usually involved a bunch of women getting together to say the Rosary, as if once a night after dinner with us wasn't enough for her.

For about an hour, Marie begged and teased and pinched Gerard, her idea being that if he punched her hard enough to leave a bruise, she could fake an injury. Gerard resisted, but you could see that the pinching was getting to him. Marie was probably poking him and threatening him with secrets he had stupidly revealed to her. She was also a pretty famous blabbermouth. By then, Marie was also doubting out loud that Gerard could hit her hard enough to give her a charley horse. She had decided she'd need a real limp to make my mother take pity on her. That's when Gerard hauled off and hit her. He punched her full force. I was there, and I was so astonished that I really can't remember if it was her arm or her thigh that he hit. Instantly, Marie started screaming and claiming she had a lifetime bruise and threatening to tell my mother Gerard had punched her.

I bet Gerard wished he had chosen her head.

Marie howled and wept all night and ended up telling the whole story to my mother, who wouldn't let you stay home from school unless you were in a wheelchair. What impressed me a couple of years later when Marie did get a wheelchair and months out of school, was how she didn't play the martyr. She never exposed you to her wounds. She barely even cried. She did milk the situation for things like private time with Joe the football player and snacks on demand, but I admired her for that.

It took a few months for her pelvis parts to come back together so she could walk again, but Marie was never the same. She was easily my most improved sister after that, but I didn't know her well enough yet to know if she considered that worth a car crash. I never did ask, because early in November, I suddenly lost some of the money I'd collected from the weekly newspaper customers. Something like all of it.

The money just disappeared. Joe still hadn't identified the criminal who was swiping dollar bills out of The Box, and instead of helping out with his investigation, I had privately started to doubt anyone was stealing from us. This basically meant that once word got around about the money I'd just lost, I would be everybody's favorite suspect for all of the previous losses. In case anybody forgot, Joe could easily remind them of my mother accusing me of padding my spiritual bouquets.

And it got worse, which would've seemed impossible if Joe hadn't asked me for The Book. In a fit of optimism about my trustworthiness, Joe had allowed me to carry The Book around by myself for a while. The money, I might have been able to repay. I'm not sure I can remember the total, but the figure $13.70 still gives me a sour stomach in a way that makes me think it is accurate. I knew I had at least $30 in my First Communion bank account. I also knew I didn't really have a plan for getting my passbook out of the blue steel box in the buffet where my mother kept it. One problem was that she'd selected a box for herself that came with a built-in lock.

I could have asked Mary Ann for a loan. Maybe I resisted putting money between us, knowing what it had done between me and my mother and me and Joe. More likely, I didn't want Mary Ann to have to suffer for my problem by admitting to her lousy public high school students that her little brother wasn't as great as advertised. Sometime before Halloween that year, Mary Ann had asked me to explain to her what was meant by her poster that said, *You have not converted a man because you have silenced him.* It had a drawing of a black man on it, which I assumed was Martin Luther King, Jr., because he was basically becoming a Catholic saint since being murdered in the style of a Kennedy. Mary Ann must have liked my answer, because she told everybody at dinner that she was going to tell her high school students that instead of giving them tests to fail, maybe she should just give their tests to her fifth-grade brother (everyone at dinner realizing that was me). Mary Ann was constantly doing things like asking you questions that really mattered and then giving you the results of your quiz in some surprising way. I didn't end up asking her for a loan.

Eventually, I confessed to Joe about the lost money. To spare him a total fit, I used the figure of $10. I asked him not to mention it to any family members at least until the end of the month. Joe calmly closed the bedroom door, and then he really let me have it. He had picked up the phrase "I don't mind telling you" by then, which got under my skin by being so obvious. The upshot was, he didn't mind telling me that he could never trust me with anything ever again. After that, he left me alone to invent a plan for digging myself out of debt. To work off my bad mood, I probably unfolded most of his T-shirts and underpants, setting him up for some problems of his own when my mother checked our drawers. I figured he had gone out to the garage to play a Beatles song on his folk guitar and pretend it was electrified, because the paper route didn't pay enough even in good times to let him buy an amplifier. I found out later, though, that Joe had unexpectedly pulled a Walter Cronkite on me. I was the evening news. My whole dinner was wasted fielding suggestions for improving my flawed character, including keeping everything I owned in one brown paper bag if I couldn't be trusted not to lose things from now on. Nobody was offering me any loan money.

Either Joe hadn't mentioned my losing The Book or nobody else in the family bought his story about how valuable it was. It never came up among the crimes I got charged with at dinner. I knew The Book was irreplaceable, obviously. Joe could barely talk about it without his head starting to shake against his will. I remember only one of these conversations. He began by saying, It's not the money. He said this because he knew as well as I did that the money would magically appear sooner or later. One of the things Joe resented most about me was that I had much more luck than he did. But after saying the money didn't matter, he added, It's that you don't show any respect for things that matter to me.

That stung. I didn't appreciate Joe's making me out to be as bad as the rest of the family on that score. I was totally faithful about calling him a professional musician. He was the one who was stingy with respect. I had about a dozen art projects going on in the basement, including an old chrome towel rack I was painting with stripes, and a selection of very unusual dead leaves I'd shellacked onto somebody's skis, and Joe was still refusing to call them art. Even after I'd discovered a stash of ancient solvents and smeared my best landscape paintings to keep up with modern art trends, Joe wouldn't budge. He did scrutinize the objects, and I could tell he was almost persuaded, but he finally said, These are still crafts. You can call yourself a craftsman, but you can't say you're an artist.

To make matters worse, Joe went out and bought a new ledger from our tips without offering me even a probation period to find The Book, which I did, a couple of days before Thanksgiving. I remember the timing because I was in our bedroom closet, trying to make neat folds in a pile of fifteen or twenty wax-paper lunch bags so they could be shoved into a pocket of my school uniform pants and stay there.

The wax-paper bags were an assignment from Sister Urban. Before every holiday, she demanded that we all bring in at least four of them. I always packed extras to try to get on her good side by having some available to lend to poor kids from bad families with no kitchen supplies. Starting at about noon, we'd be forced to take off our shoes, put a bag on each foot, and skate around our own desk in circles to wax the floor, stopping only to turn over the bag or change to a new one when you'd wiped off all the free wax.

I was packing the bags in my school pants the night before because since losing the collection money I had developed the annoying bad habit of asking everybody in the house to remind me of things I was likely to forget. My mother finally banned me from making further requests, so to avoid forgetting stuff I had to find ways to do everything I was supposed to do in advance. As a result, before Christmas that year, I read my whole history textbook and surprised Sister Urban by knowing more than she did about Saint Isaac Jogues and the Indians who turned him into the holy Catholic martyr named Mangled Hands via torture. It was around this time that I also on purpose stapled a staple directly into my index finger to know how it felt. It hurt. I didn't allow myself to scream in pain, proving I was prepared to deprive the Indians of their greatest satisfaction.

After I'd stuffed the wax-paper bags into a couple of my pockets and put my school pants back on the hanger, I noticed a raincoat among the indoor clothes. It was not mine. It had belonged to one of my sisters, and it had the buckles on the wrong side to prove it, but it had a corduroy collar I particularly admired, and I often snagged it during a downpour. We weren't expecting any rain, but I tried it on. In one pocket was the collection money. In the other was The Book, admittedly folded over the wrong way a couple of times and its cover mushed up.

I made a beeline for Joe, who was in the dining room doing homework. I had not worked out an explanation for the coat's being in our closet. I knew how that had happened. Instead of having to listen to somebody explain to me the difference between boy and girl coats again, when I'd finished the paper route, I had skipped the laundry-room routine and run upstairs to hide the evidence of my sartorial transgression.

Joe didn't ask what a girl's raincoat was doing in our closet. He told me to put the money in The Box after counting it twice and then add that amount to the total on the slip of paper with the old total, which he had taken to displaying on top of the cash in order to deter the thief. It was all very businesslike between us lately, which made me sad. However, I knew I had the antidote in the raincoat pocket. I waited a couple of dramatic seconds before joyfully producing The Book.

I remember Joe's exact words. "Show it to Mom. Maybe she'll care." He probably squinted at me at that point to underline his message of not being able to forgive me this time.

I counted my recovered cash about three times, or at least once very carefully, before adding it to the rest of the collection money. Then I counted the total cash before writing the new total on Joe's slip of paper. Then I counted all the cash again because there seemed to be an extra ten dollars in the box. I must have counted the money at least two more times before I believed my math.

There were ten extra dollars. Maybe Joe's investigation had started to make somebody nervous enough to stick the $10 in the box. Probably the thief was hoping to shut Joe up by repaying us for the most recent robbery. If so, the guilty party didn't know about my reputation for being lucky and hadn't counted on my finding the lost money, which had been broadcast by Joe as exactly $10. I was thrilled and scared out of my wits. Instead of covering the crime, the thief had proved it. And Jack wasn't living at home since he'd got married. Another one of the Downings was a criminal.

Joe had been right all along. It was like living with German invaders in the house. I said nothing, not even to Joe. It was too frightening and too embarrassing to admit. If Indians tortured me with their craziest weapons, I knew I wouldn't tell them. Even at the end of the month, even after we'd paid Mrs. K. and split the tips and our unusual profits, I didn't say anything about the extra cash, and neither did Joe. Initially, I thought he felt as queasy as I did about having a robber right under our noses. Later on, I suspected Joe was playing it cool so the criminal would finally ask some supposedly casual question about whether we ever found an extra ten bucks in The Box, thus exposing his or her true identity. But after a while, I realized Joe had stopped looking for the thief. He'd seen something else in our cash windfall that month. I think he'd been blinded by the shiny new electric amplifier he could see in his future.

It was almost forty years before Joe and I talked about this episode in our lives. He wasn't particularly surprised about my discovery of the extra $10. Maybe Mom put it there, he said. This surprised me, or maybe it shamed me—I've always had a hard time making that distinction. The point is, it had never occurred to me that someone, maybe my mother, might have been trying to do me a favor by slipping $10 into The Box.

If my mother were still alive, she could have pointed fairly to this as another of my miscalculations. If she had, Joe—to my total surprise, as usual—would have come to my defense. Unlike me and my mother, Joe never mixed up his currencies. He didn't blame me for not coming up with a benign explanation for the extra $10. He made it clear he didn't really know if our mother had put that money in The Box. But he also let me know he was pretty certain she had been our thief.

This occasioned another jolt of shock or shame.

Joe didn't level this as an accusation. It was more like a balancing of the books. She was always short on money. Joe and I weren't paying our way. So if she needed five bucks to run to the grocery store before dinner, or some small change when some kid knocked on the door selling Girl Scout cookies, it made sense that she would dip into our stash. His theory rested on a question: Why else wouldn't she let us lock The Box and put an end to the crimes?

Maybe for the same reason she wouldn't name the guilty party to spare the other kids the wooden spoon? Maybe all she had was us, her children, and she figured the older kids would survive the indignity of an unearned spanking, that Joe and I would survive the inconvenience of petty-cash shortfalls, but she could not survive if she had to admit, even for a moment, that one of us was lost. Or maybe she was sick and tired of being reminded that instead of a bunch of nuns and priests, she'd accidentally raised a pack of thieves.

I can't account for her no-lock policy. I can close the book on fifth grade. Joe eventually got what he wanted most—an electric amplifier and revenge on me. As usual, he managed it all in a businesslike way. Before he quit the paper route, behind my back he secretly negotiated a deal to buy out the paper route belonging to Lori's brother, doubling our customers, our profits, and my misery.

6. *Family Bonds*

At the end of fifth grade, I saw the future. I didn't see much of it, but I liked what I saw. It was sunny there. Across First Street, to be precise.

I'd been kept after school by my ancient teacher, Sister Urban. She made me sit at my desk while she went out into the hall and bawled out some kid who'd blown his final conduct grade by getting caught calling her Sister Hitler. I figured she wanted me there as her witness in case she got accused again of using fists or shoes to make her point. I didn't hear any physical contact before she told the kid to go home, and when she came back into the classroom she was smiling. Sister Urban was old, but she always seemed to enjoy a good workout. Totally out of the blue, she said, Your father must be very proud of you up in heaven. Then she apologized for making me stay and dismissed me. Her smile didn't fade, and on the way home I thought maybe she was proud of herself, that she had kept me there to prevent herself from doing something she'd regret.

I was in no particular rush to get home, so I stopped off at the deserted playground area of the Pittsfield Common. I passed it every day, but usually I was with my best friend, Joey T., and some other Catholic kids who lived on my street, and as a group we considered ourselves too old for public playgrounds. By myself, I could still enjoy a few minutes on a swing or even a couple of backwards runs down a decent slide. This playground wasn't the best choice. It was basically just an empty sandbox and some worn-out kiddy equipment beneath a grove of maple trees next to the real Common, a huge circle of open space on First Street that was used mostly for baseball in summer and ice-skating in winter. On the far side was Berkshire Community College, a single brick-and-granite building that used to be a high school.

I had good associations with BCC. My sister Peg had recently been forced to spend two years there to prove it was worth my mother's sacrificing to pay for her to attend a four-year Catholic college with tons of buildings and motivated students like my brother Gerard, who was being allowed to choose Providence College right out of high school that year. Part of Peg's proving herself had included giving my mother a break from "the boys" once in a while, so Peg and a friend of hers had once taken me and my brother Joe to see a silent movie in the BCC auditorium. Joe didn't mind the silent part because he said he just wanted to check out the college girls. I didn't mind because Peg was famous in our family for being easygoing and gaining weight since she'd sold candy bars for charity in grade school and you could pressure her into buying you something like a Chunky with raisins or Milk Duds. I also liked Peg because, unlike a lot of the older kids in the family, she didn't ask you probing questions as payment for taking you someplace.

Peg never even asked me why I begged her to take me to the big peace protest at the Common. This proved no matter how old she got, Peg would be happy to ignore you in public. Unfortunately, Peg also didn't bother to let me know we could've designed homemade protest signs and joined the parade of people singing some of my family's favorite Joan Baez songs. I spent the whole protest sitting near the batting cage in the Common, practicing how to participate in a sit-in, which unexpectedly included just sitting there. The big trick was to be totally silent while some old woman wearing a Chinese bathrobe claimed you were a powerful weapon against the Establishment. I doubted her. It was exactly like being stuck in a silent movie.

Of course, my whole family was well known in the Berkshires for supporting peace, unless you counted the Crusades. The only soldier in our family was my father. He'd skipped World War II but joined the Knights of Columbus. When he died, a bunch of men in military hats with feathers showed up to comfort my mother and give her a sword. To honor my father's service, and to prove to Joe and me that he was going to inherit that sword and we were not allowed to touch it, Gerard was totally pro-war until he turned eighteen. That's when he found out the Army expected him to risk getting his own head shot off. My personal objection to the Vietnam War was President Johnson's choice of the jungle location. Every summer, I got wicked bad rashes on muggy days, and usually I needed to borrow half a bottle from Gerard's private stash of Listerine to stop the itching. I didn't like my chances in Saigon.

By June of 1969, I didn't really like my chances in Pittsfield, either. I'd started to have some personal problems at the end of fifth grade. My mother was forced to bring up the topic because she'd been caught off guard by some unsightly stains on my bedsheets after she'd already pressed them in the mangle. This was called "setting a stain," and she let me know it was not her favorite thing to do. In general, my mother didn't love surprises.

Nobody in my family loved to talk about anything that came out of your body. My brother Joe was in seventh grade at the time, and he had started spotting facial hairs on himself, but nobody mentioned shaving. I don't know how Joe discovered razors, but I know that he doubted himself about how they actually worked. He didn't dare try one on his face until he experimented with shaving his legs to see the results. His leg hair grew back almost right away, which made me think he was doing something wrong. I started paying a lot of attention to magazine and television advertisements for shaving cream, looking for tips, but most of what I learned was stylish ways of knotting a bath towel around your waist. I was relieved to find no growths on my face.

I was not exactly relieved when my mother brought up my bedsheets. We were at the kitchen table. She had poured us both beverages and there was nobody else around. I think it was nighttime. I recall the blazing beam of the pendant light, but I might be mixing up the glare with my emotions. Next to my mother's teacup, my sheets and pillowcase were stacked and folded, stains hidden. Her point was that she had plenty of work to do without my extra stains, but she didn't want to dwell on the problem. My mother hadn't touched her tea. I sipped my juice. You're not a little boy anymore, she said.

I was pleased, but in the silence that followed this announcement, the congratulatory air leaked out of the room. I knew then that the beverages were just props. This was a setup.

I confessed my problem. I told my mother the wetness had woken me up in the middle of the night a couple of times recently. In my own defense, I added that I was pretty surprised to be wetting the bed by accident all of a sudden.

My mother said, You were never a bed-wetter. I must've acknowledged this compliment, because the next thing I knew my mother was saying, It's not urine.

Her switch to medical terminology unnerved me, but my mother was good at delivering bad news and forcing you not to panic and start asking questions she didn't want to answer. She did this by staring at your eyes and not turning away or even blinking. You knew if you wanted to say anything personal about your body, you were going to have to say it to her face. This made you not say a lot of the things that flew into your head. It's ejaculate, she said. Hoping to be helpful, I'm sure, she added, You had an ejaculation.

This really muddied the water. I was a good enough Catholic to know that an ejaculation was a little prayer, like *Glory be to God* or *Blessed Virgin Mary, pray for us.* Until that moment, I'd used ejaculations only to prevent being bitten by stray dogs or to thank God those fire trucks I'd just heard weren't headed to my house.

My formal introduction to human biology had begun and ended in fourth grade when I'd snagged the copy of *The Miracle of Life* my mother had given to my brother Joe. I understood the part about my being a boy with a seed that any girl would be lucky to have, but I must have skipped an essential chapter or two, because I could not figure out the injection process. The rumor at school was that it was just like peeing, but the two-hundredth time I begged Joe to confirm this, all he would say was, Girls pee; boys take a piss. He was full of information like this since he'd joined the Boy Scouts, but he wasn't offering any sex-education classes.

Neither was my mother. And she wasn't exactly smiling when she said, You didn't do anything wrong. I appreciated this, but by fifth grade I knew a sentence like that was a ticking bomb. Sooner or later, the *but* was going to explode. My mother slid my filthy sheets toward me. I probably gulped down my orange juice as a bracer. But as you fall to sleep from now on, she said, you have to ask your guardian angel to protect you from impure thoughts.

I don't know if I was still sitting at the table or if I was upstairs anchoring my sheets between the box spring and mattress with a series of crisp hospital-corner folds that would hold up to surprise inspections later in the week, but the staggering truth of my impurity became clear to me. As usual, my first instinct was to figure out how I was not to blame. For instance, the biggest problem was obviously my name. My being named Michael was why my guardian angel was so easy to mix up with the famously handsome Archangel Michael. This led straight to my other problem: I recalled having a couple of extremely pleasant dreams recently about an angel—I think he was the Archangel by the looks of his curly blond hair and breastplate, but I couldn't be sure. The wings, which could've have belonged to any angel, were the body part that had caused me the most excitement.

When my mother came into your bedroom, instead of just saying *Sweet dreams* or *I love you* like a pagan, she always said, *Good night and God bless* and flicked some holy water around, which would burn like hot oil on the skin of Satan and any of his friends hanging around to catch you off guard while you slept. Lately, she'd also been scolding me for having my arms and hands tucked in under the sheet and blanket. She never offered an explanation for this, so I figured forcing me to sleep with the blanket and sheet wedged under my armpits prevented strangulation. That night, I realized she was accusing me of sticking my hands under the covers to do the devil's work. I couldn't defend myself. All I had to back me up was the dirty secret that I was too busy dating angels.

My mother and I never discussed my problem again, but it was between us, and it was one more good reason to stop off at the Common after school instead of rushing home. For old time's sake, I climbed up the monkey bars and balanced myself at the top. It was sunny up there, but I was feeling a little blue about Sister Urban and her knowing about her bad reputation. Plus, a lot of people I knew had started dropping hints about how lonely it was going to be at home next year for me and my brother Joe and my mother.

I got lonelier the more I thought about it.

In the summer before I started fifth grade, seven of the Downing kids were at home. But Elaine got married to Bill in September, Peg finally went to a four-year college in Vermont, and Gerard was practically all packed for college in Rhode Island. Mary Ann had got married in April. Fortunately, after she and Bob went to Bermuda for their honeymoon, Mary Ann was required by contract to come back to Pittsfield and finish teaching her lousy public school kids while Bob went to the Navy's Officer Candidate School, but I knew she'd eventually run out of excuses for staying home.

Bob was well known to us by his having grown up in Pittsfield, so we didn't want to make a big deal out of his bad choice to believe Nixon's propaganda and join the war. To avoid compromising our peace-loving principles, we discussed how Bob was actually avoiding the draft by joining the Navy. That's when somebody leaked a rumor about Elaine's husband, Bill, being a retired Green Beret. We had some trouble proving to each other why this was better than being drafted into the regular Army, but the important point was, thank God Bill had been in and out of Vietnam before there were enough American soldiers to kill practically anybody.

Sadly for me, Mary Ann said she was moving to Newport, Virginia, as soon as Bob learned how to safely shell Vietnamese people from the deck of a huge ship. By next September, it would be my mother, Joe, and I. I didn't count Marie. She would be a sophomore at St. Joseph High School, and I already knew one of the subjects the Downings never studied there was How to Take the Pressure Off Your Little Brothers.

All of this was on my mind as I stared across First Street at the Rainbow Restaurant. Its design—from the front it looked like an old-fashioned diner, but made out of brick instead of aluminum—had landed it among my top ten restaurants in the Berkshires, none of which I'd yet visited based on my family's not needing to throw money around to impress people.

The Rainbow was Italian by reputation. By the looks of him, so was the man who walked out the front door in white slacks, a white T-shirt, and a prom-length white apron. He looked my way. He had dark hair, and he seemed to have lost his razor about a week ago. He lit a cigarette. He looked my way again. He took a drag. I tightened my grip on the monkey bars. I knew where this was going. He ducked his head and pulled off the top half of his apron, letting it double over at his waist. It was just my luck that his T-shirt was a V-neck and he had chest hair. He smoked and stared at me. By the time I could smell the smoke, my underpants were soaked and I was scared out of my wits. He was a slow smoker. Finally, he flicked his filter to the curb, waved at me, and disappeared into the Rainbow, which immediately vaulted to the number one spot on my restaurant list.

I didn't know exactly what that guy thought we were doing, but from the moment I saw him, I knew exactly what *I* was doing. I didn't move for a long time. There was the practical consideration of drying out before I walked home. The underpants, I knew, were going to be wrapped in old newspapers and stuffed into a bag in the garbage behind the back porch. I'd had plenty of success with this method of destroying all kinds of evidence in the past. Mostly, though, I sat up there knowing that what had just happened could not happen in my life as I knew it.

Maybe it was the confluence of departures from home, or maybe it was a testament to the value my family placed on higher education, but staring at the sunny empty sidewalk in front of the Rainbow—I can't be blamed for naming the place—I saw my future. I was eighteen over there, and I wasn't here anymore. My job was to get there. So I wrapped up the man in the apron with my delight and flicked the whole thing across the street, across the years, where I knew I would one day find that it had all really happened.

This was exactly like the $25 U.S. savings bond I had been given for First Communion, which wouldn't be worth $25 until I got to college.

On the way home, as I passed Berkshire Community College, I gave a nod to my dead father in heaven, in case he'd been paying attention while I was on the monkey bars. Like Peg, he had a reputation for being easygoing and not as curious about every detail as my mother or my guardian angel, so I let him know he could turn his attention to the older kids and just rely on me to be a student worthy of being sent to a four-year college immediately upon graduation from high school, probably with high honors.

That summer, I enjoyed my first fancy restaurant dinner. To thank us for letting Mary Ann live rent free for a couple of months after he married her, Bob took us all out to The Springs. This was known to be better than restaurants in New York City and a favorite of the rich people who stayed in motels in Williamstown all summer, wishing they lived in the Berkshires. In advance, we discussed not ordering individual appetizers and not telling Bob we would just as soon eat a hamburger in the backyard.

Despite our family values, I was totally overwhelmed by the atmosphere at The Springs from the moment I walked in. And nobody had warned me about the menu. I'd been expecting someone to just bring us the food they felt like cooking. I don't know if it was the number of vocabulary questions I asked while reading the menu or if it became obvious I was leaning toward the lobster, but my mother suddenly told our waiter I wanted Chicken Maryland. I wasn't allowed to ask additional questions about the Maryland part, and she let me know it would have been considered bad manners to keep my menu and read up about my dinner during the cracker-and-cheese–spread part of our meal.

The Springs had plenty of ways to impress you, but I don't recommend the Chicken Maryland. It tasted too much like my mother's new favorite way of preparing Chicken Shake 'N Bake. Mary Ann was the one who quietly asked me how I liked it. For her sake, I lied. For my sake, she tasted it. She smiled to let me know she was sorry it had turned out that way. She looked at my mother and back at me. I got it. We weren't going to say anything. She gave me a hunk of whatever she had ordered, which tasted unfamiliar, as I'd hoped mine would. Then we joined the discussion about how delicious everything was at The Springs and how we would miss having Mary Ann around.

When school started in September, and right through till June, I didn't really miss the older kids. They were good about calling home, which I appreciated because it meant my mother was often stuck sitting by the telephone table in the hall for hours at a time with the kitchen door closed, so she couldn't hear or see what you were or weren't doing. Many nights, my mother tried out new menus for small families involving frozen Howard Johnson fried clams or Chef Boyardee products that we all agreed were no substitute for dinners from scratch, even though they did have the advantage of tasting better than homemade food. On Saturdays, she'd often suggest we "hop in the car" and drive to West Springfield to see Roberta, my oldest sister. Marie was usually studying for a biology test. She was allowed to stay home because the sophomore science nun was prone to anger. She was the same nun who used to force Mary Ann's husband, Bob, and his tall friends on the basketball team to kneel down in the hall when she was mad at them, not so they could pray about their sins but because she was short and wanted to bang their heads between two locker doors. Joe usually came along for the rides, but he sat in the back and read up on basketball or the Nazis.

I loved these trips. Once we finished saying the Rosary, my mother would get bored and start asking for my opinions on things about Roberta that were none of my business, like why did I think an educated young woman would choose to live in a tiny apartment where most people wouldn't keep a cat, never mind a newborn baby. After Roberta and Dick bought a house, we'd try to figure out who might be able to get Dick a better job than flipping pancakes. We also discussed all the topics we weren't going to bring up in front of them, like how the cheap toys they liked were actually pretty expensive and shouldn't have been left out on the lawn overnight, and how Roberta was starting to be as fat as Dick, and how enough soda and chips could turn even the best kids into maniacs. We didn't agree on everything. I loved Roberta's food, both for how it tasted and how the whole meal she served always looked exactly like a picture in a magazine. This was fine by my mother, if you were one of those people who believed paprika tasted like something other than red dust. She'd have been just as happy with a hot dog once in a while if it meant she didn't have to leave cash under Roberta's new matching place mats.

Our only really big disagreement was about my oldest brother, Jack. He lived in Pittsfield, also in an apartment, with two kids. His wife was skinny, and their kids only had a few toys, like ring-toss and dolls with one outfit that was permanently attached, so their money problems made you want to help them out with free babysitting. But my mother was also starting to force me and Joe to spend a lot of time with Jack, including going to work with him on weekends at a state reform school for juvenile delinquents. I argued that this was not fun. My mother argued that Jack said it was fun. I argued that Jack was a liar and she knew it. My mother argued that anything she'd said about Jack's being a liar in the past was just to prevent me from becoming as big a liar as Jack was, and it was mean of me to try to use his weakness against him. I argued that being left alone in a cafeteria with a bunch of criminals eating eggs that weren't fried long enough to turn the whites of the eggs white was not fun. My mother argued that it was not supposed to be fun but was supposed to help Jack think he was repaying her for being so much trouble in high school and dropping out of college. I argued that if Jack went back to college, it would be better for both of us. My mother argued that it was peculiar for a boy my age not to want to spend time with his brother.

This was my mother's polite way of reminding me that I wasn't all I was cracked up to be. We both knew she hated my peculiarity, but neither of us wanted to be forced to admit it. In moments like this, I realized I was getting ahead of myself. It was as if I had threatened to cash in my savings bond and she was reminding me how little it was worth.

My peculiarity first came clear when I tried to skate on some patchy ice that had formed on our carport in December. There was not enough ice to practice crossovers or skating backwards, so I may have been doing more twirling than was normal on hockey skates. My goal was to complete a full axel while hopping from one island of ice to another over the exposed tar. My mother came out of the house and watched me for a couple of minutes. I thought she might have some advice for completing a full twist in midair. I never saw her skate, but I knew she was considered an expert when she was young and turned down college athletic scholarships to work in a clothing store and buy her mother coats on discount.

There's not much ice, she said.

I asked if she thought I was going to ruin my skates.

I just want you to know you look very peculiar, she said.

I knew this was a peculiar thing to say to a kid, and I knew we were talking about the one thing we never talked about, so I didn't say anything.

The neighbors can see you, she said, and so can any stranger driving down Howard Street. You have no idea what you look like.

She wasn't enjoying this any more than I was. She was standing perfectly erect, her feet touching each other, her arms straight down at her sides. She reminded me of me when I was a little kid and I was pretending that whatever was happening was not really happening. I can see now that I was trying to stand pretty still, too, probably pigeon-toed to keep my skate blades in place, my arms maybe jiggling around at my sides a little for balance, maybe reminding her of me as a kid, maybe reminding her of herself as a kid.

We looked peculiarly alike, my mother and I, and our likeness didn't stop there. We were so alike that I think it was sometimes hard for us to know in a moment like this whether it was her peculiarity or mine that we hated and were trying with all of our might not to admit into our happy lives.

We didn't discuss ice skating again. I gave myself a free pass to walk to the rink at the Common after dinner whenever I felt like it, without ever asking permission. My mother never objected. During holiday dinners that year, my habit of disappearing became another of the many examples my older brothers and sisters used to prove that I had it way easier at home than they ever did. In a peculiar way, I knew they were right. And I knew we would soon be discussing how Jack's work with troubled kids was the true meaning of the spirit of the season, and we'd be eating dozens of Roberta's superb Christmas cookies.

By then, I had perfected the art of knowing the difference between cash money and savings bonds. Something would happen, and I would decide whether it could be traded among the other currencies of my daily life or if it had to be socked away and saved for the future. This didn't take up much of my time. I mean, you didn't have to be chairman of the Federal Reserve Board to know you couldn't immediately cash in on the story of your overnight with the kid who had a backyard clubhouse and accidentally on purpose got mixed up about which bunk he belonged in, which led to a naked make-out session and another set of stained sheets. Same goes for kissing in church.

I was substituting as an altar boy for some kid who had to miss his assigned Sunday Mass. He gave an excuse about visiting relatives, which probably translated into his family's secretly going to an amusement park and not admitting it to avoid having to invite friends. The kid's regular serving partner came from a family I knew by sight, so I agreed. He was a year older than I was and about a foot taller, and after Mass, while we were taking off our cassocks and surplices in the secret room behind the altar, he said, Thanks for filling in, and he kissed me on the lips. I noticed he'd balled up his uniform. I still had to get mine onto a hanger. We were in the sacristy, so I guessed I was supposed to look away in shame so he could flee the scene. Some stuff you just know. I looked at my shoes. He suddenly hugged me and held on for about fifteen seconds. When I finally raised my face, he smiled conspiratorially, flashed me the peace sign, and walked away. We didn't see each other in private again for a couple of years.

Sixth grade was not a total sex party, but right from the start, after about ten minutes with my new teacher, I knew most of what happened in school that year would have to be converted and saved for the future. I got a lay teacher. It was no secret that Catholics were running out of nuns. We were praying our heads off at church for an increase in vocations under threat of being charged tuition for costly professional teachers. But Mr. D. was the real answer to my prayers.

He was the tallest person at Notre Dame grammar school, and one of the skinniest. He had curly hair and dark eyes, and whenever kids asked tedious questions about how wide he wanted margins to be on our essays, he would look at them like they were nuts. Mr. D. didn't mind yelling at all, but unlike nuns he also sometimes applauded you for a great answer on a quiz or a joke that caught him off guard. My mother considered him qualified but excitable. She had her doubts about people who were constantly expressing emotions. He was also the first adult I'd met who didn't get insulted when interrupted. My mother worried this might be a sign of immaturity, but my whole sixth grade loved him from start to finish.

For me, Mr. D. was obviously exactly what I was not obviously, and I don't recall a single conversation in which any of my classmates or I mentioned this astonishing fact. Mr. D. let it be known he lived in an apartment with a man of his own age. When forced to admit this, my mother referred to the other guy as a roommate, but Mr. D. always just called him by name.

Mr. D. never did or said anything to single me out from other kids unless I did something like be the last Notre Dame kid eliminated from the citywide spelling bee. I came in fourth, which was not the first time I'd made it to the top ten and then crumbled. At home, there was a sense that I wasn't studying hard enough to show much improvement. In class the next day, Mr. D. surprised me by having cupcakes and leading a big round of applause. After that, he handed me a tiny plastic trophy with a sticker on the base that said GOOD ENOUGH FOR US, which cracked us all up.

A few weeks before the end of school, I was forced into the hospital to have my jawbone sawed in half so a couple of teeth that were bugging our family dentist, Dr. F., could be removed. One afternoon, as a complete surprise, I woke up from a morphine nap and saw Mr. D. and his pal sitting next to my hospital bed. After all the introductions were made, Mr. D. filled me in on some of the best stuff I'd missed from classes and told me he'd announced an end-of-the-year party at his place for the class—and don't worry, I was invited. Then they had to leave because Mr. D.'s friend had to be at work. I think he sold shoes and often worked at night.

The visit's being cut short was my fault for having been asleep for most of the time they were there, but they promised to come back again. I couldn't believe they'd been willing to waste their free time on me in my sleep. This was the detail that bugged my mother most when she arrived a few minutes later. She let me know she couldn't believe they'd stayed in the room while I was asleep, either, but we both knew we disbelieved it for different reasons. She started asking a lot of questions designed to trip me up, like exactly where each of them had sat and what "the roommate" had said to me. I faked being sleepy, but my mother knew it was impossible for anybody to sleep when she was conducting an investigation. About twenty times, instead of waiting for me to make up some lie, she answered her own probing question by saying, That's very peculiar.

Aside from random interrogations, my mother was a good visitor if you were sick. Most of the nurses knew her and would bring you as much ginger ale as you could stand once they knew she was your mother, and she usually showed up with a couple of get-well cards from my sisters to spread around as decorations. After my silver-domed dinner came on a tray and we agreed on which parts no normal person would ever eat, my mother wondered out loud what kind of job Mr. D.'s roommate had that allowed him to take time off in the middle of the day. I knew the shoe gig was not going to impress her, so out of loyalty to Mr. D. I told her I'd try to remember to ask when he visited the next day.

He won't be back, she said.

I didn't say, He said he would. I realized I had already said too much. My mother didn't say anything. She never mentioned Mr. D. or his roommate again. Mr. D. did not visit me again. The party at his house never happened. And though it never occurred to me then, if Mr. D.'s career at Notre Dame seemed as unnaturally brief to him as it did to me, I think I might now know what happened. Admittedly, his crazy ties and plaid jackets were probably not in his favor.

A savings bond of any kind is not a great investment, but it does eventually pay out. It was the third night of my college career. Classes had not yet started, and I was still having trouble sleeping in my assigned bunk bed, so I wandered out and landed on one end of a vast circular granite bench near the center of the Cambridge Common. There, drawing on my extensive experience in musical comedies, I exhausted my repertoire of theatrically exaggerated gestures to attract the attention of a black guy wearing a pair of peg-legged corduroy slacks. His performance was subtler, and thus lost on me. It was not until he had walked almost a block past the northern boundary of the park and turned, raised his hands shoulder high, and held his palms skyward—he performed the whole routine twice—that I was certain he expected me to follow him. I trailed him for several blocks and then stopped. I'd never been around this block before. I was lost.

He walked back to me and extended his hand. I'm Tim, he said.

He was one of the handsomest men I'd ever seen, a distinction I awarded for years on the basis of proximity. I shook his hand, hoped he might want to kiss immediately, and finally had the presence of mind to say, I'm Rick.

Some stuff you just know.

As we walked to his apartment, he told me he was a lawyer and I told him I was a sophomore majoring in biology. I don't remember much else but his pants and dodging a question about long labs by saying I really loved horticulture, though I couldn't come up with a single plant name except for maple trees.

He lived in the basement of a brick building, and instead of turning on the lights or offering me a snack or beverage, he held me and kissed me, and by the time he made it clear it was time to get undressed, I was done. It took him about four seconds to figure this out. Because I didn't know him, I felt more disappointed than embarrassed. He let me know he felt pretty much the same way. He offered me a beer, but I said I had to go. He didn't try to stop me. Before I left, I said, How should I get in touch with you?

He said, We'll run into each other.

I said, Wouldn't it be easier if I called you?

He said, We'll run into each other.

I said, What if we don't?

He said, Grow up. You're here now. Stay and have a beer.

I finally got the message. I left. And then I wandered around North Cambridge for about an hour. I wasn't sad. I wasn't scared. I was actually lost. The only person in town I knew well enough to call was my brother Joe, and if I'd called his dorm room at that hour, he would've wanted to know more than he actually wanted to know. I walked back to Tim's place and knocked.

He was handsomer than ever in his bathrobe.

I said, I'm really sorry. I'm lost. I'm a freshman. My name isn't Rick.

No problem, he said, Rick works for me.

A couple of hours later, he pointed me in the direction of Harvard Yard.

Tim and Rick ran into each other several times during my first semester, always in the Common, always after midnight. I didn't see it then, but it is obvious now that we were going to some lengths not to disrupt each other's lives.

Most of the kind, generous, and gratifyingly eager men I met in the next couple of years were, like me, liars. It wasn't always our names, but we typically withheld or misrepresented something essential about ourselves. For me, and maybe for many of them, this was one of the unforeseen costs of my adolescent savings plan. I'd bought a ticket to the future, but I'd spent everything else on the rent and maintenance for my place in the family. I couldn't afford to let anyone into my new-found life.

7. *Second Verse, Same as the First*

On the bone-chilling late afternoon of Thursday, 18 December 2003, I drove along Pomeroy Avenue in Pittsfield toward the house where my brother Gerard and his family had lived for many years. The street was narrowed and slick. A recent fall of snow had been shoved aside by city plows, banked up like breaking waves. Daylight was failing. The wooden houses in the neighborhood floated like boats in a swollen bay, and my brother's seemed to be adrift until I drove directly past the dugout driveway, a slender pier tethering his house to the wider world.

It is one thing to drive by your brother's house in the dead of winter and not stop your car. It's another thing if your brother's wife and their kids are huddled in the driveway, shivering halfway between ship and shore, well on their way to freezing to death.

I didn't ask them if they needed help. I knew what their problem was, and I knew I wasn't supposed to let them know I knew. They were on their own. This was a test. They had to navigate the length of that dark driveway and walk into that dark house. They could do it. They were Downings.

In my family, your eyes eventually adjust to darkness.

I circled around the block and drove by one more time. They were still there, but I was suddenly mindful of a time long ago when their house had belonged to the family of two pretty, dark-haired girls named Paula and Judy, and I'd heard a rumor that Gerard had a wicked crush on Paula or Judy or both, which started when he was high school and might still be affecting him in college. Maybe Gerard had dated them and maybe he hadn't, depending on who you asked. Gerard was able to date girls at will and keep most of the details secret. I felt I had a right to know this time, though, because Paula and Judy were first cousins of one of my sister Mary Ann's friends, Julie, and Julie was my piano teacher, and meanwhile Judy and Paula and their parents were paying customers on my paper route, so there was a good chance I might run into one of them and be expected to know how to treat her.

Unlike the seven older kids, who took piano lessons from the nuns at school by paying an extra quarter, Joe and I were exposed only to the tambourine at Notre Dame grammar school and, once in a while, the maracas. We were forced to have piano lessons at home. To make up for this, my mother hired Julie, who was an ex-nun. Besides dropping out of the convent, Julie had also dropped out of Juilliard, which made her affordable.

Julie's father was a dentist who didn't offer discounts to friends and neighbors, so my family didn't give him our business. He returned the favor by not letting me and Joe deliver his newspaper for the longest time, even though his house was right near the beginning of our route. My mother tried to cover for him by explaining that he had loyalties to another paperboy, but she finally admitted he could be gruff. His wife died before I got a chance to get acquainted with her, but by reputation she used to smooth things out so you could be friends with that family.

I was fond of Julie, but I wasn't allowed to ask her half the questions her weekly visits raised. For one thing, she had a lot of hair for someone who'd been a nun just a couple of years ago. For another, unlike my sisters, Julie kept all her hair in a huge bun, which constantly reminded you of a papoose in the wrong location. She also chose to wear dinner dresses and silk scarves and matching high heels to lessons, and my mother refused to admit this was interesting, even though I'd already overheard something about Julie wearing clothes that used to belong to her mother.

You had to take piano lessons until you got to high school. My family was very musical. We were apt to burst out singing on holidays and during any party after somebody received another sacrament. Sometimes temporary guests or cousins would join in, but they usually couldn't keep up after a couple of hours, so we would happily let them stick around as audience members. Our specialty was lyrics. We knew all the words to sentimental favorites like "I'll Be Seeing You" and "In a Shanty in Old Shanty Town," as well as rock-and-roll hits like "Going to the Chapel" and "Leaving on a Jet Plane." I think the music craze started with my father, who loved to sing before he died, and back then it often involved one of his sisters playing the piano, which was the best explanation for our owning one. All of the Downing kids, no matter how old they were, could play about one complete song on the piano—unless someone accidentally started singing along and threw off their rhythm. Luckily, like the Von Trapps, our family singing style didn't rely on accompaniment.

The one exception to our musical talents was Joe. About the time we were forced into piano lessons, he was diagnosed with perfect pitch, which caused him to do things like teaching himself how to play a guitar that one of the older kids got as a present before we were born. Perfect pitch was a gift from God, so Joe couldn't expect any compliments on his ability, but he could expect to be loaned out for family weddings and baptisms, and to the St. Teresa folk choir, and even just for background music when one of our older brothers or sisters had volunteered to head up the social committee for some good cause.

The total time for our weekly lessons was exactly one hour. This gave Julie a few minutes to warm up the piano with some classical music that made you wish you'd practiced your scales; twenty minutes for Joe's lesson; twenty minutes for my lesson; and just enough leftover time for tea so my mother could demonstrate how to ask Julie polite questions without getting stuck in a real conversation. People with no children of their own could talk your ear off.

I can remember only one particular piano lesson, but our weekly arrangements are unforgettable because they never changed. Almost nothing ever changed in our house because my family had a tendency to get things right the first time. If it ain't broke, don't fix it, as people with bad grammar liked to say. We said, If somebody did break it, try applying some glue or Scotch Tape for looks, and just don't pull down that window shade again, or choose another chair and from now on sit up straight instead of leaning back on two legs.

For lessons, we got together in the parlor, where we kept the good sofa in a space created by a bay window. Julie had the whole sofa to herself. At one end of it was the piano, which you played with your back to Julie while facing the wall of photographs starting with my father and including anyone who'd graduated from high school, except my mother. She chose to be represented around the house by paintings of the Sacred Heart and statues of the Blessed Virgin Mary. At the other end of the sofa was my mother's upholstered rocking chair, which came with a footrest and a brake, both operated by real mahogany hand levers. I sat there, facing Joe's back during his lesson, and I was usually forced to keep the brake on.

Joe got to go first, meaning he didn't have to stay in the parlor during my lesson, which also meant he didn't have to sit there afterwards while I was stuck on the piano bench watching my mother and Julie drink tea in front of me. But going second did give me the advantage of having my lesson short-changed by five or ten minutes almost every week, because Julie enjoyed asking Joe to improvise, especially after he learned how to turn almost any song you knew into a boogie-woogie version of itself. Julie always sat at the piano end of the sofa during my lessons, sometimes attempting to make me aware of the metronome by holding it next to my head like a ticking grenade, but during Joe's lesson, she usually stayed near me so we could discuss how to persuade Joe to devote less time to his guitar and more to the piano.

The lesson I remember was our last one with Julie. It must have happened when Joe was in eighth grade, near the end of my sixth grade, because Julie was asking me to confirm a rumor she'd heard about Joe's quitting the piano any day now. Joe was spreading that one everywhere. I was secretly hoping I could quit, too, and I'd mentioned this to my mother in terms of saving her some money. I had a sense my timing was good, because out of nowhere my mother had recently announced she was going to get a paying job as an assistant teacher in some public school in the fall. Joe heard from one of the older kids that the job was based on our Social Security running out. The four oldest kids were married by then, Peg was graduating from college, Gerard was in college, and that left only Marie, Joe, and me earning checks every month. Joe kept saying, The government is cutting us off at the knees.

Julie had a lot to say that last day, a lot of it in whispers you could barely hear over Joe's playing, so I finally had to put the footrest down, release the brake, and lean toward the sofa. I think I might have missed the part where Julie introduced the topic, but all of sudden she asked me if I'd ever seen the inside of a spaceship. I mentioned that my family had access to top-secret photographs for our science fairs as a result of an uncle who worked at NASA for a while. Probably I also mentioned he was the one who was now Ted Kennedy's right-hand man. There was a cup and saucer with shamrocks in the china cabinet to prove my uncle had forced Ted to visit our house and use some of our dishes so we'd have souvenirs, but before I could offer to show her the teacup, Julie said she'd been inside a spaceship, and she added, Not one of ours, one of theirs.

I knew instantly she was talking about a UFO.

I must've looked alarmed, because Julie assured me nothing painful had happened to her while onboard.

I was riveted. I wanted to hear everything Julie had to say, and I didn't want Joe to overhear us and stop playing and risk attracting the attention of my mother, who got suspicious during any periods of silence in the house. I looked up at my father's smiling black-and-white face. Usually, I considered that smile his friendly way of forgiving me when I was praying to him about my latest attitude problem or *Sports Illustrated* leading to sudden erections and some other stuff in the bathroom. That day, though, his smile seemed more like a wince. He knew perfectly well that I already didn't believe in UFOs based on some pictures of gas clouds NASA had sent to us with captions about amateur telescope operators trying to claim they were alien spaceships. Nonetheless, I asked Julie where she'd made contact.

That's when she mentioned the golf course. For months, she and her father had been going out at night to a golf course, looking for aliens. I tried to get her to tell me if it was the course at the Pittsfield Country Club or the Berkshire Hills Country Club, because I had a pretty good story about my father getting invited to join the Pittsfield Country

Club and my mother fighting it tooth and nail based on its banning black people and Jews—people we would happily associate with if they ever decided to join our parish. But Julie wanted to tell me about how she and her father brought lawn chairs to the golf course and stayed awake all night. For a while, her details seemed so normal and easy to picture—they packed late-night suppers in a picnic basket and brought a thermos of coffee to make sure they didn't fall asleep—that you sort of doubted she could have made it all up. She started to lose me with her description of the spaceship as a huge, hovering dough-nut and the predictable blinking lights, and then she mentioned wear-ing antenna hats and armbands made of aluminum to attract radio signals.

I asked where they got the hats.

Julie said you could make them out of aluminum foil.

I accidentally cracked up. Remember, the whole time she was talking about the foil hats, she still had that huge bun.

I could tell Julie was offended, but instead of reprimanding me, she started talking louder about being forced onto a cot and strapped down and probed. She claimed it was frightening but pain-free due to their alien fingers' having suction cups. I immediately thought how those fin-gers would nix piano lessons, and that's when I realized Joe had taken off and my mother was standing near the piano bench.

This was fine by me. I was bound to tell her about it eventually. Most of the alarming or unpleasant one-on-one conversations you had in my house ended up being three-ways with my mother in the middle. I really don't know how she felt about being used that way. I think it started out when we were just little kids who needed her to step in and settle arguments or explain things, and she probably expected us to break the habit when we got older. But most of us never did. With nine kids, it saved you time to mention moral concerns or potentially damaging rumors about somebody else to my mother and let her figure out how to get your point across. Whether she liked it or not, as the person in the middle, she usually had the last word.

In a crisis situation, you appreciated her interference. Once she'd intercepted your radio signal, my mother could let you know every-thing you needed to know without moving a muscle. One minute, she was standing by the piano bench, smiling at Julie. Maybe she raised her eyebrows one millimeter to admit to me that this was not her idea of fun. Maybe she adjusted the angle of her head by one degree to indicate the obvious exit for me to use. I know she said something to Julie like, John's friends were always trying to get him to take up golf. The next thing I knew, I was in the hall and she was leaning forward in her rocking chair, talking some sense into Julie.

Julie said something like, John would've enjoyed golf, letting me know my mother had already intercepted her radio signals, too.

John was my dead father, but you had to remember he'd had eternal life granted unto him and was apt to come up at any moment in our conversations. I was pretty sure Julie was going to hear the country club story before somebody called her father to come take her home.

My mother basically took it as a compliment when people unrelated to us decided to have their nervous breakdowns in our house. As she said to me later that evening, Julie feels comfortable here. She knows we'll never mention her problems to anyone.

That was all she offered by way of explanation for the aliens, besides something about Julie's being exhausted, which I took as a cover story. It was well known that Julie and her father had a cleaning lady doing their chores for them.

I didn't mention this episode to anyone for at least ten years, not even Mary Ann, my favorite and most trusted sister and Julie's true friend. Mary Ann had heard about it from my mother, but she hadn't mentioned it to me, either. I doubt she ever mentioned it to Julie. I know I never did. There was no need.

I was looking forward to a summer with no piano lessons and a decimated population in the house when I started seventh grade in the fall, probably with my own private bedroom without Joe, which would mean less time wasted on night prayers and more time with *Sports Illustrated*. June and most of July lived up to my expectations. Marie had turned sixteen and got a job as a lifeguard, like all of my sisters did in high school, at one of the two lakes where I spent my afternoons swimming while my mother read the newspaper and Joe complained about wasting his precious time where there was no basketball court. I also had my lake friends, mostly rambunctious public school kids who were also always broke but willing to admit it. For some obvious reasons, including rough language and Advanced Swimmers having nothing in common with kids still hanging on the lifeline, I kept my lake friends separate from my neighborhood friends, who were mostly not allowed to overlap with my school friends, who never got mixed in with my cousin friends. I could make myself at home with almost anyone as long as I knew I wasn't exactly who they thought I was.

There was a lot more yard work every morning those days, since it was divided only between me and Joe, who was famous for spending more time finding gloves to prevent blisters than hoeing the garden. He also wore long pants and long-sleeve shirts as a method of embarrassing you in public, claiming he hated sunburns and got plenty of vitamin D through his head. Instead of random inspections and monitoring us from the kitchen window, though, that summer my mother had started to shake things up by coming outside after supper when I'd be watering the garden while Joe was in the cellar, claiming he wanted to find a new rubber washer to install on the outdoor faucet so we didn't waste God's precious resources with drips. This gave my mother and me a chance to discuss Joe's inability to enjoy life's simple pleasures, like sitting in the grass you mowed that morning eating a carrot or a raw tomato like farmers, or why Peg was working in a New York state-park concession stand with a new college degree, or how Gerard's being away for the summer working was no skin off our backs. Being just like my father, Gerard's biggest contribution to gardening was buying bleu-cheese dressing to slather on the tomatoes.

Nobody in the family was admitting it yet, but I could tell everything was changing, and this suited me just fine. The disappearance of the older kids made me less obviously the baby of the family, and without them constantly reminding her, my mother often forgot my bedtime. Also, I figured once she started that job she could afford some better bikes. I did sometimes overplay my hand. Once, I wondered out loud if we wanted to add a little flower garden in the front yard. This forced my mother into bringing up my history of peculiarity. The point was, I had to guard against sending mixed signals to the neighbors. Possibly as punishment, or possibly because Joe reminded her I hadn't served out my sentence at the piano, my mother suddenly announced Ann from next door was going to be my new piano teacher.

At first, I thought she was kidding. I knew it was impolite to bring it up, but besides not being classically trained like Julie, and besides being non-Catholic, and besides having a personality that didn't always rub you the right way, Ann was blind. My mother argued that she played piano beautifully. I argued that Julie spent half of our lessons using her eyes to stare at my hands so she could criticize my style. My mother argued Ann was already in the house constantly to use our piano. I argued I could probably find that piccolo I'd bought off some visiting missionaries who were desperate for money, which came with a song-book and finger illustrations.

I had about six lessons with Ann. She'd be seated next to me on the bench, showing her inexperience from the start, and she'd order me to play the C scale. I'd get out two notes, three at the most, and she'd hol-ler, *Start again!* like I was deaf. Same with, say, my G or F scales, if we even got that far. Each time, Ann's voice would get louder, and she'd eventually be physically stuck to me by her sweat. My mother would have to interfere and calm her down with cold beverages.

By the end of August, my mother had had just about enough of me, Ann, and my sister Peg flipping hamburgers in a state park. Ann was forced to admit the lessons weren't working out. Peg was forced to move home and search for a decent job. Mary Ann convinced her husband, Bob, to quit the Navy and move back to Pittsfield, and they became regular visitors with their baby. Jack and Jerry had had two babies by then and had to get out of that hot apartment they rented for some reason, so they dropped by to use our windows and yard quite a lot. That's when we started being targeted for weekend visits by Elaine and Bill and their two kids, and Roberta and Dick with at least three kids. This was perfect if you happened to like babies and volunteer-ing as a busboy and dishwasher every night, plus spending Saturday with a brother-in-law teaching you how to paint the bulkhead. Best of all, one of my sisters knew another unemployed mother with her own piano who lived a couple of miles away. As a distraction for my mother, I started hoeing the peppers and tomatoes like crazy, but she hired the piano teacher behind my back. The weekly commute to her house gave me a perfect reason to hate my old bike while all of the profits from my mother's new job went into guest meals and baby showers.

In the family, my life was basically right back to where I'd started as a kid. My new piano teacher, Patty, said so was my playing. Without Joe to make up for my lack of practicing, my only useful strategy was being late for lessons. Since there were suddenly plenty of older kids around to check my departure time, I had to bike all the way to Patty's house and then go right past undetected and down to Elm Street, where there were a couple of useful drugstores with clocks in their windows to help you gauge how to be late without being so late Patty would panic and pick up the telephone. A watch would have helped, but you didn't get one of those till you were in high school, which is when you could quit piano lessons and would have no possible use for it.

Most of the rest of that year is a foggy blank in my mind. If my suspicion is right that my seventh-grade teacher ended up also being my eighth-grade teacher, that might have caused my blurred memory. I do remember I stopped reading, partially in protest for being banned from reading the books discussed at dinner by the older kids, and partially because no one noticed, including me after a while.

I spent a lot of time hovering above my life, held aloft by other people's ideas about what I was doing, waiting to be engaged. You can call it adolescence. You can call it diffidence. If the sidewalk still hadn't been shoveled, my mother usually referred to it as laziness.

I still have bouts of hovering, though I like to think of them as scientific experiments. I was in the midst of a long one near the end of 2003. On Monday, 15 December, I was standing beside the dining room table in my home in Cambridge, repeating the protocol I'd set up after the last day of the fall semester at Tufts University. On one side of the table I'd arranged six boxes of meticulously culled and filed research for a book I was supposed to be writing on the history of daylight saving time. On the other side, I'd stacked the twenty-four portfolios of original fiction I was supposed to be evaluating for final grades in the two creative writing workshops I'd taught.

I didn't move. These were the two halves of my professional life. I was hovering, waiting to be drawn to one of them. For the seventh day in a row, I noted, those boxes and that stack of portfolios continued to exert precisely the same degree of anti-magnetism.

The telephone rang. It was my sister Peg. She was calling to tell me that earlier in the morning our brother Gerard had walked out of his home in Pittsfield and dropped dead.

My sadness was vertiginous.

Gerard was fifty-two, the father of four, and the long-time district attorney for Berkshire County. Peg told me the local news was reporting that Gerard had been shoveling snow, but she had been assured this was not true. He had simply dropped dead.

I was still dizzy. Plus, my view of my furniture and walls had changed, as if instead of seeing, I was watching a broadcast of familiar objects projected in relief, backed by blackness. Something—I figured it had to be blood or air—was being pumped and drained too forcefully between my chest and head. For the first time in my life, I wondered if a heart attack would hurt or feel like this, an instant, heady, exhilarating exhaustion. I accused myself of melodrama. I sat down so I wouldn't do something really peculiar, like passing out or moaning into the phone.

This was my story and it wasn't. Gerard was a ringer for my father, minus six inches in height. Unlike me, they both liked just about everybody. They were gregarious optimists, overweight, drawn to public life and Mass on Sunday, and their likeness even extended to a shared taste in associates. Gerard's first assistant district attorney was the son of one of my father's close friends, a former mayor of Pittsfield. I resembled my mother physically—right down to a single, shared allergy: walnuts. At the time, she was eighty-six and upright, which tallied with my plans for my life. I was forty-five and I was an atheist, and in coronary terms, I had every reason to believe I was safe.

No one saw my brother die. More than an hour passed before his body was found by his wife, Pam, in the driveway. Somebody called an ambulance, which necessitated the dispatch of a fire truck—just the sort of expensive, union-negotiated superfluity that my family endorsed as a down payment on the debt owed to the working class. I don't think there was a doctor in either vehicle. None was needed. No autopsy was performed. None was needed. Peg apparently knew, as everyone

I spoke to during the next week apparently knew, that Gerard's heart attack had been sudden and massive. It was common knowledge my brother had not suffered for a second. The official diagnosis was God's will.

We knew this song. It was 1961, and one block away from Gerard's home, in the house where I grew up, when my father got out of bed in the middle of the night, walked into the bathroom, coughed, and died. He, too, was a beloved public figure in the Berkshires, president of the Association of Business and Commerce. He was forty-four. No autopsy was performed. None was needed. He'd had an instant and painless death, thank God.

So, yes, it had snowed last night in Pittsfield, but Gerard had gone outside this morning with a broom, not a shovel. Just like Dad, just like Gerard, we agreed, talking ourselves into believing a familiar version of this story. Household chores were not their forte. The point was, Gerard was not responsible for his own death. He died. God's will.

If you believe in God and you are forced into laying bets on who in the world knows God's will, you'd be crazy to bet against my family. We prayed so much that one of the older kids gave my mother a kneeling pad for her birthday to use during the family Rosary so her knees wouldn't give out and force her into a chair. Even leaning back on your heels would set a bad example for any strangers kneeling bolt upright among us in the parlor, like one of the rookie in-laws or somebody's astonished date for that night or a new kid in the neighborhood who hadn't figured out yet not to drop by right after dinner. I'd heard my parents used to get out of bed at 3:00 AM to pray as part of a club my mother had joined that was dedicated to the perpetual Rosary. I'm not sure if this was my father's idea of a good night's sleep, but my mother was a tireless innovator.

By the time I was in high school, my mother and my three eldest siblings suddenly started having visions. They spoke in tongues. Prophecies sometimes popped into their heads, often involving useful advice for people like me, who obviously weren't getting any gifts of their own from the Holy Spirit. Occasionally, they prayed so hard they passed out—though they lobbied hard for the rest of us to use the phrase "slain in the spirit."

I didn't know it at the time, but when people I loved and admired took to toppling over in rapture, the foundation of my faith was shaken. I did know I was gay, and I knew my private raptures were unlikely to improve my status in heaven or at home. So when I went away to college, I kept going and going until I felt I had escaped the centrifugal force of my family. I turned up for the occasional holiday, forged genuine friendships with Mary Ann and Joe, and often talked on the telephone to my mother. In a family of nine children, someone else is usually madder or crazier or more troublesome than you are, so I was never the furthest-out outlier. On the family radar in 2003, I and my partner of twenty years, Peter, probably registered as benign UFOs blinking somewhere in the middle distance. It felt right, this orbital posture—responsive to, but not governed by, the pull of the past.

By midday on that Monday in December, I was somewhere west of Springfield on the Massachusetts Turnpike in my old Saab. Peter would soon be in his car on the same road, but he was at least a few hours behind me. Ahead of me was the first soft rise of the Berkshire Hills, bruised blue spruce shot through with silver maple boughs. I floored it, and then I opened the windows and breathed in the intoxicating atmosphere of my youth, the bracing air of tragedy infused with the odor of sanctity.

I really believed I was acting out of free will, that I was traveling to Pittsfield to honor my past. I wouldn't know what had really happened for many months. I couldn't yet see that the bottom had fallen out of the family history, leaving a black hole. It was irresistible. Against my will, I was being drawn back in.

I drove directly to Gerard's house. His wife, Pam, was in the kitchen. His youngest son, sixteen-year-old Nick, came and went several times while I was there, often returning with another bouquet of flowers so Pam could pluck the card and he could find a surface not yet bedizened. Their grief was total, and it was instantly evident that my brother had been loved this way, totally, by these people whom he had loved best in the world. This made me deeply happy—an emotion of dubious utility, under the circumstances. But of all his siblings, I probably knew Gerard least well, and besides a bag of comestibles from Cambridge, I wasn't bringing much else to the table, which was already stacked three stories high with doughnuts, deli platters, and Danish pastry.

I drove around the block to my mother's house. Peg met me on the back porch. We hugged. We were both weepy. It usually took something tragic to get my family into emotional unison.

Except for her last two years of college, Peg had lived with my mother all of her life, making it easier for the rest of us to go when we felt we had to, as her sometimes puzzlingly pacific demeanor and inalienable affection sometimes made it easier for me to come home. Peg was paired with Gerard in my imagination of the family before I was born. He was sort of surrounded by sisters, and Peg had been a tomboy when she could get away with it, according to the stories I'd been told. She was also the principal of the high school all of Gerard and Pam's kids attended, as had I and all of my brothers and sisters except Jack, who got the privilege of being sent to a Jesuit prep school so he could fail to fulfill my father's social ambitions and my mother's moral expectations without cracking a book.

My mother was seated at the kitchen table, taking up about as much space as a cardigan sweater. She had lost her beloved husband, and now she had lost her most beloved son. She was inconsolable. The only relief I brought her was the news that I had stopped first to see Pam.

If my mother was reliving her own history in this moment, she wasn't letting on. I knew she was. The many loyal friends of my father who spoke at the Berkshire County courthouse ceremony the next day said they were. Almost every one of the thousands of people who came to Saint Teresa's church for the marathon wake on Wednesday (the funeral parlor had correctly predicted that people would be standing outside for hours in the freezing cold if they didn't find a place for the wake in which you could snake the line and get several hundred inside at a time) said they were sure she was when they finally made it up to the altar, where Gerard's casketed body was flanked by Pam and their four children, Pam's parents, and a kind of seven-hour tag team of Jack and Jerry, Mary Ann and Bob, Peg, Joe, Peter and me, and my mother, until she wisely retired to a front pew backed by several dozen grand-children, her one living brother, nieces, nephews, and great-thises and great-great-thats, but neither the two oldest nor the youngest of her five daughters. At one point in the festivities, there was a rumor flying around in the sanctuary about a confrontation in front of the church involving those three aggrieved sisters and one of Jack's angry daughters. At any one time, there were usually two or three raging civil wars being waged by factions within my family, and Mary Ann and I had a policy about not taking sides, which that night just meant taking our cigarette breaks outside a basement-level side door.

But from the moment I first saw my mother on the afternoon of the day Gerard died, all she really wanted to know was what was being done, what could be done, what hadn't been done for Pam and her children.

You couldn't help admiring her. You couldn't help pitying her. And if you were apparently exactly like her—which was constantly conflated with being her favorite by people who were not like her and didn't instinctively understand that she didn't really approve of herself—you couldn't help wishing she had died before any of her children.

Jack and Jerry had invited everyone to dinner on Monday night. Jack or one of his many children had mowed my mother's lawn and shoveled her vast sidewalk and heaving concrete driveway for years. Jack brought her the Sunday papers every week. Jack was her most provocative and persistent partner in piety. If Jack had died instead of her favorite, Gerard, we'd have starved, unless Mary Ann and Bob had already made reservations and promises to pay.

"Nobody said we were perfect," is what I'd like to say, but people said it all the time, and they didn't get any arguments from us.

I was staying at the Hilton hotel six blocks away with Peter. Mary Ann and Bob and their three kids and grandkids would be there, too. Home away from home away from home.

It snowed constantly that week. In December, Pittsfield is basically Buffalo without the Bills. The weather didn't prevent the state's elected luminaries and dignitaries from turning up for the funeral. It didn't interfere with the state police leading a mile-long cortege from the funeral Mass to St. Joseph's cemetery. It did prevent the digging of a hole, so when we retreated to St. Joseph High School for a reception, Gerard's body was still balanced above the dirt in which my father's body was interred. This tallied with my own sense of being there and not being there, belonging there and not belonging there.

The relentless wind hadn't prevented a nearly broken-down old man none of us knew from walking to the cemetery in the snow to honor Gerard for being "a really fine man, the best I ever knew." I met him at the reception because a few people had noticed him arriving at the gravesite just as the rites ended and then saw him walk away without a word. Someone among a busload of Gerard's colleagues had passed the old guy and insisted the driver stop to pick him up and invite him to the reception because, as one of them later told me, That's what your brother would have done.

That's what my father would have done. Maybe my mother would have done the same, but I have to admit I can easily picture the two of us in a car, not stopping as we passed the old guy, so as not to invade his privacy or bring attention to his not owning a car, and then discussing for days how much we admired him.

After the dinners, civic ceremonies, religious rites, and more finger sandwiches than you have fingers, at some point you realize it's over. It comes on you like evening. You have entered the aftermath. After the reception, Peter and everyone else with a car drove a lot of people somewhere. He was driving back to Cambridge. I was going to meet Mary Ann at the hotel and then head to my mother's house to prepare for a few hundred more visitors, who were in for a lot of donated deli meat, Danish, and every word of the American songbook. Gerard's eldest son, Ben, had a car; his brother, Nate, wanted to walk the mile home alone; I dropped Pam and Nick and his sister, Maggie, in their driveway on Pomeroy Avenue. I waited. They waved. I backed out and paused. They waved. I drove to my mother's house to be sure she was not already swamped.

She was at the kitchen table alone.

I made coffee and poured us both a cup. I don't remember either of us saying a word until I sat down.

She said, Did Pam get home?

I said she did.

She narrowed her gaze.

I said, I'm sure. I drove her.

Thanks, she said.

She raised her chin about an eighth of an inch—a request for additional details.

She didn't go in the house, I said. I waited. She didn't go in.

She's afraid. I don't blame her, my mother said, but she has to go in. She has to go on.

We didn't say much more than that. My mother did let me know that Pam had told her about already being so nervous without Gerard in the house that she'd locked every door and window at night. She didn't want anyone to know Pam had told her this. My mother reminded me how infrequently Pam had been alone. Gerard had been famous for never staying in a hotel when he was in Boston for business. He always drove home, no matter how late he was starting out, no matter how exhausted he was. It must have been a point of pride. He'd worked this into his last conversation with me.

On my way to the hotel, I drove by Gerard's house. Pam was still standing in the snowbanked driveway, where I'd left her, but now all four of her kids were huddling with her. More than any of my many reproductive siblings, Gerard had made a singular, cohesive, self-contained family. Even as the kids became adults, the six of them turned up places like a successful team—spirited, engaged, alert to the ground rules, and happy to retreat to their home field. I wondered if that was the family my father had had in mind.

I circled back past their house. I could imagine standing there, forestalling the onset of the aftermath. I knew one of them was going to have to screw up the courage to lead them into the dark future. I was certain they didn't need any coaching from me.

I waited for more than an hour at the hotel for Mary Ann. Someone had called her or Bob. Somebody else was trying to rouse somebody who worked for the city and would be happy to have a chance to do a favor for Gerard Downing's family. Nobody had wanted to disturb my mother by calling her house. Somebody else claimed he'd already gone straight through the yellow pages without any luck. And somehow

Mary Ann and Bob had ended up at the fire station to ask a crew to take another fire truck to Pomeroy Avenue and find some way to help Pam and her four kids because they were freezing cold and had been trying for twenty minutes to find a way to get into their house, which they'd locked up before the funeral, having left all of their keys inside.

In the end, something had to be smashed. Or the firemen saved the day. Or a locksmith turned up. Eight or nine of my relatives were present, so there are probably a few more authoritative versions of the story. All I know is somebody told me that all the emergency personnel on the scene were initially directed to a little window in the cellar, which a couple of Gerard's kids had been forced to kick in years earlier to sneak in after curfew without disturbing their parents. It was the one window everyone was certain Pam hadn't bothered to lock. They found the window easily enough. Instead of glass, the frame sported an old pine board, and the sash had been nailed down to the sill by Gerard, a home-repair job my father would have been proud to call his own.

8. The Other Lazarus

One month after my brother Gerard died, I got together with my family for another wake and funeral in the Berkshires. Mourning always makes us happy to see each other. At a wedding or graduation, our casual greetings are often inflected with uncertainty, and even a genuine embrace is apt to be electric with ambivalence. But put a corpse in the room, and we are immediately recognizable to each other and instantly at ease.

Mary Matthews was ninety-five when she died. She was the mother of Mary Ann's husband, Bob, and we had tracked her long and slow decline for several years. We had loved her because we loved Bob since he had fallen in love with Mary Ann. Still, most of our sadness was residual. Maybe most sadness is: At appropriate moments, you reach into your past, tug the coil of private grief, and momentarily extend your sympathy to someone else. Then you hope for decent food and an open bar at the reception after the burial.

Mary Ann and Bob had booked bartenders, caterers, and a big, windowed room at the Berkshire Hills Country Club. It was the third week of January 2004, and like every new year in Pittsfield, most of this one was still buried beneath several feet of snow. The golf course was entirely under wraps, which kept to a minimum the number of rhetorical questions about people who devote themselves to knocking a ball into a hole eighteen times. If you admired the view, though, one of my siblings was quick to point out that the snow made you aware of how beautiful this land must have been before the country club had bought it up and groomed the good out of it—almost as beautiful as the land at the two public lakes where we swam for free as kids, instead of crowding into an overchlorinated private pool jam-packed with spoiled brats whose fathers were paying attention to their putters instead of their kids, who were probably peeing in that pool.

At some point, I was seated at a round table with my mother; Gerard's widow, Pam; my sister Peg; my brother Jack and his wife, Jerry; and a few other relatives. They were done eating. I was done as soon as I'd seen the chafing dishes. Almost any food in quantity is automatically promoted to my least favorite food. My family credits my peckishness in public to food snobbery, but it has a more venerable history.

Before I was old enough to attend school, I would often wake early to join my mother in the kitchen before the troops assembled and breakfast was served. Typically, she'd have a double boiler full of steaming oatmeal or a poacher full of eggs on the stove beside a cauldron of hot chocolate. Buttered toast would be cooling somewhere. While her coffee percolated, she'd assemble brown-bag lunches. On the counter next to the sink, she'd have twelve or fourteen slices of bread arranged in pairs; an open jar of mayonnaise; sliced cheese, sliced tomatoes, and sliced bologna or ham; and an assortment of bananas, apples, and oranges. Long before I saw her, usually as I hit the landing halfway down our long run of carpeted stairs, I would get a whiff of what she was up to. The elements of the many meals she was preparing always cohered into a single, unlikely stew in my imagination. More often than not, this would occasion a detour into the half bath under the stairs, where I would vomit, wash out my mouth, slather a little toothpaste on my tongue for freshness, and then happily join my mother for a few quiet moments in the kitchen.

I got over this during first grade, as if the habit of carrying my lunch to school taught me a kind of sensory discretion. It was not until I was in eighth grade, though, after she had started making lunches for Marie, Joe, and me the night before, that I mentioned my old morning ritual to my mother. She nodded. She had a way of making everything seem normal. That's normal, she said, adding, I feel that way at those buffets where they put the fish next to the blueberry pie.

Not that any sane person who'd ever tasted a crust made from scratch would bother with that pie.

It took a while, but by sunset, even Bob's closest relatives had conceded the party was over at the country club. Mary Ann was finally able to pull a chair up to the round table and join the rest of us, who'd been waiting patiently for the crowd to clear and the noise to die down.

Mary Ann said she wanted to discuss something. Who didn't? After we'd spent a full day surrounded by people unrelated to us, she hardly had to prime the pump.

Mary Ann said it was about her heart.

This was greeted by silence. In my family, illness was discussed after you'd recovered, typically by offering up your suffering for the souls in purgatory or taking a swig of Coke syrup from the medicine cabinet, or applying some unlikely topical treatment. I'd been controlling my eczema with Listerine since I was tall enough to reach up onto Gerard's bureau and experiment with his private stash of personal-hygiene products. (In a pinch, aftershave will get you through an itchy night, but the odor raises questions.) When you were desperate, you could mention your symptoms to a sibling to prevent exposing your weakness to a doctor, but these humiliating consultations were usually cut short with the provision of cotton balls and hydrogen peroxide. And there was always a little bottle of St. Joseph's chewable orange aspirin in the house for people who weren't able to sweat out their fevers after twenty-four hours. If you were ever going to require an office visit or surgery, you definitely put it off until it could be handled as an emergency with only seconds to spare.

It was typical of Mary Ann to ignore the old taboo. She was prone to controversy. She was also getting to be known as an overreactor. Years earlier, when she and her family lived in Pittsfield, Mary Ann had been known as the reasonable one, the person to go to before you went to my mother with any special requests or embarrassing questions. She got this reputation because my mother developed a habit of cutting off unpleasant conversations and sending you to Mary Ann's house for a pre-interview. But then Mary Ann had a couple of bruising fainting episodes, which she insisted on calling "seizures" instead of admitting she was high-strung and drank too much coffee. She opted for medication, totally ignoring the prescriptions for joining a prayer group or, at the very least, attending Sunday Mass like a normal person instead of constantly harping on the coincidence of one of her fainting episodes occurring in a church. Finally, she up and left the Berkshires—basically just so Bob could keep working for General Electric, which was shutting down its huge transformer business and pulling the plug on Pittsfield's economy.

After she moved, Mary Ann's advice and opinions often showed her reliance on outside experts, including doctors and the *New York Times*. She was constantly accused of taking everything too seriously and analyzing it, an intellectual way of emotionally overreacting that appealed to me. It was no help to her moral standing that Bob made way more money than any of her siblings and spread it around. The rest of us understood that my mother could've afforded to pay for two weeks in a cottage on Cape Cod—or one week, anyway—and her fourteen-year-old Chevy probably had a few more years in it, but we also understood that Mary Ann had a need to write those checks.

Evening was smoothing the shadowy swales and swells of the snow-bound golf course. I probably broke the silence by saying something like, What about your heart? I knew what was coming. Mary Ann had tipped me off. In the months ahead, however, I would know what it felt like not to know what was coming. I would feel precisely as I had during those morning moments on the landing of the stairs, overwhelmed and slightly sickened by the complicated stew that my family history had stirred up.

Several months earlier, Mary Ann's primary-care doctor had noticed evidence, in a standard diagnostic test, of a slight thickening of the wall of her heart. He deemed this age-appropriate but said it would merit attention in his analysis of future test results. In a subsequent conversation, Mary Ann mentioned Gerard's death, and her doctor urged her to see a cardiologist immediately, preferably a doctor associated with a university teaching hospital. During her search for a specialist in New Haven, New York, or Boston—all within a couple of hours of her home in Connecticut—Mary Ann recalled that she and several of our siblings had sent blood samples to a laboratory in Boston in the early 1990s. At the time, one of Gerard's children was being treated for an unusual and severe case of hypertrophic cardiomyopathy, a thickening and stiffening of the heart muscle that can occasion cardiac failure. Mary Ann never received any follow-up information from the laboratory about her blood sample or how it was used. But her doctor's alarm and her own confusion after Gerard's death compelled her to cast a wide net in January 2004, so she contacted the laboratory.

On the same day that her mother-in-law died, Mary Ann received an email from the clinical coordinator at the laboratory, an affiliate of the Harvard Medical School department of genetics. Mary Ann spoke to the laboratory's director, who expressed her sympathy and sadness about Gerard's death. She'd read his obituary in the *Boston Globe*. She briefly described her role in the identification of genetic mutations in specific contractile proteins, which she believed had direct bearing on the health of the entire Downing family. Even without a DNA test, the geneticist warned Mary Ann, the presence of detectable heart disease combined with a family history of unexplained, sudden death in successive generations dictated immediate treatment.

At the time, I didn't know my ventricle from my atrium, and I wasn't alone. Somebody at the table wanted to know exactly how many centimeters of thickening constituted a problem, as if we might as well find a tape measure and figure this thing out. Somebody else suggested it would have to be millimeters. What was Mary Ann's cholesterol count? She ought to have an EKG. She had. Somebody bragged about taking an aspirin every day, just in case. What about an ECG? Somebody prescribed beta blockers. A vote was cast against light mayonnaise. What about an echocardiogram? Was an ECG the same as an EEG?

All Mary Ann knew for sure was that the Harvard laboratory was willing to foot the bill for testing DNA from the eight living siblings, and no matter what the results were, she would probably end up with a defibrillator implanted in her chest.

Pam said she couldn't take any more of this conversation, and she didn't want to hear another word about defibrillators.

I said we weren't talking about defibrillators; we were talking about Mary Ann staying alive.

My mother said, Gerard is not even dead one month.

I knew what she meant. She meant it was insensitive to talk about hearts and death in front of Pam. She also meant it was typical of Mary Ann to spend her time shopping for experts who didn't know the first thing about our family but would happily turn us into guinea pigs to advance their careers at Harvard.

To my surprise, it was Jack who said that was the point—Gerard died. And Dad died.

Maybe Jack was looking at Mary Ann. Maybe he was looking at me. I don't remember. I do know that this was the first time it occurred to me that the deaths of my father and my brother might not be eerily corresponding or suggestively parallel tragedies but two events in an unfolding sequence.

I am pretty sure I quickly and probably too vehemently added something about not wanting Mary Ann to die, because I remember Peg cautioning me about being melodramatic. Fair enough. I had crossed the line. In my family, there was a simple distinction. Drama was you died. Melodrama was you were alive and expressed an emotion.

We eventually dragged this conversation to my mother's house—that evening, I think, as I can't recall anyone else dying that winter and occasioning another reunion. Joe volunteered to inform absent siblings. Jack and Mary Ann plotted to press for inclusion of their children and that entire generation in the free testing pool. I reminded myself that I was more like my mother even than Mary Ann, who looked a lot like us but had a couple of varicose veins and wasn't committed to bananas and other simple fare that sustained our superior veins, hearts, and mutual sense of superiority on health issues. You got good genes, my mother often said to me. In return, she got recipes for fish and vegetables Peg wouldn't eat and my cure for weird rashes. She'd happily reported that none of those wildly expensive prescription unguents did the trick like Listerine.

We were oddly alike, my mother and I. We were not identical. And more than gender distinguished us. Her hair was black, mine brown; she was way shorter than I. And yet our bodies were the soul and spirit of our relationship. Our physiological peculiarities and the preferences they engendered were an unstinting source of relief and delight. This singular solace survived the miseries of family life and the miseries we inflicted on each other. You can call this love, but trust me, that will fuck you up. My mother and I both lived long enough to understand that we had loved other people better and had been better loved by others, too. What we had was the singular authority to say, I know you. It was an assurance and a recrimination, an acknowledgment and an accusation. It was a relief.

I know you.

As we discussed our hearts in her kitchen, I tracked my mother's tired, narrowed gaze. You didn't have to know her very well to know that she had seen enough. You did have to wonder if she was wondering why she was alive. She had tried to die not long before Gerard had died.

My mother often boasted about her uncommonly strong heart muscle. It amazed doctors. Her chronic high blood pressure, however, didn't surprise anyone who'd spent more than an hour in her company— during which time she'd probably washed the kitchen walls, ironed a dozen shirts and blouses, and made lasagna for ten while you drank your coffee and complained about how busy you were. Late in her life, she was told she had a leaky heart valve, but she was eighty and frequently short of breath while vacuuming before she was willing to contemplate surgery. By then, most of the doctors who knew her were dead, and the younger guys didn't have the expertise to see that her old heart could easily muscle its way through the surgery. In the late summer of 2003, she went to Boston, to one of the Harvard teaching hospitals, where she figured they'd do anything if you had insurance. She got nowhere with her heart, but somebody noticed a huge cancerous tumor on her lower spine and scheduled a consultation with a surgeon. After the surgeon delivered the tumor news, my mother thanked him for his thoroughness and got ready to go home.

I was in that consultation room with Peg and Mary Ann when the doctor recommended removal of the tumor. It was growing, he said. It was cancerous.

My mother thanked him again. She didn't have much tolerance for know-it-alls.

Peg was her healthcare proxy. Since she'd been old enough to talk in full sentences, Mary Ann had been my mother's one trusted confidante on matters she didn't want to discuss with her children. I was there to ask provocative questions peppered with vocabulary I'd googled, and to take notes. I think we all felt like failures for not having dug up a doctor who would give her the goddamn heart valve she was finally willing to admit she needed.

My mother said, What will happen if I don't have the operation? She had already made it clear that she was not opposed to dying.

The doctor said the tumor would soon grow enough to cause such utter, relentless agony that no amount of morphine would relieve it. Somewhere in my notes is the phrase "screaming in pain."

By the time the surgery was underway, Jack and Gerard had driven to Boston to join us. As it ended, we were called from the spacious public waiting room to a tiny cubicle in the deep basement, just outside the operating room. There was a window onto the corridor, and we'd been instructed to watch for my mother, who'd be rolling by at any moment. She had insisted on seeing us.

The cancer excision was a complete success, thanks to an innovative approach the surgeon had invented for lower-back tumors, which involved hanging my mother over a stainless-steel bar. Unfortunately, it hadn't occurred to anyone that folding an elderly woman in half and hanging her like a towel for an hour might put a strain on an eighty-year-old heart that was already working overtime to compensate for a faulty valve. Had they asked, I really think we might have inquired about alternative positions.

Instead, they asked us to persuade her to let them perform an emergency quadruple bypass surgery. Otherwise, she would die.

Mary Ann produced a copy of my mother's Do Not Resuscitate order.

The heart specialist looked at it like a bouncer examining a fake ID. His point was, Your mother is awake and breathing now.

Mary Ann's point was, Since when?

I had a file full of notarized documents describing my mother's expressed intentions not to be kept alive by extraordinary means.

The doctor's point was, I do this surgery five days a week. For him, this was ordinary, and that was good enough for him.

Then my mother zipped by on a gurney, her body bent and bolstered to protect the incision on her back, her hair matted to her head. An attendant had been instructed to park her by the door of another operating room so she could speak to us.

How could she speak?

She did. I heard her. Mary Ann heard her. I can't account for anyone who was in that hallway not hearing her. She said, I don't want them to do anything else. A doctor explained the surgery that was being proposed, and she shook her head. The doctor expressed his exasperation. I don't recall what she said next, but before she was wheeled away, she made it clear to the doctor that her children would make the right decision for her.

Somebody in a mask told us that without the surgery, she would die. The corridor was lousy with doctors, so it was a relief when we were herded back into the little room. For a while, we approached the dilemma like good Democrats accustomed to being in the minority —we basically filibustered, talking to forestall any action. Time was short, however, and it was soon being counted down for us by a new doctor who'd watched too many NASA launches.

Mary Ann was the first to voice her vote: No more. She said she was representing what my mother had made clear in many discussions in recent years, what my mother had articulated when she had signed her living will, and what my mother had said when we stood beside her gurney. My other siblings voted for the surgery. The doctor looked relieved.

I trusted Mary Ann. I trusted my mother to know what she wanted. But I didn't trust myself.

I voted for the surgery. Peg signed the consent form, and the doctor left.

My mother lived to see more grandchildren and more trouble in her family; she lived to see another surgery and another summer and to see her son die. She lived to know that she would not have lived if, like Mary Ann, her other children believed and respected and represented her wishes.

I now understand that my mistake was not really a failure to trust myself. My mistake was considering my feelings worthy of consideration at that moment. Instead of endorsing my mother's expressed desire, in my own peculiar way, I chose to intercede. Of all people, I was playing God.

In eighth grade, I'd spent a lot of my time trying to explain why Jesus raised Lazarus up from the dead. The obvious answer about Jesus and Lazarus being best friends was obviously wrong because it made Jesus look like someone who played favorites with his miracles. Lazarus had a couple of sisters, Mary and Martha, and they begged Jesus like crazy to do something about their brother's being in a tomb, but that was no excuse. My dead father had two emotionally unstable sisters at his wake, plus a wife and nine kids and dozens of Catholic best friends, many of them Knights of Columbus, who all prayed their heads off and didn't get any surprising results.

Honestly, I didn't consider Lazarus all that interesting. I did first bring him up, but that was in a religion class, or maybe a religious discussion to fill in time at the end of a history or English class. I know a nun was forcing us to answer a survey question about our favorite miracle and why. I'm sure she had a name. Sister Rose Helen has a familiar ring.

I don't remember much about eighth grade. Except for the arrival of some new kids and a surprise visit from my brother Jack, my last year in grammar school was sort of what I expected, another whistle stop I'd heard about from brothers and sisters who'd blown through before me. By then, I liked being the caboose of that long train.

The pop quiz on miracles was not a total surprise. A couple of other schools in Pittsfield had been forced to shut down due to lack of Catholics, and the nuns at Notre Dame tested out the imports when the school year began. Some of these kids were still lacking Confirmation, and some of the girls in particular had to be singled out for tips on modest ways to hide their puberty, but I'd also noticed several of the transfers were trained math whizzes and had been given information about footnotes, making you nervous every time you copied anything out of an encyclopedia. These newcomers had no problem asking to see your grade on the latest test—another modesty lesson their old schools had skipped. To avoid being creamed by them on the first-quarter report card, I figured I had to build up extra credit in Religion and Conduct and pray it spilled over into my other subjects.

A lot of kids voted for the Loaves and the Fishes (mostly girls, based on the predictable idea about spreading the wealth, except for one genius who took it as a parable about not eating meat on Fridays) or Walking on Water (boys, probably based on Jesus' finally doing something with his superpowers just for fun). Some new kid stole my idea for Water into Wine but blew it by making a joke about getting drunk. Hoping to score some bonus points for originality, I voted for Lazarus. I backed myself up by arguing this miracle showed Jesus giving the Romans and Jews proof he was God (power over life and death) so they would convert and save their souls. My point being, they were so hard-hearted they ended up choosing to crucify him under false pretenses.

I don't remember any applause or anything, but my miracle must have gone over well, because I took the story home. We were getting pretty desperate for dinner conversation. Most weeknights, the four married kids ate at their own houses. They covered for you after dinner and the Rosary with phone calls so my mother could let them know that rash they'd just found on the new baby was known as a rash, not scarlet fever, or how to force-feed a two-year-old without the kid ever knowing it. But at the table, we needed new topics.

Peg was teaching at St. Joseph High School and living at home, but she was often absent with no explanation, forgetting that we weren't running a college cafeteria where you could drop in for meals only when you felt like it. Marie was a senior at St. Joe's and able to convince my mother that she had to eat her pork chop on the way to play practice or a meeting of class officers or a study group. More impressive, my mother had convinced Marie that all this extracurricular activity would mean Marie would be allowed to go away to college for all four years, like Gerard, instead of having to save money and put in two years at Berkshire Community College, like Peg and Mary Ann. This was known as "saving money for the boys," and it tended to make Joe and me even more unpopular and likely to be targeted for free babysitting.

Joe was a sophomore at St. Joe's and rode to school every morning with Marie and Peg in Peg's car. I didn't resent being the only one who had to walk to school every morning. My reputation had definitely improved ever since Joe started high school and stopped filing daily reports on my commute. I didn't resent being the only kid at home not at the high school, either. Joe let me know what it was like in high school by constantly pointing out which annoying habits or stupid ideas of mine would never fly there. Joe was scrupulously honest, so if you didn't mind having your feelings hurt, it could be useful to hear what he had to say. Had they dined with us more often, Peg could have avoided a ton of mistakes Joe had noticed in her method of teaching history, and Marie would've known which of her friends not to bother naming as references when she was trying to get permission to go to a party or some out-of-town school trip.

I don't know if my mother was sick of hearing about high school or still hoping my peculiarities might indicate I was being called to the priesthood, but she really latched on to Lazarus. She started firing off questions, her main interest being why him, of all people? I'd been having a lot of luck in school with the answer *As a symbol,* so I gave it a shot.

Joe immediately accused me of not knowing the difference between a miracle and a parable.

To prevent a fight from breaking out, my mother claimed I was allowed to use Lazarus as a parable in my life as long as I admitted the miracle really happened in the Bible.

Joe claimed this was fine by him, but she had to admit I was basically turning Lazarus into a non-Catholic figure of speech, like comparing Lazarus to Richard Nixon.

My mother immediately said, Helen Gahagan Douglas. This was a reflex, like saying *God bless you* after someone sneezed. Also, telling the famous story of how Nixon cheated Helen Gahagan Douglas out of her rightful seat in the U.S. Senate forced you to mention the nickname invented by Helen Gahagan Douglas for him: Tricky Dick. This was my mother's favorite use of a footnote.

Joe claimed people should have more respect for the presidency. I think he also secretly believed people should have enough respect for the Senate not to allow women in there.

I doubt I was asked for my opinion. My political views were well known to be direct quotations from Mary Ann ever since my mother had discovered I hadn't read a book since the summer of sixth grade and she'd forced Mary Ann to start a weekly book club at her house for me. This was, by far, my favorite punishment ever. Unlike the other Downings, Mary Ann turned out to be a person who read books with no obvious point at all. My mother had at first demanded I hand in book reports, something she'd probably picked up at her new teaching job, but Mary Ann had a college degree *cum* lots of *laude* and was able to argue for a list of questions instead. This was just one of the tricks she had for sparking good discussions.

I had stopped reading when I first figured out I was what we called "homo" and therefore didn't have much of a future as a Downing. Until I graduated high school and went my own peculiar way, though, I knew I had to act like a normal passenger and not make any sudden moves that might annoy the conductor or throw the whole train off track. Not reading wasn't an act of rebellion; it was an experiment. I was trying to calibrate exactly what I did and didn't have to do to stay onboard.

I might never have read another book except for Germaine Greer. I'd overheard several discussions about *The Female Eunuch* started by Mary Ann and focusing mostly on what was wrong with it according to my mother and some of the older kids who refused to read it. I'd long since looked up the meaning of *eunuch*, which was hair-raisingly clear, but after a few weeks of fruitless research, I was forced to ask at dinner how you'd know if a female had been turned into a eunuch. Holy Helen Gahagan Douglas. My mother started accusing me of secretly reading that filth, or at least the filthiest pages—the way most Catholic kids had read *The Godfather*. I panicked and started listing all the books I hadn't read, including school assignments and *Captains Courageous*—somebody's idea of the perfect Christmas gift. That's when she invented the book club.

My mother must have brought up Lazarus at least ten more times that year, always in a way that made me think she hoped I would be able to explain him to her. We'd be driving up the turnpike after visiting Roberta or Elaine, or we'd be rolling back the carpets to paste-wax the floors, and she'd ask if I'd had any new ideas about him. These conversations never really went anywhere. I'd end up not saying what I had really been thinking—that there might be a medical explanation. Like Lazarus being only half-dead and Jesus using mouth-to-mouth resuscitation while no one was looking. Or a coma. She'd end up saying something like, I wish your father could let us know what it all means. He couldn't. It was common knowledge that people in heaven had perfect understanding but could not use it to your advantage, no matter how much they loved you.

The meaning of the miracle escaped me. As a parable, though, the meaning in my life was clear. My oldest brother, Jack, was Lazarus, and he was likely to pop up in my life when least expected.

Sometime during seventh grade, my mother had started dropping hints about the shortage of male role models around the house. I mentioned my father, and she said I could probably use a living role model. I mentioned my basketball and swimming coaches. She claimed they weren't related enough. I mentioned my brother Gerard. I liked the idea of him as a role model because he didn't know Joe and I were alive. My mother reminded me about Gerard's high IQ and everyone having high hopes for him, so we weren't going to create burdens to weigh down his potential. Joe didn't get this message, and kept naming weekends he could clear his schedule for a visit to Gerard at Providence College. Joe also wrote letters, forcing Gerard to waste his energy ignoring them.

Unlike me, Joe was constantly advertising for role models, but even Joe was shocked when Jack got the job. I thought there were three basic reasons my mother recruited Jack. First of all, he had a reputation for terrifying my older sisters when he was in high school, which might come in handy as a skill in dealing with me. Second of all, he was chronically underemployed, living in Pittsfield again, and had only two kids after being married long enough to have at least five. He and his wife, Jerry, had started to take in orphans and juvenile delinquents— fine, because Jack had a new job working with these outcasts and probably got some help from Welfare to feed them, but considering how much she'd done for Jack financially and morally, my mother figured it was about time for him to learn that charity begins at home, meaning her home. Third, Jack had recently allowed himself to be interviewed for the local paper and claimed his new work was inspired partly by being a punk when he was a kid. This was called "going to confession in public." It gave people the correct impression that my parents had been unable to control him, which was called "giving people a false impression." By forcing him to spend time with his two youngest brothers, my mother could give Jack the false impression that she considered him trustworthy, while using Joe and me as informants.

Joe did his share of complaining, but when it came to the stuff that could really bury Jack, I did most of the heavy lifting. Joe had a loyalty streak for brothers older than him. Plus, I think Joe really believed if we played enough Go Fish with Jack's kids, Jack would finally introduce us to some of the cops and probation officers who were his latest friends, and a game of pickup basketball would suddenly break out. I was a better spy because I had no loyalty. I'd betray myself for an orange soda. And I knew which details would really bug my mother— cold macaroni passed off as macaroni salad for dinner; an argument involving the landlord; specific examples of curse words; his kids' knowing biological words for peeing and body parts.

Despite my good work, a few months after I started eighth grade, without any advance warning, Jack was allowed to call an assembly at Notre Dame for the seventh and eighth graders. I knew he'd been doing this to public school kids who were prone to felonies, but I was caught totally off guard by the nuns' admitting him. We were in the cafeteria, which was in the basement and held up by cement pillars but was otherwise as good as the public school facilities, except for having no food or service people.

The intro went off fine. Jack was identified as my brother, and though he was wearing his typical disrespectful clothing, he was over six feet tall, with sandy hair and no visible gut, and I had to admit he was handsome. Plus, he had given them a version of his résumé that set him up as an expert.

He warmed up the crowd with some pretty funny insinuations about kids who broke somebody's window or bullied third-graders and figured they could get away with anything. Then he asked who'd tasted beer but warned kids not to raise their hands, which they appreciated. Without using any transition, though, he went right into the heavy stuff—teen sex acts, imported marijuana, skipping school. And next thing you know, he was confessing sins from his prep school days, including being one of the biggest goons on a hockey team I'd never heard about and trying cocaine. I'm sure he padded his résumé with even worse stuff, but I couldn't hear the end of his presentation from my new location in the boys' bathroom.

Your brother never tried drugs, my mother assured me that evening. We weren't sure, but we both thought cocaine hadn't even been invented till after Jack was out of prep school. She estimated he had experimented with beer twice—three times at the most. She couldn't verify the sports references, but she did mention that most of Jack's friends at prep school were South Americans who played cards. We were seated at opposite ends of the kitchen table. She was ignoring her tea, and she had put her eyeglasses on the table so she could pretend her winces were just squints to see better. To her credit, she apologized for Jack's going to confession in front of all my friends and teachers. She promised it would never happen again, which made me think Jack might be physically incapacitated in some way by the time she was done with him. I'm sure I described the sweatshirt he'd been wearing as I was rolling the stone to seal Jack in his tomb. My mother nodded, and then out of nowhere she came up with this smile and said, Life will never be dull with your brother.

Lazarus was out on bail again.

The point was, my mother wasn't giving up on anybody based on disrespectful outfits or sins of the past. She didn't care how deep you dug your own grave; she'd happily haul you out and hand you a shovel to clean up the mess you'd made.

I didn't tell my mother the whole Jack story. I left out the part about a couple of big transfer kids I barely knew who came into the boys' bathroom after Jack left that day.

He's cool, said one of them.

The other one agreed and added, Must be nice to have a brother who's so with it.

I immediately tried to detect whether they were being kind to Jack or to me. I failed, but that's not why I didn't repeat their comments. As the three of us walked back up to our classroom, like friends, I realized those two guys didn't mean anything special by it. They were just nicer than I was. Out in the world, I was ashamed by the comparison. Once I was at home, though, I realized it was no use complicating my mission. My job wasn't to be a normal eighth-grader. It was to let my mother know the chances were even better than we knew that Jack might be headed straight to hell.

You don't have to be an atheist to behave like a normal person, but in my family it helped. Three months after Gerard died, Mary Ann was sporting an implantable cardioverter defibrillator (ICD) in her chest. More than a few people in the family considered her new device the equivalent of a Rolex—an extravagant accessory for the spiritually impaired. Worse yet, it was an impulse purchase. Many of the rest of us hadn't even contacted the Harvard laboratory, and there was better than even money on Mary Ann developing buyer's remorse. She hadn't used it yet.

In another family rocked by sudden death in successive generations, news of a plausible means of preventing further tragedies probably would have generated more enthusiasm than it did in mine. Perhaps we should have spent a little less time with scripture and a little more with Darwin. Adaptation was not our long suit. In many ways, the organism of the family simply stopped evolving after my father died. Maybe we couldn't bear to leave him behind. Maybe that's why we opted for endurance.

Publicly, we were admired for our perseverance. Privately, we darkened every celebration with my father's absence and diminished each accomplishment with reminders of his towering shadow. I was happy as a kid, but I always understood that no lived moment would ever be as important or impressive as the moment my father died. I think this might be why we prayed so much. We were lonely without him, and often frightened, and surprisingly short on money. We prayed to persuade ourselves that what apparently mattered did not matter.

I'd been at the hospital in Boston when Mary Ann had her surgery. It was the same hospital where my mother's two surgeries had been performed. I had called my mother after it was clear that Mary Ann was going to be fine.

My mother was happy. And curious. She asked, You're not getting one of those things, are you?

I told her I didn't know if I needed one. I did tell her I had finally Fed-Exed some of my genetic material to the Harvard laboratory.

You don't need one, my mother said, as if she'd intercepted my DNA, run it through her old electric mangle until she'd straightened out the twisted strands, and noticed nothing that merited a medical intervention. You're just like me, she said.

She knew me.

A few weeks after Mary Ann was implanted, I got a call from a nurse, the laboratory's clinical coordinator. She offered me the option of speaking to a genetic counselor before I received my results. This didn't sound good, but I figured it wasn't definitive. It reminded me of the early days of blood testing for HIV, when clinics postponed your results until you'd been talked into a stupor by an insanely optimistic nurse so you wouldn't kill yourself on the premises if they handed you a death sentence.

I declined the counseling option.

The nurse said, I'm sorry to say you do have the mutation.

I made an appointment to meet the director of the laboratory.

I didn't call my partner, Peter, as I knew I soon would. I didn't call my sister Mary Ann, as Peter would urge me to do before he hung up.

I roamed around with the telephone in my hand. Peter and I live in a generous slice of an old warehouse, which offers plenty of options for the aimless. I had two impulses. The first was to climb up the two long flights of stairs and get outside, onto the roof deck—just the sort of precarious position I knew my genetic counselor would have counseled me to avoid. My other impulse was to call the nurse, not because I believed she had made a mistake—though I did want her to know that there would be no hard feelings if she ran those tests again and proved the laboratory wrong—but because I realized suddenly that I didn't know what *mutation* meant to me, or what it would mean for me.

My familiar sense of self was a fiction.

I put the telephone back on its base to juice up for the workout it was soon to get. I put myself on the sofa to contemplate my good fortune. I thought of my father and thanked him for bequeathing me a screwy protein instead of something normal, like a house on the beach. I thought of my brother Gerard and the cruel month between that morning he was found in the snowy driveway and Mary Ann's success at tracking down the doctors who might have made it possible for him to survive his untimely death.

I probably should have called my mother. But I really didn't know how either of us would respond when I revealed this unexpected twist in my DNA, this kink in the only cord that still connected us. Plus, it was never easy to tell her you'd flunked a test.

The good news was, I might soon be the electronic Lazarus, buzzed back to life every time I tried to die. The bad news was, I'd have to put my life in the hands of doctors to achieve this miracle, and that bunch had a lot of other tricks up their scrubs. The sad news was, that happy Lazarus story was just for kids.

I got the adult version of the Lazarus story when I was thirty-six or thirty-seven. I'd spent a rare weekend at my mother's house—maybe it was her birthday, maybe we'd had a particularly benign run of phone calls and I was inspired to bring her some decent bread and olive oil. I remember only the moment of departure, the moment just before I should have left. We were at opposite ends of the oval kitchen table, coffee cups between us. The day was darkening, but neither of us turned on a light. We were both really happy I'd been there, which was rarer than real bread in that house.

As I stood up, she said, You know I love you, son.

A declaration of love between us was not a salutation. I had been challenged to a duel.

I said, You know I love you, Mom, and always will.

We'd both managed to make it sound like a bit of a bother.

Game on.

Next time, she said, maybe Peter will come with you.

I said, That's never going to happen. I sat down. Thank god there was still some coffee in my cup.

I think the world of Peter, she said. I want him to know he's always welcome here.

He knows that, I said. More to the point, he admired her, as did almost everyone I knew and admired. But I had a standing policy: day visits, yes; holidays with the cooperation of a nearby hotel, occasionally; overnighting in separate bedrooms in the family home in the Berkshires, no.

She said, It's not normal, you know, to avoid your family. She tossed in Gerard and Jack and their kids wanting to spend time with me, but they were just handy fuel. She was firing up to launch us into the stratosphere. She said, You have no idea how hard this is on me.

I said, For me, it's easy. And this part was. I said, I promised myself that Peter would never feel the force of what you really feel about me.

You could call this policy shame or sanity, fear or fortitude. I called it love, but frankly, given my training, I was shooting in the dark.

I went on and on and on, and we went back and forth, and then my mother began to weep.

My mother was seventy-six or seventy-seven, and well below her fighting weight. Her curly hair had gone gray and wiry, and when she finally raised her head out of her hands, her hairdo didn't recover. Even to me, this seemed a Pyrrhic victory. But I could not unsay what I had said, and given the chance, I wouldn't have. I would have twisted the volume knob back several notches.

I said, I am sorry to make you sad.

She waved that off. You don't understand, she said. This isn't about you. And though I can't vouch for every single word she spoke next, I am confident an X-ray would reveal that most of what followed is branded on my cerebrum: If you don't listen to me now, I won't be able to help you. I'll be dead someday. So will you. This is what I have to live with every day. You will be begging me for relief, and I won't be able to do anything for you. That's what I'll have to live with for eternity. All those flames, and I won't be able to give you even a drop of water.

I don't know how we did it, but my mother and I conspired to get me out of that house in less than five minutes with a hug, a *God bless you,* and a thanks again for the bread.

I'm not sure, I said to Mary Ann when I called her the next morning, but I think Mom is mad at me for being damned to hell and disrupting her eternal rest in heaven.

I hoped that I had missed the point of the parable.

Mary Ann said, I am truly sorry she said it to you. Did you get the bit about the dipping the tip of her finger in the water?

I told her I was not even getting a drop.

That's the point, Mary Ann said. My mother had laid out my incendiary future for Mary Ann several times. It was bad enough during the daytime, but apparently the smell of my roasting flesh had started infecting my mother's dreams, and she'd been waking up in a sweat.

I said, I am in hell, burning to a crisp, and she's got problems?

She's Lazarus, said Mary Ann, and she let me know this was not the happy-go-lucky guy who crawled out of his tomb to eat lunch with his sisters, Martha and Mary. The other Lazarus, said Mary Ann. He was a poor, holy beggar who couldn't get so much as a crumb from the rich man's table and ended up in heaven while the rich man roasted in hell and begged god to let Lazarus "dip the tip of his finger in cool water to cool my tongue: for I am tormented in this flame," according to St. Luke.

Also according to St. Luke, Lazarus the beggar was covered with sores—unlike my mother, but she had left out that part of the story, presumably so I wouldn't start demanding a pass to purgatory on the basis of a few liters of Listerine.

Medical School

1. Occupational Hazards

Listerine, my beloved antibacterial beverage and bath splash, was named in honor of Joseph Lister, an English surgeon who tried to persuade doctors to sterilize their surgeries. This earned him an honorary title, Father of Antisepsis, though you probably know him better as that weird hospital smell. That's Lister's lingering legacy.

Lister didn't invent the mouthwash. His liquid of choice was carbolic acid. Until Lister came along, carbolic acid was being wasted on sewage, which it effectively deodorized. Lister figured it would also clean up hospitals, and in the middle of the nineteenth century he started spraying the stuff everywhere—on surgical instruments, bandages, and incisions. He convinced doctors to wash their hands with a solution of carbolic acid and to put on clean gloves before they got to work, and he even forced them to wash up again with carbolic acid when they were done.

You'd think doctors would have always known enough to scrub their hands before sticking them into your business, but until Lister pointed out that the best way to deal with infections was to prevent them, doctors didn't think there was any relationship between their germs and their patients. Even today, a lot of doctors have more important things on their minds than germs and patients.

On a sunny day in late March 2004, I was trying not to think about becoming a patient, so I was happy to have occasion to think about germs as I scouted for an open parking meter on Avenue Louis Pasteur.

This short, broad boulevard was named in honor of the French chemist whose pioneering experiments confirmed the germ theory of disease. Pasteur was Lister's inspiration, and though an enterprising salesman tried to cash in on his reputation with a mouthwash named Pasteurine, his legacy has been better served by milk and the popular lexicon's embrace of the verb *pasteurize.*

Avenue Louis Pasteur is a gateway street, a transitional corridor from the museums and colleges gracefully spread out along Boston's reedy and willowed Fenway to the main campus of the Harvard Medical School, an emblematically self-contained and self-important granite quadrangle at the center of a vast and expanding pile of concrete and tinted glass known as Longwood Medical Area, the inexplicably ugly empire created by Harvard, five prestigious teaching hospitals, training schools, research laboratories, clinics, and the $10-an-hour parking garages I was trying to avoid that morning.

Instead of entering the medical-complex maze, I did what any normal person would do: I pulled a U-turn and started begging Jesus for a break. I'd acquired this habit of praying for parking spaces as a child after my mother bought the green Bonneville. Before our little pink Rambler wagon died, my mother would just zip into a supermarket parking lot, say something nice to St. Teresa, and no problem. But the new car was a Pontiac, an extrawide three-seater that sometimes forced my mother to knock small parts off the cheap sedans parked next to spaces St. Teresa had opened up for us. Until she got the hang of the wagon, we often needed two parking spaces, so my mother started assigning me the role of praying to Jesus for those rare doubles. I had a knack for it.

I prayed for parking spaces long after I'd stopped practicing my religion, based on the lapsed-Catholic fairness doctrine. If there was a god out there, I was not about to be out-Jesused for a meter by some Protestant. After that phase, I kept it up because I don't have many good habits, and I'd noticed that I was one of the only drivers I knew who was never frustrated while hunting for a legal parking space. If I end up being late, or blocks away from where I want to be, I chalk it up to god's will, and god doesn't exist, which defeats the purpose of investing any emotion in the relationship.

Plus, I constantly get primo parking places.

As I passed a maroon minivan, the driver waved and pulled out, and I backed my old Saab into the space. I locked my car. I had inherited fifty free minutes on the meter. Directly across the street was the biggest building Harvard had ever built, more than half a million hulking square feet of conference rooms and laboratories clad in glass that was supposed to reflect the sky. I bet it looks great from a MedEvac helicopter, but at ground level, that towering glass left me with a radically foreshortened horizon and something dark and faceless in my immediate future—an intimation of what it would mean to cross that street. Adding to its charm was the fact that the building was essentially nameless.

On the second floor of the so-called New Research Building was the laboratory of the geneticist who had identified me as someone I didn't know. I was, according to her, identifiably my dead father's son. My father had passed on to me his myosin-binding protein C gene, a missense mutation named GLU 258 LYS.

I am not on a first-name basis with my DNA. I am cribbing from my medical record. Even the geneticist didn't mention the name or serial number of my peculiar protein that day. She also didn't mention that she'd met my mutation years ago while investigating my brother and his family. This familiarity with the secret story of my life might account for her disarmingly informal demeanor, which I credited at the time to good manners in someone so obviously out of my conversational league. As it turned out, though, this meeting was not the beginning of a relationship but a formality.

About a month earlier, following my sister Mary Ann's lead, I had contacted the laboratory about having my genetic material tested. I'd received a handwritten note from a nurse, a kit with mouthwash (not my brand of choice) and a swab, instructions for performing the DNA protocol, and a Federal Express package with a return label. I'd read the nurse's note informing me that she had alerted a cardiologist at the hospital that I would be calling for an appointment. I hadn't made that call. I was forty-five years old, five feet ten inches tall, and I'd weighed 150 or so pounds since I was eighteen. The few times anybody checked, my blood pressure was reliably in the range of 120/70.

And though I've never believed that cholesterol is a useful measure of anything, I did have mine tested once: 167, despite a lifelong devotion to dairy products.

I didn't have a heart problem.

A few weeks later, in exchange for my soggy swab, I got a call from the nurse, some bad news about that mutant protein my family had taken to calling by the scientific name *Daddy's gene*, and an invitation to meet the geneticist. And had I called that cardiologist yet? Instead of making that call, I decided I should get a second opinion. About what? Unclear. And from whom? Also unclear. I thought about calling my primary-care physician for a referral to a heart specialist, but that seemed a little presumptuous, as we'd never met. One of my principal strategies for staying healthy was to avoid getting into conversations with people who were qualified to dispute my personal sense of well-being.

I didn't need another opinion—I needed to make a choice. Was I sick or was I healthy? Should I carry on as usual or seek medical intervention?

I had my opinion. My DNA had expressed a different opinion. One or the other would turn out to be the story of my life.

I cannot accurately account for the time I spent in the New Research Building. I know I was alone in the lobby, in the elevator, and in the corridor on the second floor. This, combined with the deluxe fixtures and finishes, made me feel I'd wandered into the wrong hotel. The first human being I encountered was the nurse. I remember her seated at a desk a long way from the door I'd opened, but that distance is more profound the more I dwell on it, until she seems to be seated several city blocks away from me, as if Luis Buñuel is directing the movie. All of my attempts to recall the sequence and details of this appointment are similarly distorted.

Fortunately, I took notes. Unfortunately, something the geneticist said early on really threw me off my game, and most of what I wrote down is a jumble of isolated words or phrases, as if I had been standing on a platform with a notepad while she shouted information from the window of a train that was leaving the station. Near the top of the page, I wrote, *first symptom = sudden death?* I don't know if that is a quote or my own transliteration of what the geneticist said, but I am pretty sure it follows from my asking her more than once to explain how my inherited genetic mutation would manifest in a person who, despite expectations to the contrary, turned out not to have any heart disease. I must have pursued this line of questioning in various ways. My page is shot through with arrows leading from other phrases and numbers back to *sudden death?* The rest of what I left with was *father, Boston Globe* (how she first heard about my brother Gerard's death at the age of fifty-three), *9* (number of Downing siblings), *44* (father's age at death), *remarkable/must be* (referring to my mother, I think), the phrase *hypertrophic cardiomyopathy* and its abbreviation, *HCM*, as well as *family history, call any time,* and *great woman*—the cardiologist, presumably, as the next word I wrote was *vigilance*, followed by a telephone number.

Standing on the steps of the New Research Building, ignoring my reflected self behind me, I contemplated my future and my faded green Saab on the other side. I appreciated the geneticist's time, but I was a little insulted. She hadn't asked many questions. She seemed perfectly content to use some gunk extracted from my cheek as the basis for a totally new story of my life. I especially didn't appreciate her dropping hints about a possible surprise ending. She also showed a total lack of interest in my theory of heredity, which aligned me with my mother's side of the family—physically robust people with an aversion to walnuts and other people's opinions, who weren't prone to dropping dead without warning.

I'd spent many years sorting through my inherited sense of self, cultivating the qualities I admired and ditching the stuff that made me miserable. I didn't appreciate some stranger's revising the story of my life. If anyone was going to pluck one weird little detail out of context, stick it under a microscope, and blow it up out of proportion, it was going to be me.

That was my job. And until my DNA had started blabbing, and Harvard had started poaching on my territory, I'd been the principal researcher in this neighborhood.

Avenue Louis Pasteur cuts right through the story of my life. Had I taken a few steps to my left, I would have been on the campus of Emmanuel College, which I first visited when I was ten, to watch my sister Mary Ann receive her degree. She went on to teach and marry, and raise three children. I eventually wound up across the street from Emmanuel on the tidy urban campus of Wheelock College, where I was hired after I'd published my first novel, a story narrated by a woman with three children. I was hired by a woman named Marcia to teach basic writing skills, and from Marcia I learned the habit of copious note-taking. She did it in meetings, during telephone conversations, and when students spoke in class, and now so do I. It makes things memorable.

I stayed at Wheelock until I wrote a novel about a man who teaches grammar at a little college in Boston and inadvertently ignites a political firestorm that gets him fired. It turned out all right in the end. Marcia and I remain great friends. I next wrote a novel about a peculiar little boy, which begins in the Isabella Stewart Gardner Museum, my favorite sanctuary in Boston and home to Giotto's *Presentation of the Infant Jesus in the Temple*, my favorite painting in America. The Gardner, with its Renaissance masterpieces tucked into elegant and homey furnished rooms arranged around a mesmerizingly serene central courtyard, is just one block the other way along the Fenway from where I was standing that morning. I probably could have seen it through the transparent glass on the second floor of the New Research Building had I looked. I'd seen it in my mind's eye from San Francisco four years earlier. I had been out there to read from that novel about the peculiar little boy when my partner, Peter, had called from his office at Boston's Healthcare for the Homeless to say he had an interview for a job—at the Isabella Stewart Gardner Museum. And as I stared at my Saab across Avenue Louis Pasteur, Peter was sitting in his office at the museum, overlooking the courtyard, waiting for a call from me. I was hoping I had not yet used up the inherited time on my meter.

We're all preprogrammed to die. That's what I told Peter a couple of days later when he forced me to admit I still hadn't called the cardiologist.

Peter reminded me that the warranty on my Saab had expired but I still took it in for tune-ups.

I said the prospect of having a defibrillator implanted in my chest raised all sorts of issues. From the cosmic to the cosmetic, I added, having saved that one up for him.

He said, You had a new clutch put in your car.

I called a psychologist. I've never been in therapy, which after forty-five years at the tail end of a vast and voluble family had all the appeal of a busman's holiday. But I get along very well with shrinks. There's something deeply familiar to me about people who doubt every word you say.

The psychologist (another trustworthy man named Peter, so I'll distinguish him as P.) worked at one of the big teaching hospitals in Boston. I told him I was shopping for a primary-care doctor with referral privileges at the hospital that was home to the cardiologist I'd been avoiding. P. gave me three names. At the top of his list was a woman, an internist, who was his doctor. That evening, I mentioned my doctor search to my friend Marcia, who highly recommended her doctor, the same internist.

I didn't mention the coincidence to either of them. Marcia and P. knew each other well, but I didn't think they'd want me to draw back the curtain in the examining room and expose them to each other. If I hired that internist, would I be obliged to tell P. and Marcia? Would I be obliged to tell them about each other seeing her, too? Where was the line between disclosure and discretion? If Marcia and P. and I were comfortable with this medical ménage à trois, and I told the internist how I had come to strip for her, I figured it would be considered perfectly normal for her to ask, How is Marcia? But, at the following visit, would it be okay for me to ask the internist the same question? Next, I wondered whether the answer to any of these questions would change if P., Marcia, and I were all seeing the same shrink.

I was in a muddle over medical ethics, and I didn't even have a doctor yet.

The next night at dinner, Peter asked if I had called the cardiologist.

I said Avenue Louis Pasteur had become my Rubicon, and I wasn't ready to cross it.

Peter said he thought I'd crossed it when I agreed to swab my cheek.

I said, Hypothetically. Or maybe I'm halfway across.

I regretted the Rubicon reference. I knew it had forced us both to imagine me in the middle of the real river at the Fenway end of Avenue Louis Pasteur, a stagnant swamp known as the Muddy River.

Since we were speaking hypothetically, Peter asked what I would say to him if he were the one with the bum gene.

I called the internist. She was full up and not taking any new patients. I quickly called the second doctor on P.'s recommendation list. I got an answering service. I panicked. What if I was having a heart attack? I called the third name on the list, another internist. His nurse said he was accepting new patients, which didn't inspire confidence. I told the nurse I needed a referral to a cardiologist. She said the doctor would probably like to meet me first. *One of those*, I thought. *A real stickler*. It got worse. With new patients, he also demanded complete physical exams.

I let a lot of time elapse before I said anything. I was eleven or twelve, wearing nothing but my underpants and a wicked itchy rash behind my knees. To spare me embarrassment, my mother and the pediatrician were ignoring me while they discussed my claim that I was allergic to wool. I'd developed the annoying habit of breaking out in rashes every time you turned around. I tried blaming chlorine in swimming pools, but my mother said bleach was about the best thing for a rash. I told the doctor about suntan lotions and insect repellants, but he said those fell into the category of luxuries I could easily do without. I'd also had some bad outbreaks after an experiment with somebody's shaving cream recently, but I wasn't going to be offered any sympathy for stealing. The doctor pulled a sheet of paper out of his filing cabinet.

We could test him for allergies, he said. There were three printed columns of potential culprits.

I think we'd find he's mildly allergic to most of them, he said.

My mother reminded the doctor that you have to be careful about where you look for trouble because you are apt to find it. She studied the allergy list. She wasn't one to ignore facts that supported her opinions. She read *dust,* aloud, twice, as a question. The doctor said I might be one of those lucky allergic kids who just outgrow things. My mother said I was due for some growth spurts. We all agreed to skip the tests and opt for more of that ointment that didn't require a prescription and always worked for the older kids in the family. On me, it mostly had the effect of spreading a rash to unexpected places accidentally scratched during the application process. I knew exactly where we kept that ointment—in the bathroom cabinet, right in front of my brother Gerard's private bottle of Listerine.

The internist's nurse asked how long it had been since my last physical. After another long pause, she added, Or your last checkup.

I said, Not counting eye exams?

No problem, she said, your insurance company will send us those records.

This occasioned another pause.

She said, Are you currently a member of a plan?

Oh, yes, I said. I was delighted to give her the number on my HMO card. I thought of it as a gift certificate to a department store that typically stocked nothing in my size.

The nurse told me the doctor didn't have an opening until the middle of April.

It was reassuring to know I wasn't his only paying customer. I flipped through the pages of my daily planner. I asked if he had an opening on the third Monday of June. That's the first day of summer, I said.

Summer, said the nurse, that seems a long way off.

I had a lot of work to do before I could take on the job of preventing my own tragic death. I'd been commissioned to write a play by a theater in San Francisco, and I had to deliver the final draft by the end of April. At the same time, the students in my writing workshop at Tufts expected me to show up on campus until classes ended in the beginning of May. I was also meant to be writing *Spring Forward*, a social history of daylight saving time, and the final manuscript for that book was due on July 1. It got worse. In a fit of optimism sometime in February, I'd convinced myself I had written the last draft of that play and would complete the book with time to spare, so I'd bought a nonrefundable ticket to travel with Peter, whose job was taking him to London and Florence for a week in May.

I did call the cardiologist's office. I booked a date with her soon after my scheduled appointment with the internist. I squandered the rest of that day bemoaning my various deadlines. One week later, daylight saving arrived, and I lost another hour of my precious time.

I love deadlines. They are my best defense against nihilism, which is how I like to characterize my tendency not to do what I am supposed to be doing.

By the end of spring, the play was out of my hands, my final grades had been delivered, and I was sitting on the completed manuscript of my sixth book. I should have been in the catbird seat. Instead, I was naked as a jaybird on the internist's parchment paper–upholstered examination table. The internist was young, and we hit a couple of rough patches in our relationship during the first fifteen minutes. For starters, he asked me about my family history, but as I launched into my theory of matrilineal heredity, he said he'd read my answers on the health questionnaire already. What he really wanted to know was the name of my mutation. When I couldn't deliver, he brought up smoking. I'd admitted to it on the questionnaire— a rookie error. I'd reduced my intake radically, but I was not prepared to give up cigarettes entirely, which he memorialized as "hasn't tried to quit" on my permanent record, right above "denies having firearms, denies fever, denies sputum production, denies STD risk factors," as if he wasn't convinced I wasn't a public-safety risk.

Fortunately, he'd caught me on a day with no inexplicable rashes, my blood pressure didn't betray me, and by the time I was naked, he was very complimentary about what he was and wasn't picking up on his stethoscope. We were finally getting along really well, so we started discussing my testicles—"normal volume, nontender, no masses" was how he described them to the cardiologist in his report, probably to save his friend from having to waste any time down there. He told me he knew the cardiologist and the geneticist. I think he said he'd met them while he was doing a rotation or residency in the genetics lab, but I was not in a position to take notes just then.

He did point out one other problem, two little distended veins on either side of my lower abdomen. I'd noticed them every day after my exercise routine, which concluded with two hundred sit-ups. They went away when I lay down, so I figured they were muscles. I was happy to

have something to show for my efforts. He said they were latent ingui-
nal hernias—not an immediate problem, but something to monitor. I
immediately volunteered to quit exercising. He said it wouldn't help.
He said they had nothing to do with anything I did.

They're hereditary, he said.

It was clear nobody was going to dig up anything good from my
past, so I went home, dug up the notes from my meeting with the geneticist, and googled *hypertrophic cardiomyopathy*. From the first batch
of results, I learned it was a common killer of cats. This made perfect
sense. There was never a single cat in my house growing up, but all of
us in that house were constantly announcing we hated cats. I've since
met a number of allegedly likable cats, but I have not warmed up to any
of them. I'm sure I have an innate antipathy for anything that reminds
me of me.

I must have mentioned the cats during my first meeting with the cardiologist, because among the door prizes I left with were a couple of
printed primers for laypeople on the human form of the disease and a
warning about the Internet. I didn't say a word. By then, I was effectively auditing introductory courses at medical schools in Minnesota,
Texas, and New York and fact-checking advice and prognostications
I picked up in heart-related blogs and chat rooms with links on the
National Institutes of Health website.

The cardiologist and I didn't get off to a great start. That was my
fault. She shared a large waiting room in a cardiac-specialties cove on
the second floor of the hospital. To get that far, you had to pass several
signs, including one in the elevator, reminding you not to discuss private information in public spaces. There were several other people in
the waiting room when I got there, one of whom I thought I recognized.
If he recognized me, he didn't let on. As happened every time someone
left the waiting room, when he was called away I learned his name and
the name of the doctor he would be visiting, which didn't inspire confidence in the hospital's vaunted confidentiality policies.

After my name was called, I met the cardiologist halfway down the
hall to her office. She shook my hand and mentioned she'd recently met
one of my sisters. She was a compact woman with dark hair and a reassuringly direct demeanor that would occasionally yield to a sudden,

bemused smile—like when she closed the door to her office and I told her that several of my siblings would not want me or anyone else in the family to know anything about them unless it came from them.

She had an idea about family that did not apply to my family.

I got the sense she felt like apologizing, but she didn't. She did take notes while I delivered my gimcrack theory of family history. I didn't apologize, but I must have felt like it, because her follow-up letter to the internist mentions my interest in smoking cessation.

Her physical examination of me was a revelation. She was a font of useful facts about the structure and operation of the human heart. She was happy to field questions in WebMD vernacular ("So, the problem with hypertrophic cardiomyopathy is that the thickened wall of the heart defeats the electrical charge?"), and she responded with her tribal language, peppered with translations ("The cellular disarray—those sarcomere proteins I mentioned—creates chaos in the fibers of the heart muscle, which are normally linear"). She also inserted long pauses for the note-taker to absorb the idea that the thickened ventricle wall could disrupt the normal rhythm of the heart and instantly, unpredictably, produce a fatal arrhythmia.

Something like that. I also several times wrote the phrase *sudden death?* My notes are strewn with question marks—indiscriminately marking moments of confusion and disbelief. She told me my electrocardiogram was interesting but not alarming, though she did let me know I hadn't done her any favors by arriving with no previous EKG results for comparison purposes. She assured me that nothing she heard or saw alarmed her. This tallied with my long-standing prognosis. I knew I was healthy. I know her examination confirmed what I knew. As she wrote to the internist, I was by then "a 46-year-old gentleman in excellent health, and with no symptomology suggestive of active cardiovascular disease." And I know we both knew I was not who I appeared to be.

I had become a patient.

This was a Thursday. I left with a follow-up appointment on Monday for an echocardiogram and a stress test. I also left with a supply of stick-on nodes and a Holter monitor—a portable EKG device designed like a CD player on a belt—which I had to wear for forty-eight hours.

I hate accessories. Most days, my watch is a desk clock. The only compensatory benefit I could exact was the suspension of my daily exercise routine, which I figured would generate a false record of wild cardiac mood swings. Stupidly, I said this aloud and was ordered to push up and sit up as usual. Any hope I harbored that I might pass the test and recover my status as a normal person was crushed when the cardiologist mentioned one other assignment for Monday. As she later wrote to my internist, *I will arrange for him to see* (make an appointment and turn him over to) *our electrophysiologic colleagues* (surgeon and staff) *for consideration of* (becalmed explanation of the urgent need for) *ICD therapy* (an operation to insert a defibrillator in his chest so he doesn't suddenly drop dead) *pending results of these tests* (as soon as we get him off the treadmill).

When I left the hospital, I started to run—an unprecedented impulse. The farther I got from the hospital, the more I felt like Matt Damon in the Boston version of *The Bourne Conspiracy*. I urged myself on with the thought that I had to talk to someone who would help me escape— and the vague memory of having left my cell phone in my car, which was parked in a metered space about a mile from the hospital. I slowed to a jog, which soon gave way to a brisk walk, and that didn't bode well for the stress test. Before I reached my car, I saw the red band of a parking ticket tucked under the windshield wiper.

My luck had run out.

I called Mary Ann for a second opinion. I told her I suspected we were part of a research experiment.

She said, We are.

I said, I don't have the disease but I'm going to be given the cure.

She said, I thought the gene was the problem.

I said, I think the gene is a potential problem. I tossed in something about proteins and my sarcomere.

She apologized for not getting her PhD in microbiology.

I said, The geneticist told me to call her if I had any questions.

Mary Ann gave me the number.

I got the nurse, who hadn't heard my last name and asked if I was part of the so-and-so family from such-and-such town. This accidental breach revivified my conspiracy theory. I imagined thousands of citizens being implanted and monitored all across Massachusetts. I spelled my name and, to her credit, the geneticist took my call. However, that was about all she was willing to take from me. I explained my confusion about the lack of physical evidence of cardiovascular disease.

She said, Why are you calling me?

I started from the top, but I didn't get far.

The geneticist said she didn't have my EKG.

With just a few more words, we managed to make it seem something important had been cleared up.

I talked to a lot of very opinionated people over the weekend. None of them could believe I needed a defibrillator, but only one of them was willing to go on the record with her objections to the surgery. My mother said, You should do what you think is best, but I just think this whole gene thing has gone too far.

By Sunday night before the stress test, I had persuaded myself I had the authority to write my own life story. I was no longer a child. I was a man with a medical condition that could be rectified. Even if I needed surgery, I needn't become a chronic patient. I was a writer. To assert this, to make it all seem true, I decided I should treat surgery like a little freelance job that had to be fitted into my existing work schedule. I convinced myself the operation was a deadline I had to meet, something to be done—and done with—before I left town and turned my attention to the premiere of my play. And this plan almost worked.

2. Other People's Parties

I first met the surgeon on the last Monday of June 2004. Of all the doctors I'd encountered, he was the most straightforward. Maybe his role was the least complicated. Maybe I had become better at being a patient by the time I met him on that Monday morning—my resistance worn down by his colleagues, my recalcitrance exhausted by the stress test the cardiologist had arranged.

I had been assigned two spotters during my time on the treadmill, which was not encouraging. After eleven or twelve minutes, one of them said I was passing with flying colors and shifted the machine into high gear. After a few more minutes, I was flagging. Nobody invited me to join the hospital's Boston Marathon team, but my blood pressure got kudos for rising and falling like a normal person's.

As a reward, I got to lie down and watch a half-hour television program starring my heart. For the first few minutes of the echocardiogram, I stared out the window while a friendly young woman stared at a monitor and traced a handheld wand over my lubricated torso. She had a short, spiky hairdo that seemed to involve some of the same cold gel she'd slathered on me.

After I'd agreed to lie on my side and hold my breath a couple of times, she asked if I wanted to watch the monitor.

I said, May I? I knew the hospital had strict confidentiality policies.

She smiled and said, I'm doing this for you. With her free hand, she helped me get comfortable.

Maybe it was because my heart was exposed, but her kindness momentarily overwhelmed me. This was the first time I sensed that someone in that hospital was not working from a script.

At some point, a doctor attended by a couple of silent interns showed up with no need to introduce himself or his footmen. A few minutes later, he pointed to the monitor. There's nothing there, he said. He sounded miffed, as if I'd dragged him to my bedside under false pretenses. He barked a few commands at the young woman, as if I were a video game and she was operating the joystick for his amusement. He doesn't have it, he hissed in a stage whisper, and then he and his attendants hurried away. The young woman with the wand smiled. I watched the black-and-white real-time movie of my bewildered heart: normal-not; healthy-sick; life-death.

The sequence of that morning is not recorded in my notes, but I must have seen the cardiologist again after these tests. I know I forgot to ask her what the disappointed doctor who'd dropped in during the echocardiogram didn't see. Maybe I sensed it wouldn't matter to her. The cardiologist made it clear I had flunked the test. I felt I was being graded unfairly on a curve that made sense in a laboratory but not in the world. My protest is recorded on the next legible page of my notebook, which begins with an equation: *nothing there ≠ significant.*

My heart had responded well to everything they'd thrown at it. My blood seemed to be getting in and out without any problems—no apparent obstruction at rest, excellent preserved pumping function, and no significant valve disease. This didn't matter. I had demonstrated clinical expression of the mutation, not extreme but identifiable thickening of the ventricular wall. As far as I could understand, some greater degree of thickening, which could occur sometime in the future, could be associated with unstable electrical-signal processing. By then, the cardiologist was applying her stethoscope to my back and chest again, allegedly confirming her grim prognosis. I was a prime candidate for "prophylactic therapy," which meant someone was going to stick a defibrillator into me.

I began to suspect I was being scared into buying a backup generator for a furnace that had never failed to circulate hot water through the pipes. I'd been assured from the start that my insurance company would pick up the tab, but I did wonder whether I was the principal beneficiary or the mark—the only thing standing in the way of a profitable collaboration among researchers, manufacturers, and installers.

I didn't air my conspiracy theory. My conversation with the cardiologist was interrupted, and my notes disintegrated into a series of exclamation points, a cheap trick I'd never tolerate from the students in my creative-writing workshops. This began with a knock on the cardiologist's office door.

I was seated on a table with my shirt unbuttoned. The cardiologist said she hoped I wouldn't mind, but the genetics laboratory had sent someone over to clear up any concerns I might have. I figured this was compensation for the answers I hadn't gotten when I'd called the geneticist after my first visit with the cardiologist, so I was pleased to meet the young woman, who immediately asked if I had any questions.

I said I did but I would have to think about what they were.

She said maybe we could start with her questions, and she opened up a folder.

I had spent the weekend at the University of Texas website, brushing up on basic physiology. I was not prepared for a pop quiz in genetics.

She asked me to confirm I was the youngest of nine Downing siblings, and I said we were eight since my brother Gerard had died. So noted. She mentioned one of my living siblings by name and asked me to name that sibling's children. I didn't say anything. She kept her pen pointed optimistically at her folder. After a few silent seconds, she tapped the pen. She smiled. She was willing to prompt me with a few hints. She looked at her notes and recited a couple of my nieces' first names and even speculated on birth order, obviously hoping I would correct her.

All of my siblings had been informed of the possibility that they and their offspring had inherited Daddy's gene after Mary Ann had uncovered this fact in the wake of Gerard's death. I even knew, inadvertently, that the sibling in question had recently visited the cardiologist in the office where I was seated. The nieces and nephews I was being asked to discuss were all adults.

Confidentially speaking, I was confused.

I said I wouldn't answer questions about other adults.

The genetic counselor took this as an insult and left.

I was starting to feel right at home in that hospital, the youngest kid in a family whose mystifying behavior had less to do with me than with the untimely death of my father.

The cardiologist adroitly shrugged off the episode. Clearly, someone had botched somebody's attempt to be helpful. She wasn't thrilled, but no harm done. I asked a few more questions. She answered each one coherently, and at the end of every response she made it clear she wasn't going to raise my grade, that I was prone to total heart failure and my best and only hedge against suddenly flunking out was a defibrillator, and then she sent me on to the surgeon, whose office was conveniently located across the hall.

The surgeon had excellent credentials. He had implanted my sister Mary Ann, and she was alive. He was a married man with an appealingly metrosexual haircut and a manner to match. And he talked a lot—an admirable quality we shared. There was one tentative moment early in our conversation when he inched forward on his chair and uttered the phrase *sudden death*. He made it sound like a flat tire—unlikely, but a real pain in the ass. I nodded. He nodded. This sealed the deal: We were going to err on the side of caution. Then he introduced me to his cool, ironic nurse practitioner. Together, they let me know I was younger, healthier, and thinner than almost anyone he'd implanted. It was clear we were all going to get along. When he pulled out a diagram of the heart to explain his plan of attack, I got a lot of compliments for all the studying I'd done. Half his patients didn't know they had ventricles.

We didn't discuss the past. This guy was all about the future. For two weeks after implantation, I wouldn't be allowed to pick up anything weighing more than ten pounds, and for two additional weeks I'd have to avoid repetitive exercise and lifting my left hand above my shoulder, and after that I was basically carefree except for powerful magnets at airport security gates and in car batteries. He handed me some brochures with pictures of old geezers playing tennis and riding recumbent bikes to prove his point. You'd never know by looking at those happy people they'd almost died any number of times.

Luckily, I'd dropped by on the day he had a brand new device on offer as part of a clinical study. Like all ICDs, it was basically a three-part system: a microprocessor and voltage generator with a battery in a case about the size of the pagers the surgeon and his sidekick were wearing, which he would stick into a pocket in my chest. I asked about how much tailoring this would require, and he said he'd just make a slit and slide the thing in. He claimed I was anatomically outfitted with an empty pocket between my pectoral muscle and my collarbone. The device would be attached to wires—*leads*, as they say in the trade— which he would snake through a vein so he could screw them into the muscle of my heart and wait for scar tissue to seal them in permanently. The third piece of apparatus looked exactly like a laptop computer, which I was happy to know would live in his office, not in me. This was the programmer he'd use to set up my system and to monitor me during quarterly checkups and data dumps.

The new-fangled test model I was going to get had a super-fast response capability, so it could deliver a life-saving shock just a few seconds after it detected a heart-stopping electrical problem, long before my brain had been deprived of blood for time enough to make my life not worth living. It also had a pacing function that kicked in during those few seconds the generator needed to charge itself up and deliver a shock to my stalled system, and that pacing function alone might restore my heart's natural rhythm, obviating the need for that annoying shock.

Not that I expect you'll ever need it in the next forty years, he added.

Manufactured by Medtronic, my test model was brand-named Entrust. I signed a ten-page consent form. I did not read every word. Evidently, I considered the surgeon entrustworthy. Months later, I read the document and realized I had absolved Medtronic, the hospital, and "the physician conducting the study" (this was the surgeon—really) from any responsibility for injury or illness the study might cause.

The point was, I was lucky. Otherwise, I'd have ended up with "a commercially available ICD," which sounded to me like the sort of thing anybody might have purchased and returned to Target or Radio Shack.

It was all very confidential. Of course, Medtronic had to share my data with its employees and business partners abroad—but they would be urged to use "all reasonable efforts" to protect my privacy once the study data and my existing medical record were made available to Medtronic, their business partners, relevant employees of the hospital, all affiliated hospitals and staffs, other interested researchers, oversight boards, all entities that felt they needed to know something about me that was somehow related to issues of treatment, payment, or general health-care operations, plus the hospital's data-storage companies, insurers, and legal advisors, and Medtronic's subcontractors and all of its agents, as well as federal and state agencies galore, hospital-accrediting agencies, and probably some data- and safety-monitoring boards, but not to worry. There were strict policies in place to protect confidentiality all along the line. Naturally, "some of those who receive protected health information may not have to satisfy the privacy requirements" and might "redisclose it" under certain circumstances, which basically boiled down to *on a whim.*

There was no expiration date on my consent because "research is an ongoing project." If I had any concerns, I could in no uncertain terms withdraw my consent at any time, though I could not expect anybody to waste time trying to withdraw information that had already been used or shared.

Two weeks later, on 8 July, I met the surgeon for the second time. I was on a gurney in pre-op. Peter was with me, and so were a lot of johnnied people not looking forward to this day, most of them attended by sniffling partners, rheumy parents, sneezy children, and hospital staffers zipping around and redistributing the available germs from one bed to the next. The sanitation and privacy standards were exactly what you'd expect in a mosh pit. Only the staff had access to rubber gloves and masks.

I was introduced to a lot of the surgeon's colleagues as they introduced intravenous tubes into me, plastered me with electrodes, and helpfully held their index fingers where I had to sign my name on lines I couldn't see since I'd packed away my eyeglasses.

The surgeon was reassuring. Peter was reassuring. Mary Ann and Marcia and many of our friends had reassured me they would be waiting upstairs with Peter or by a telephone or beside a pot of homemade chicken soup when I awoke.

I was calm, as I am when I board an airplane. The truth is, I can sleep through anything. Plus, someone slipped me a mickey, and I was delightfully dizzy as I was rolled away. I remember waking up in post-op, which is pre-op with more monitors beeping. Peter was there. I ate some crackers and drank something advertised as apple juice. I knew enough to ask immediately for Percocet.

I was awakened often during the next eighteen hours. Each time, somewhere deep below the smooth, narcotic ice of my mind, I was aware of something ominous roiling beneath the surface. Under there, my chest was sore, my left shoulder ached, and it didn't matter. The worst was over, and the night nurse was rich in Percocet.

My only complaint was something bugging my back, something small, something I told the nurse might be the quill-end of a little feather. It didn't occur to me at the time that the mattress was not stuffed with down and my so-called linens were basically thin, impermeable sheets of linoleum. I hated to bother the nurse, and I certainly wanted to stay on her good side, the side where she kept her supply of painkillers, but I eventually asked her to have a look back there.

She said I had a little scar.

I said I didn't remember a scar. I didn't really remember my name.

She said, Not a scar. A pimple.

I said, I get a lot of weird rashes, but never pimples.

She said, Not a pimple. A little black dot.

I said, A dot?

She said, Not a dot. It's healed over. It's nothing. It's been almost four hours since your last Percocet. You want to stay ahead of the pain.

The next morning, I racked up a lot of compliments and congratulations from the surgeon and his colleagues. My device was working like a charm, and after I was wheeled down to X-ray for a couple of mug shots with my newly installed accessory, I waited around for my discharge and my parting gift of Percocet. The day nurses were already trying to wean me with over-the-counter painkillers.

As Mary Ann said, Would you like that headache with or without Tylenol?

Fortunately, Peter had arrived with two large lattes long before the breakfast we both knew I wouldn't be eating.

That was Wednesday morning. The following Thursday, I saw the surgeon and the nurse practitioner. I'd obediently removed the bandage, and the surgeon flicked away the few tiny sterile strips that hadn't come off the incision in the shower. As he wrote to the cardiologist, "He has residual discomfort at the surgical site, which is typical." He added that the "site itself looks perfect"—a compliment to both of us, if he did say so himself—"the incision is healing nicely, and the pocket is totally unremarkable."

Honestly, the fact that I had a spare anatomical pocket and that it had been stuffed full of electronic equipment seemed sort of remarkable to me. As the outline of the device was evident on my chest, I figured other people might remark on it as well. I didn't begrudge people their curiosity, but it did dim the prospect of a day at the beach. I could already hear myself during a fortuitous encounter with old friends or casual acquaintances, yelling into an onshore breeze about myocin-binding proteins and my dead relatives. For the rest of my life, I'd be an ad for the past.

The next day, I flew to San Francisco—but only after I got felt up at Logan Airport for the first time. The security guard wore gloves and said I was awfully young to need a pacemaker. He meant I was awfully young to have had a heart attack.

I said it wasn't a pacemaker, and I didn't have any heart problems.

The guy shoved his hand further down my pants. He said, What do you call it? By then he had tapped the palm of his hand against the ICD, alerting me to my unbandaged scar, and he was tapping his way down my abdomen.

I said, It's a defibrillator.

He said, Have a nice day. His point was, No matter what you call it, you're still young to have racked up your first heart attack already. He pointed to my shoes. They had been conveyed through the X-ray machine, which would be a perfectly safe and much more pleasant way for me to bypass airport security gates.

A few days later in my hotel room in San Francisco, I didn't really feel like myself. It wasn't my unfamiliar surroundings. It was something else. Of course, I had a four-inch scar and a something the size of a beeper half-embedded in my chest. I hadn't understood it would stick out.

That's normal, the surgeon had assured me, on someone as thin as you.

I didn't think it was a great fit. And from the start, I had frequently felt something like a wire in my chest.

That's normal, the surgeon had assured me. You know you have a wire from the defibrillator to your heart. But you can't feel it. You don't have any nerves in that vein.

I was sure he knew where my nerves were, and I was sure I didn't feel like myself. It wasn't psychological. It was an accumulation of small physical miscues—a momentary loss of balance; an intolerance for alcohol; that little blackhead on my back that resisted even Listerine; an occasional spasm of pain in my back or neck; a nip from that wire I couldn't feel.

I called Peter in Cambridge. He asked how I was doing. I told him I was fine. As reassurance for both of us, I reminded him that every day at noon, I dutifully went into a bathroom, closed the door, and listened carefully. My surgeon had told me my ICD would beep at noon if it had been activated during the previous twenty-four hours. Although most people who'd received a shock from their devices compared it to a kick in the chest, some people actually slept through the event. Moreover, the device was programmed to alert me to other problems, including a sudden depletion of its battery.

The point was, I hadn't heard a peep out of it.

Peter said, I'm sure you are fine. But maybe you should listen at 9 AM. Isn't your defibrillator set to Eastern Standard Time?

I'd probably missed my own death. And since I was stuck in San Francisco, I wouldn't know if I had attempted to die until I flew home and the surgeon downloaded my data. If I did have a personal power outage in the meantime, I wanted to know it had happened. I made a mental note to find a quiet bathroom every morning. This reassured me and Peter. Later that week, my friend Jeanne called from New York City for a report on my health.

I told her about the play.

She asked about my heart.

I said I was fine.

Jeanne said, You sound tired.

I said I was fine and told her about my 9 AM appointments with my device, which had been reassuringly silent.

Jeanne said, I'm sure you are fine.

I said, I know I am.

Jeanne said, Okay. But nine o'clock is really eight o'clock. Are you sure your device was smart enough to spring forward for daylight saving time?

When the lights go down for the premiere of a play, the one superfluous person in the theater is the playwright. Your name is attached to the story, but over the course of a couple of hours, the cast, crew, and audience make something else of it. You're there because the play is yours—you wrote it, and you will live with it long after everyone else involved in the production and its premiere has moved on. But there is absolutely nothing for you to do.

It's a lot like surgery, minus the benefit of general anesthesia.

If you are a playwright or a patient and you don't die, you can't help but be grateful and a little dazed. You know it is good luck to be surrounded by talented professionals, so you'll be happy to oblige when you are asked for your opinion afterward. You'll even be congratulated, incongruous as that seems with your static performance. In the hospital, you are rolled out of surgery to post-op for a glass of apple juice, and then you're wheeled away to a rented bedroom while the doctors take off their masks and relax. If it's a stage play you survived, you are carried with a crowd for champagne in the lobby and then whisked off to a smaller, boozier, louder, altogether better all-night party somewhere else. But you don't stay all night. You go back to your rented hotel room. It is a cast party, after all. You are not a member of the cast. And tomorrow and tomorrow and tomorrow, a spotlight will brighten that stage. These shows go on without you.

By the end of August, I was back in Cambridge, facing the start of the fall semester at Tufts. I saw the surgeon for the second time since he'd operated on me in early July. I knew something was wrong. Instead of thinking about my next book, I was spending way too much time thinking about my chest, my heart, and my dead father. Despite my best efforts, I felt more like a patient than a writer.

After calling me an ideal patient, the surgeon restored my unrestricted license for physical exercise, and then he asked how I was feeling.

I said I still felt vulnerable.

He said, Do you mean you or the device?

I was very grateful he was observing that distinction, which was unsteady in my mind.

He said, You are healed. Get some exercise. And don't worry. The device—it's encased in titanium. You could get run over by a bus and it would be fine.

Again, the distinction was lost on me.

I was certain my medical drama was not concluded. The surgeon assured me it was and urged me to get on with my next project. "He has been entirely well since the last visit," the surgeon wrote to the cardiologist. "No symptoms of arrhythmia or symptomatic therapies from his device." The surgeon reported that his comprehensive interrogation of my ICD was "totally unremarkable."

It wasn't the review I would have written. The device was still too prominent on my chest and in my life. I wanted it to disappear. The surgeon didn't want to see me again until October. One of us would get his wish.

For the next two weeks, I consulted my chest every morning in the bathroom mirror about the prospect of push-ups. I was behaving like a closet atheist in a world of believers, looking for evidence that would prove my suspicion that all was not right in the invisible world beneath my skin. Everyone I had consulted, everything I had read, and everything I knew about my recalcitrant appetite told me exercise was the best medicine. Day by day, the scar was fading. The swelling had receded. All the signs were good; all systems go. However, I hadn't gained back even one of the ten pounds I'd lost, and the device was now articulated in high relief. If I stared long enough, I could see an inch or so of the electrical lead arching out of the top of the ICD and disappearing into the nether regions. And every day, the signal from my happily atrophying pectoral muscles—the secret message only I could decode—was the same: Do not disturb.

On the first Wednesday after Labor Day, I taught the first classes of my two workshops at Tufts. Unlike every previous semester, I'd been assigned to a classroom down the dreaded hill from my office in East Hall, a handsome brick building on the flat and favored Green, a cross-hatchery of grass and paths designed for strolling and lollygagging and the other liberal arts. My assigned classroom at the bottom of the hill was in the Pearson Chemical Lab. I tried not to take this as a sign. I also tried not to take it as a sign that there was an illuminated sign suspended from the ceiling outside the classroom. DANGER. After my second class, I did take it as a sign that the muscles in my legs were complaining before we were halfway up the stone steps set into that unnecessarily steep hill. I was unfit for normal life.

By Saturday, I was ready to reclaim my body. I rolled out my exercise mat. I started with some tentative stretching and bending, just to make sure I wasn't apt to empty that pocket. I turned on the TV. Normally, I'd get started with three or four sets each of seventy-five push-ups and seventy-five sit-ups and then attend to my lungs and legs. I did three push-ups and my arms quivered. I forced myself to keep going, working slowly this time, and when I was fully angled up and off the floor, I stopped. I felt the device responding a little too eagerly to the gravitational pull of the earth.

The sit-ups went better, but eventually my brain began to behave like a random Internet search engine, tossing up grim images of the leads straining against the thin walls of that vein every time I thrust my shoulders toward my raised knees. I rolled up my mat. Two young Russian women were banging away at the baselines of Center Court at the U.S. Open tennis tournament. Who was the old geezer now?

On Sunday, to spare myself the embarrassment of comparisons, I waited until Peter went to the gym, turned on Chopin, and did much better on my mat. As a reward, I turned on the TV and watched two young men romp around Center Court. Clearly, a good workout had altered my attitude. My brain immediately started generating spurious images of me at midcourt, executing overhead smashes.

That night, my ICD started to disappear. I was brushing my teeth, and I noticed my push-ups had puffed up my pectorals a bit. The device was less prominent, more implanted. I felt a little rush of pride, and it wasn't only in my head. My upper body was looking a little flush with its success, a lot less pasty, which made the knotty line of stitched and folded-over skin above the device look a lot less red, a lot more like a scar and less like a gash.

I woke Peter as I got into bed, a favor I do him almost every night. I told him the good news. He sat up to have a look. I was wearing a T-shirt. It was dark. And I was certain I had exaggerated my progress. I promised to show him anything worth bragging about in the morning.

I don't keep a tape measure in the bathroom, but the preliminary results of my Monday morning inspection were very promising. A good night's sleep had not deflated my new muscle mass.

Before he left for work, Peter turned on all the lights in the bedroom and bathroom and looked at my chest, then right into my eyes, and then back and forth like that for a couple of anxious seconds. He said, It is definitely less visible.

I was thrilled. I would have dropped and given him one hundred push-ups right there had he asked. It's amazing, I said.

This confirmed one of my cherished theories, which was based on the wonders of workouts that involve lifting and resisting nothing but your own body weight. Actually, it wasn't my theory. It was based on advice I'd gleaned from a book I borrowed from the Pittsfield Public Library a couple of days after I graduated from high school. The book was called something like *So You Think You're Marine Material?* I knew I wasn't, but I could tell I would've gotten along well with the short-haired guys who were Marine material, based on the black-and-white pictures of them doing chin-ups and deep-knee bends in T-shirts. The point was, during a high-school graduation party at my house, which was making me feel sad for some reason, my brother Joe caught me with my fist in the onion dip. He was a rising junior at Harvard, where I was headed. Without warning, he said, One of the first things I noticed when I got to Cambridge was how few fat people there are. By *Cambridge,* Joe meant *Harvard.* He treated the name of the place like the name of god and never said it around heathens.

Like everybody in my family but Joe and my mother, I had acquired the habit of gaining about five pounds every winter, and then every summer, to balance things out, I'd gain a few more.

When you do see a fat person, Joe said, he's usually alone.

In my family, this and a biography were considered a decent graduation gift.

I became a closet Marine. To avoid accusations of fanaticism from my immobile older siblings, I did most of my sit-ups in bed, and I swept out a space for push-ups in the basement, where the cement didn't creak like the floorboards in my bedroom. I rode my bike five miles to and from my job as a lifeguard that summer. On days off, every branch, beam, or rafter became an opportunity for another ten chin-ups. Even in the middle of dinner, I'd be doing isometrics until my mother started accusing me of developing tics associated with a guilty conscience. I lost thirty pounds that summer, and I stuck to a version of the same routine for almost thirty years.

Before Peter concluded his examination of my disappearing device, he asked if my chest had gotten redder.

My word for this was *rosier.* I said I was finally getting my color back.

Peter said, Since we've been standing here, has it gotten redder?

I couldn't say, though from some angles, the situation suddenly did not look entirely muscular. It looked puffier.

Peter said, Is it tender?

I said, I'm fine. I was really ruing those push-ups.

Peter said, Is it tender?

I touched it. Who was I to judge? My discomfort scale had gotten fouled up as a kid when I'd stapled my own finger on purpose and hadn't flinched. I said, I'm fine.

Peter urged me to call the surgeon.

I said, I probably overdid it with the exercise.

Peter said, Call the surgeon.

I said, It's too early.

Peter said, Call the surgeon.

I said, He's the one who encouraged me to exercise in the first place.

Peter said, What's his number?

I called the surgeon. He was not available. This didn't surprise me. He looked like a guy who spent a lot of time at the gym. I left a message at the reception desk, which is like leaving your business card under somebody's windshield wiper. At Peter's urging, I called the nurse practitioner. She wasn't a doctor, so she had voicemail. I left a message. Peter went to work. I went right back to the bathroom and took off my T-shirt. It was getting redder under there. I called the nurse practitioner again and left another message. I said something weird was going on with my device. It was disappearing. I mentioned the pushups and the redness. I gave her my cell phone number.

A lot of people in my family inherited the power of prayer. I got the power to make things worse by thinking about them. Thank god I had two classes to prepare. Otherwise, I'd have been dead by noon.

Instead, at noon I put on a button-down shirt, called my friend and colleague Michelle, and told her I was leaving the house. We were both headed to Tufts. We lived equidistant from the Central Square subway stop on the Red Line, which runs directly into Davis Square, a good walk or a short shuttle bus ride to the campus. To justify eschewing public transportation and riding to work in my old Saab, Michelle and I used the term *carpooling* for our twice-a-week trips. Michelle is a novelist, so we both shared the capacity not to crack a smile when we referred to our four-mile jaunt in the middle of the day as *the commute*, which gave us the impression we were working people.

When she got in my car, I warned Michelle I was carrying a cell phone. She thanked me for the tip-off. She was as incompetent with those devices as I was, and typically we treated them as backup answering machines best left at home. Plus, we'd had a bad experience at the end of the spring semester. We were on a trafficky patch of Mass. Ave. when a phone rang in my car. Immediately, we both started yelling and straining against our seat belts, as if somebody had tossed a live grenade into the car. We were each hotly denying we carried a cell phone while we searched the least likely places—the ashtray, the dashboard, the wells behind our seats. Before I managed to drive us into oncoming traffic, the ringing stopped. The next morning, Peter remembered he'd left his cell phone in my car.

Fortunately, I had explained to Michelle why the phone might ring before the phone rang, so she was content to eavesdrop on my conversation. I pulled over and parked in front of a pharmacy, which seemed almost as ironic as the way the nurse practitioner said, *You're having a problem with push-ups?* I got the sense she had been dragged out of her routine for more important questions. I described the redness and puffiness, and she asked if I had a fever or dizziness. I didn't. Was the site sore? I said it must not be bad, as I was wearing a shoulder strap. I did mention Peter's concerns, and I said the word *swollen*, which I remember because I remember Michelle's expression changed at that moment, and her gaze darted to the pocket hidden beneath my shirt pocket.

Before I hung up, I got a ten o'clock appointment for Tuesday morning. We drove on. After a few blocks, Michelle said, Tomorrow morning? It sounded a lot more futuristic coming from her than from the nurse practitioner. Michelle said, They don't want to see you today?

I said, I'm fine.

Michelle said, We could drive to some hospital right now and have somebody look at you.

I said I had to teach.

Michelle said she knew how to write a sign and tape it to a classroom door to cancel my classes.

I said, I'm fine. I was thinking, *Tomorrow? Tomorrow? Tomorrow?*

That evening, the device was nowhere to be seen. Aspirin didn't make a dent in the swelling. I think I prescribed the aspirin, but maybe it was the nurse practitioner. By then, a circle of skin on my chest three times the diameter of the pocket was red and sort of glowing. It's no credit to me, but I am pretty sure I did not call that evening. According to my medical record, though, I called and reported the swelling that evening for the first and only time.

You can call that a mistake or mendacity, confusion or a cover-up. Either way, that's the official version of this chapter of the story of my life.

As usual, I slept like a baby. When I awoke, my chest was redder, no question about it. And though it wasn't tender, it was almost too hot to touch. Plus, just below my skin I had sprouted a few bright red lines, as if something were streaming out of the area of my body I was trying not to think of as my heart.

As soon as I put on a shirt, I was able to convince myself that I was overreacting. It was actually reassuring to imagine the nurse practitioner had picked up on my childhood diagnosis of being prone to exaggerating.

I persuaded Peter to go to work by underreporting my symptoms and promising to call from the hospital. The next thing I remember is standing face-to-face with the nurse practitioner with my shirt unbuttoned. She'd taken my temperature twice, as if she suspected me of withholding information. When she said my temperature was normal, I got the sense she would've appreciated a little more effort on my part to gin up a fever. Then she warned me she was going to touch me. She put a gloved finger to my pectoral stew and winced. I took this as a bad sign. She did momentarily recover her sense of irony. She asked if I'd recently spilled something on myself. Lye, for instance.

I said, What is it?

She looked at her feet. She said, It's very hot.

I said, What is it?

She said, Not good. She called the surgeon.

The surgeon took one look at me and said I was infected. He asked me if I'd been swimming in the ocean.

I said I'd taken a pass this season on the beautiful beach in Ipswich where I normally spend the better part of every summer day.

He said, While you were on the West Coast?

I said I'd been in San Francisco, not San Diego.

Somewhere during this interrogation, I tossed in the push-ups. Nobody bit.

He said, Hot tubs? Jacuzzis?

He seemed to have formed an opinion about my social life based on my shirt, which was always unbuttoned when I was visiting him. I assured him that my only maritime adventures had been in the shower.

I don't remember much else until the moment the surgeon raised his hand and spread his fingers wide. He slowly moved that hand closer to my chest, the way you might test the readiness of a glowing electric burner on a stove if you were me. He said, We have to get that thing out of you.

I bent down to drag my datebook out of my bag on the floor. I was certain this operation was going to mess up my schedule for the fall. I was hoping against hope I'd written in the deadline for returning the page proofs of my new book so I didn't end up delaying the publication with a stroke of my own pen. When I was upright again, calendar open, the surgeon smiled.

He said, Today.

I said, Today is Tuesday, the fourteenth.

He said he had to get that thing out of me today. The lifesaving leads he'd threaded through my vein were basically a superhighway for any infection hoping to take a quick trip to my heart. He told me to go home and get whatever I might need to be in the hospital for a few days and immediately go to Admitting. He had located an available operating room, and he was going to remove the device, extract the leads, and try to get to the bottom of the mysterious mess in my chest, which I was still blaming on the Marines.

3. False Pride

No one at the hospital told me exactly how long it would take the infection stewing in the swollen pocket in my chest to travel from the device, along the electrical leads, through the vein, into my heart, and kill me. It was ten thirty in the morning when the surgeon sent me home to pack a bag. He had reserved an operating room for twelve thirty. I'd have to pass through Admitting and pre-op before the fun began, so I knew I had about an hour to make the ten-minute drive home to Cambridge, call Peter, and be back at the hospital.

Since my father's death in 1961, I had learned to live with the knowledge that people I love might suddenly die. Since my genetic diagnosis in March 2004, I had learned to live with the idea that I might suddenly die. By the time I was seated in my Saab again on that sunny September morning, I'd had about fifteen minutes to get accustomed to the notion that my death might be imminent. I found my cell phone on the dash, dialed Peter's direct number, and got his voicemail. I left a calm message with no alarming details, presumably for the same reason my family didn't bawl at my father's wake and funeral. Tragedies and emergencies are excellent opportunities to teach other people how to behave.

I instinctively pulled the shoulder strap across my chest and felt the sting. I wasn't sure about the physics of that puffy pocket, but I knew the strap was putting a lot of pressure on the situation, and the infection had nowhere to go but south on the highway to my heart. I remember thinking it would be ironic if I hastened my own death with a safety device, so I slowly retracted the belt. This was the first time it occurred to me that the surgeon was proposing to prevent my imminent death by removing the device he'd inserted to prevent my sudden death, an emergency surgery which—if all went well—would leave me at risk of sudden death.

I called Peter's assistant for the first time ever and asked if she could locate Peter and tell him to meet me at home. I told her it was urgent. She seemed as surprised as I was by the request, but unlike me, she didn't doubt me. As soon as I hung up, I was peppering myself with questions about the accuracy of my characterization of the situation as *urgent* and accusing myself of overreacting.

More than the infection, I regretted that call, which registered on my venerable family scale of emotion as an incendiary outburst of melodramatic panic. On the drive home, I reminded myself I was lucky my chest hadn't blown up while I was scuba diving in Belize. Suppose I was one of those people who weighed 550 pounds and couldn't even lie down on an operating table without suffocating myself? If I were blind and lived alone on a farm with no electricity before the discovery of antibiotics—that would be urgent.

I got home, and to fend off another panic attack I downed a cup of cold coffee—an old family remedy. It worked. In a fit of rationality, I sat down and googled *ICD* and *infection*. Was I ever lucky. Some people ended up with exploding pustules on their chests, and lots of others never even knew they were infected before it was too late. I glanced at my shirt to confirm my good fortune. No bloodstains. There was a noticeably warm updraft of air rising under my chin from the open collar of my shirt. I undid a couple of buttons, then a few more, and the next thing I knew, I was standing shirtless in front of a bathroom mirror. This is known as pressing your luck. There were several new circles of hell surrounding the device, and just beneath the surface of my skin, cherry-red streaks of something were streaming from my shoulder past the elbow of my left arm.

I had a really hard time killing the rest of that hour. I did locate an overnight bag. Packing wouldn't take as much time as I hoped it might.

I didn't need any slacks, shirts, shoes, socks, or underwear, and even on a good day my personal-hygiene kit is basically what you'd find in any hotel bathroom, minus the skin lotion, conditioner, and shower cap.

I had a momentary flirtation with an open bottle of wine, but I remembered the interrogation the admissions nurse had conducted about my food and beverage intake before my implant surgery. I wasn't convinced I could lie about not drinking anything for as many hours as were required with anything other than coffee to back me up.

I went up to the roof deck to get some air. I carried the telephone, in case Peter called. It was pleasantly breezy up there, but I found the air to be of no help whatsoever. I gave it a few minutes, and breathing deeply did prove effective after I added a cigarette to the mix. I called my sister Mary Ann. I explained the situation.

Mary Ann said, Oh, Michael.

That was permission to feel sorry for myself, which I appreciated.

Before she asked any questions, she guessed I was feeling scared and frustrated.

I said, Scared and discouraged.

She said, Where are you?

I said I was outside, but I wasn't sure she'd heard me. The wind was picking up and I could barely hear her, so I ducked back inside and apologized for the intrusive breeze.

Rather loudly, Mary Ann said, Outside where?

I said, Now I'm inside.

Through a window in the clerestory, I saw Peter's car approaching.

Mary Ann said, Why are you at home?

I said, To pack? It was the first time my assignment seemed a little dicey.

Mary Ann said, Why aren't you in a bed with sedatives and antibiotics? She is constantly saying things that make you wish she were your doctor.

I mentioned Peter had just pulled in.

Mary Ann said, Then you're fine. Tell him I'll call him later.

I was walking down the first of two long flights of stairs to our living room when Peter began to call my name, which stirred up the first real air I'd breathed all morning. I stopped. He was coming up toward me two steps at a time. His reassuring presence made me dizzy, as if I'd had the courage to look down and noticed that I was walking on a thin and wavery high wire.

I said, It's infected. They're taking it out.

Peter said, Let's get you to the hospital.

I said, I haven't packed.

Peter said, That's not your job.

I said, This isn't going so well, is it?

Peter said, Are you in pain?

I said, A little.

Peter said, So it really hurts.

I said, Uh-huh. The pocket was hot and throbbing, a steady thunder occasionally shot through with a little lightning bolt, a sharp spasm with a thrumming, metallic half-life inside my chest cavity.

When we were in the car, Peter said, You drove yourself home from the hospital after you saw the surgeon?

Instinctively, I thought how lucky I was that my car battery hadn't died.

My little curtained bay in pre-op was abuzz with orderlies, nurses, and unidentified people in scrubs. I pitied the sick people in the neighboring bays who were basically being ignored.

I'm a big fan of frantic activity, especially when I don't have to do anything and can't be blamed for any disasters. I was propped up in the gurney, so I had a good view. For the first ten minutes, it was a lot like being five years old and watching the rest of the family rush around to get a holiday dinner on the table. Nobody's asking for your opinion, but, Oh, my god, does she realize that thing is plugged in? Did anybody else see him drop that and wipe it off on his pants?

Peter was standing beside me, one hand on my shoulder. A nurse came by with a portable supply of saline solution, and somebody explained I'd also be hooked up to a couple of bags of IV drugs, a broad-spectrum antibiotic and a supplementary sulphur-based antibiotic. Together, they would kill anything in my body, good or bad, and I'd be hydrated— if only the nurse could get the first needle inserted into a vein without bumping up against my ulna, radius, or metacarpals. She'd already complimented me on the size of the veins on my arm, and since she'd started stabbing, those veins had only gotten bigger and juicier, and yet she continued to plug away at my wrist and the back of my hand, ignoring the obvious targets. After her third failed attempt, Peter tightened his grip to let me know we were past the point where a normal person in my position would complain.

I said, Wouldn't it be easier to aim for a vein?

She said, Much.

Peter squeezed my shoulder again.

I said, Feel free.

She said, We aim low to preserve easy access for emergencies.

Nothing from Peter. He'd heard enough.

I probably wouldn't have said anything, but the heat on my chest was ramping up and making the skin prickly and itchy, and I was eager for any distraction that would prevent my suddenly tearing into it with my fingernails. I said, Like what?

The nurse outlined a couple of bad scenarios in which serial IVs had to be inserted into patients' arms. I think emergency transfusions were involved. I know she was the first person to alert me to the simple fact that no one yet knew what was causing my infection. Whatever it was, it wasn't going to cure itself. So, she said, I'm sure those veins won't go to waste.

Another nurse, a man who claimed to remember me, came by to prove her point.

Then the surgeon showed up. This was a relief. His presence signaled progress. Plus, he had the grace to grimace when he caught my gaze. He moved behind me to greet Peter, and he put a hand on my other shoulder. He racked up a few more points for establishing normal human contact. But his presence meant more than immediate reassurance. I really believed he understood what I was feeling in this moment, what it meant to have acceded to a prophylactic implant and all its implications in my life, only to have the whole process reversed.

The surgeon said, How are you feeling, Michael?

Right question.

I said, I've had better days.

He grimaced again. Again, right response. Unfortunately, he didn't stop there. He said, This is a bad day for you, but it is a really bad day for me.

I was a blot on his record.

Nobody in the crowded little bay said anything. I did register a renewed, steady pressure on my shoulder from Peter's side.

The surgeon mentioned he had to fly to D.C. tomorrow and testify before Congress to persuade Medicare to pay for more implant surgeries. Plus, something almost as annoying as my infection had already happened to him this morning—maybe one of his patients had been late for an appointment, maybe he had gotten a parking ticket. I wasn't listening very carefully. I'm sure the bay was still abuzz with preparations, but I was no longer bemused. I was busy recalibrating my circumstances.

In the few hours since the surgeon had told me I was infected, I had invented a math to make sense of the situation: The infection was to the hospital as the mutant gene was to my family. These were endemic risks. In my mind, the equation was balanced. I figured no one was to blame for my inheriting the mutation along with the rest of my DNA, or for my picking up an infection along with my ICD. I thought it was just bad luck times two.

I had miscalculated. Over the next few days, I learned my lesson again and again. It was peculiarly familiar.

If the hospital = the family, then my infection = my homosexuality.

I had introduced something dark and dirty into a bright and pure project. The best practitioners available had lavished their talents on me, and I had squandered their time and tarnished their reputations. They were compassionate people, and they would not ignore me in my hour of need, but they had a lot of other souls to save. If I didn't see the error of my ways, at some point, for the greater good, they'd have to wash their hands of me.

I think we were all grateful when the anesthesiologist appeared. She arrived with a tailwind of good spirits, and the frantic, sober activity around me instantly acquired an antic charm. We all cheered up. If the hospital staff was my adoptive family, this woman was Mary Ann.

Evidently, everybody liked her. Within a few minutes, my bedside was really crowded, like a dinghy with too many people hanging on the gunwales. Peter must've noticed I was having a little trouble maintaining my balance because he offered to leave. The anesthesiologist assured him he was essential ballast and should stay onboard right up to the threshold of the operating room, which she referred to as a laboratory. This destination sounded more experimental than reassuring, but she explained that implant surgeries were typically handled not by surgeons but by cardiac electrophysiologists whose so-called laboratories were outfitted specifically for these procedures.

So noted. But as long as he was wielding a scalpel and plucking things out of my heart, he was a surgeon to me.

The anesthesiologist told me not to expect to be knocked out. She wasn't planning to put me under with general anesthesia.

This really woke me up.

The surgeon reminded me I hadn't had general anesthesia when he implanted me. I reminded him the leads had been embedding themselves in my heart since then.

He said, Only for a couple of months. If it had been years, we'd be concerned. Trust me.

What were my options?

The surgeon said he always used conscious sedation. I think it was then that he mentioned the lidocaine, a powerful topical anesthetic applied to the area of the incision to freeze out all feeling.

Somebody—maybe the surgeon, maybe a nurse, maybe a patient in the next bay—said, But the infection is so hot, so acidic, that the effect of the lidocaine might be neutralized.

I said, Neutralized? I was really regretting my decision to pass up that half bottle of wine.

It was the anesthesiologist who spoke next, but first she engaged my gaze directly. To her credit, she never looked away. She said, You are going to be awake—not fully aware, but you might know you are awake, and for a few moments you might feel what is being done to you.

Nobody said anything.

The anesthesiologist smiled and raised one of her hands.

She said, See this? She held a little glass vial by its lid and wagged it back and forth. She said, This is an amazing drug, very strictly regulated. It is kept in a locked cabinet. You're going to get this, and about a minute and a half into the procedure—I promise—you are going to feel better than you've ever felt before.

I think she mentioned the name of the wonder drug. I know she moved toward me, the little bottle still swinging, her thumb and index finger clasping the cap, but before I could read the label, the bottle slipped out of her grip and smashed on the floor.

Again, nobody said anything.

I was awake when we left Peter on the far side of the swinging door. I was wide awake after a board of some kind was fitted under me and I was lifted from the gurney onto the operating table by two friendly guys who laughed every time I answered one of their casual questions.

When I asked what was so funny, one of them said, Your teeth are chattering.

I said I was freezing.

One of them warned me that the surface of the table would be colder. He was right. And then the other one warned me I was about to feel something even colder on either side of my torso.

I closed my eyes. The first thing I felt was something on my wrists. I can't vouch for this, but I think the guy on my left told me to relax as he strapped my wrists into restraints. I was going to object, but right then it occurred to me that I was not feeling any heat or pulsating pain from my chest for the first time all day. I was going to mention this to the guy on my left, when he and his buddy slapped something like blocks of ice against my rib cage. I opened my eyes, but the two guys were blocking my view. I said, I know it isn't ice, so what is that?

One of them said, Defibrillator pads.

They explained that I was being hooked up to an external defibrillator, which would remain in place while my device and leads were extracted.

I said, Just in case?

A woman somewhere behind me said, Standard procedure.

I was keenly aware in that moment that I had been through all of this just two months earlier and had no memory of any of it. The

defibrillator hookup, the arctic climate, the transfer from the gurney—
it was all news to me, and it all heightened my awareness that I was
way too wide awake.

Another nurse arrived with a sheet, which seemed to have been bak-
ing in an oven. She carefully arranged it over me.

I said, Is that really warm or am I really cold?

Both, she said. Then she smiled and said, You can close your eyes,
you know.

I closed my eyes. That helped. A wave of illumination was followed
by a wave of darkness, and I thought I was probably dreaming until I
opened my eyes and noticed that the general expanse of the room was
dimmer and some lights suspended right above me were glowing more
intensely than ever. I closed my eyes again, and I heard what sounded
like a change of shift on the factory floor—a lot of comings and goings,
until someone, maybe the surgeon, said my name.

Then someone said, Can you feel this?

I didn't feel anything. About three seconds later, I felt an intense
pain radiating out from the device. I connected this to the question,
but instead of speaking, I opened my eyes. I saw nothing but a gauzy
brightness. Again, I thought, *I am asleep*. But the longer I stared, the
more apparent it became that I was seeing through a sheet. It seemed to
be about six inches from my face. I heard a monitor beeping. Someone
said, *Yes, now*. I could identify the intense circle of one of the surgical
lights near the center of the sheet, and when I rolled my eyes around I
was charmed by the tentlike structure surrounding my head. I got very
interested in how it was framed and supported, but my attention was
diverted before I was able to figure it out.

I felt something alarming. I didn't feel it in the normal way. I felt it
happening a few feet above me. And I felt it had already happened by
the time I registered the unpleasant sensation. But I was certain my skin
had been sliced open.

The sequence of the next few seconds was confusing even as I experienced it, so I've never really known the order of these events. I thought
the sentence, *He has made an incision*. The light got brighter. I felt an
astonishing pressure that I translated into the widening of the incision,
as if my chest were being split open. I invented an image of the surgeon

with a handheld axe, gazing into my innards. I had several bouts of intense breathlessness, as if someone had begun CPR on my open chest, which I knew was impossible. I felt my back arch up, or that's what I felt my back meant to do. The surgeon said either, Michael, it is all right, or, Michael, are you awake? I think I responded aloud. I know I was awake enough, or alert enough, or myself enough to assure myself that he was not using a hatchet and he was not splitting open my chest. I felt a dull, sad pain, as if someone had deposited a fifty-pound weight on my chest. And then a viscous stream of something—I thought of honey—swept me down into darkness.

I spent the next four days in the hospital, but before I could be bothered to get out of bed to pee like a normal person, three doctors bothered to tell me why it was impossible that I had picked up the infection in the hospital.

Before the results of the bloodwork were in, the suspected culprit was MRSA, methicillin-resistant *Staphylococcus aureus*, a strain of staph resistant to the commonly used broad-spectrum antibiotics. It is a particular plague in hospitals and other health-care settings. The first doctor said, You couldn't have got the infection while you were hospitalized here. He explained to Peter and allegedly to me—I was in an oxycodone bliss at the time—that only someone with a super-human immune system could have picked up as virulent an infection eight weeks ago as my presenting symptoms evidenced and not become symptomatic much sooner than I had. So you didn't get infected in the hospital, he said. The next doctor told me they suspected I was cross-infected with staph and strep, and basically there was no way I had picked up two infections at once in this hospital, and it was even more preposterous to imagine that both infections had managed to survive the one-week dose of antibiotics I'd been given after my implant surgery. The third doctor said he'd never seen anyone present with an overnight explosion such as mine. He cast suspicions on my immune system, which he said must be compromised, based on his assertion that the infection was something I'd ginned up in the last few days.

By then, my infection had been identified. It was an old-fashioned strain—*Staphylococcus aureus*.

So you didn't get it in the hospital, the doctor said. Do you understand?

I said, But it's a staph infection.

Even I knew it was easier to pick up staph than a bunch of flowers in most hospitals.

He put his hands on the end of the bed and leaned in very close. Until that moment, this guy had been my favorite among the many doctors who'd dropped by to tell me what was wrong with me. It's not the resistant strain, he said. So you couldn't have got it here. Do you understand?

I understood that no doctor was going to take credit for my infection. You can call that false modesty, or you can call it false pride.

I didn't say anything. I considered myself lucky. Those doctors would have been impossible to live with if I had died.

4. *Negative Capability*

If you want to endear yourself to the many doctors who drop by your room during an extended hospital stay, just play dead. You might be starved for conversation, but they've spent the morning chitchatting with your neighbors and had their fill. And though appearance isn't everything, did you really think not bathing for two days and slicking down that cowlick with saliva was going to make you the most popular new kid on the block?

Doctors do ask questions. Don't worry. They already know all the answers. If you're a rookie and a good sport, you'll be tempted to swing at the first pitch, an apparent softball like *How are you?*

You won't be hitting this one out of the park. For starters, you can't see it, but your reliability as a witness is undercut by the silly sedative smile on your face. No one is seriously looking to you for answers. Are you still talking? Maybe you didn't notice, but the doctor is looking at your chart, and doctors do not like to be interrupted while they are trying to get to know the patient. Just because your surgical bandage seems to be bleeding through, and you are scared out of your wits about tearing something sharp out of your flesh if you move a muscle, and you are still unable to master the remote control for your bed and get your knees back where they belong, that's no excuse for ignoring the rules of common courtesy. If you absolutely can't wait, there is a protocol for requesting relief or reassurance while a doctor is visiting your hospital room. Hit the button that says NURSE.

If you can't fake a deep sleep, nodding and smiling are your best bets. Trust me, everything you say will be used against you. I was visited by many doctors on rounds, doctors who had participated in one or both of my surgeries, and specialists from the department of infectious diseases. According to my medical record, I almost never spoke to any of them like a normal person. I alleged, claimed, complained, denied, failed to recall, and basically behaved like a hostile witness under cross-examination.

This prosecutorial approach to patient records is known as *good practice*. In theory, doctors do no harm. In practice, doctors incur no liability.

During my first two days in the hospital, I told every doctor I spoke to three features of my story—the prickly pimple the night nurse had seen on my back after my implant surgery; the discomfort I'd experienced during the two months that first device was in my chest; and the push-ups I'd done the day before the infection puffed up. My goal was to identify a source, understand the significance of the time lapse between infection and visible symptoms, and get some advice about avoiding a repeat.

Every doctor seized on the push-ups and gave me a lecture on the basics of bacteriology. The last version was delivered by a frazzled woman with a beeping beeper she tried and failed to silence the entire time she spoke to me. Like her predecessors, she had taken off her listening ears as soon as I said the word *push-ups*. Maybe gym mats are the new toilet seats, the favorite scapegoat of patients who turn up with embarrassing infections. I was just wondering if repetitive exercise could account for the suddenness of the inflammation I'd experienced. She clearly believed that I believed that I had infected myself with calisthenics.

When she stopped talking, I said, I don't think the push-ups actually caused the infection.

With a smile of genuine compassion, she said, You can rest assured, Mr. Downing, they didn't. She was serious. She was still beeping.

I dropped the push-ups portion of my story.

The next doctor who dropped by glanced at my chart and said, So, you were never really able to adjust to the device. I guess that means you're more comfortable without it?

I had seen this guy before. He was the most vociferous of the three doctors who'd told me I hadn't picked up my infection in the hospital. Sometimes I suspect he might be two of those three doctors because one of them has no face in my memory and I only remember his barking at my bedside in the middle of the night. He was young. I described him to Peter as the kind of guy who wears wingtips to the beach. He had a face like a hatchet, and slicked-back hair, and he smelled of something old-fashioned and barbershoppish. He appears in my notes as Dr. Bay Rum.

This was early Thursday morning, I think. I know it wasn't Wednesday, because when I woke up on Wednesday morning I saw my mother, my brother Jack, my sister Peg, and Peter seated in a semicircle at the end of my bed. Peter had arrived with two large lattes for me. Mary Ann was not there. Probably, to prevent a tussle, she had left to procure coffee for everyone else. It's a tough crowd when it comes to caffeine. I wasn't a great host, and Peter didn't take notes on the conversation, so all I remember clearly is one thing my mother said to me. As she bent over my bed and kissed my forehead, she said, I wish I could wheel you out of here with me. And before she left my room, someone whispered, *He is in pain. And look at that left arm of his. It's badly swollen.* Maybe this was a nurse, maybe a doctor, but most likely it was my mother, as she liked to prove that paid caregivers were overpaid.

I had not yet reported it to anyone, but I was being bugged by a new pointed and occasionally piercing pain emanating from the center of the recently emptied pocket in my chest. And when I glanced down past the tubes connected to the port in my left arm, I noticed that my hand looked like a semi-inflated surgical glove.

The nurses I asked about the swelling told me it was a normal reaction to the stronger of the two antibiotics being pumped into me. By Thursday morning, my hand was fully inflated and there was a half-inch-wide red stripe below the bloated skin of my arm, from my elbow to my wrist. Peter tried and failed to stir up some attention to this problem, and I tried to convince us both it wasn't as bad as it looked from that angle.

Peter said, Which angle? We're looking from different angles.

He took a couple of digital pictures to prove his point.

I asked Dr. Bay Rum if it was phlebitis. I didn't have access to a computer, but our friend Jeanne is an incurable researcher, and it was probably she who'd communicated to Peter that phlebitis is often associated with the antibiotic vancomycin.

Dr. Bay Rum never even glanced at my arm. I don't have a transcript, but I know he used the word *fanatic* more than once. His point was that only a fanatic would worry about overexposure to antibiotics when he had a life-threatening infection. He also compared me to the fanatics who don't immunize their children. I am sure he mentioned tuberculosis.

It was weirdly gratifying to talk to Dr. Bay Rum. He was always as mad as I should have been.

I said I wasn't angling to avoid antibiotics, but if he would look at my arm, he would see the problem this particular drug was causing. He could also have seen evidence of my childhood vaccinations.

He never examined my arm. Before he left, he did tell me that a little bit of knowledge was a dangerous thing.

Then the surgeon turned up. I hadn't seen him since Tuesday. My mood hadn't improved considerably. To my discredit, I said, How's Congress?

To his credit, he said, You look lousy.

A crack like that goes a long way with me. I told him the vancomycin was killing me. He looked at my arm and said I'd be off it by Friday. I didn't know if this was a promise he was making or something he knew about standard procedure. It was a relief either way. I would've asked for clarification, but he was staring at my pocket.

He said, What is that thing still doing there?

I didn't fully understand what that thing was, though I suspected it was the source of my latest pain. My johnny had a chest pocket, and in it was a rubber ball, which was attached to a flexible tube, which was somehow connected to the pocket in my chest.

This rudimentary turkey baster goes by the vaunted name Jackson-Pratt drain. The nurses had used it several times, hoping to siphon infected fluid and blood from the pocket, but they kept coming up dry and eventually abandoned the project. I didn't really know how it was attached to me until the surgeon pulled down my johnny. He said, Look at me for a minute, Michael. With his thumb and index finger, he plucked the tube out of my chest.

When I glanced down, I saw a puncture hole in myself about the diameter of a pencil. The surgeon said he'd installed the pump, but he was not happy that it hadn't been removed on Wednesday, per his instructions. Untended, that tube was basically a covered bridge for any infection hoping to visit my insides.

In case he was looking for a fall guy, I gave the surgeon a detailed description of Dr. Bay Rum.

The surgeon told me we were going to have to talk about another device. My options were three. He could open up the unused pocket on my right side after a long course of antibiotics, and use extra-long intravenous leads to make contact with my heart on the other side of my chest. Alternately, he could reopen the used pocket after I'd cleaned it out with an extra-long course of antibiotics. Both options seemed to involve extras, which I considered double trouble. The third option was to do nothing.

Before I was discharged on Friday, I told the surgeon I definitely did not want to open up a second pocket. I didn't agree to be reimplanted. I knew it was the option I would exercise, but while I was alone in my room with my many pockets, I'd found some notes taken by Mary Ann. I didn't know if they were transcripts of a meeting I'd slept through or data she'd dug up on the web and didn't want to spring on me until I was healthy. I read two sentences several times.

1. Pocket infections increase the risk of death associated with ICD implant surgery by %? (The figure is 300 percent.)

2. The risk of infection more than doubles every time the pocket is reopened.

I was trying to convert these statistics into a reasonable plan for my future when a woman about ten years my senior burst in with six or seven young people tagging along behind her. This is known as *bedside manners*—an arcane code of etiquette based on the theory that things go much more smoothly if a doctor acts as if the only object in the room is an empty bed.

The woman, a doctor, said she was required to ask if I had any objections to an intern performing this procedure.

I said, What procedure?

She said something I didn't understand.

I took a breath. I said, Are you seriously not going to introduce yourself?

She said her name was Dr. Something.

I said, My name is Michael, and I was given a staph infection along with a prophylactic ICD in this hospital two months ago.

I could tell by the way she kept her gaze fixed on the floor that she was really happy to have made my acquaintance. She said, to her shoes, that she had an order to insert a PICC line.

I said, A what?

A peripherally inserted central catheter, if I must know. She made it clear she had a lot of other equipment she had to jam into other patients, and then she pointed to a shrink-wrapped coil of plastic tubing that someone was going to insert in a vein in my arm. It looked long enough for both arms. She asked again if I had any objection to an intern performing the procedure.

I got the sense she was sort of itching to do it herself, so I chose the kid.

A young man with a crazy, conspiratorial smile set to work on my arm. I remember him better than I remember the procedure. In my memory, it took something less than five minutes, start to finish. He puffed up the veins in my arm, smiled at me, numbed one vein, inserted a needle, smiled, and then, instead of feeding the tube in by hand as I'd anticipated, picked up a kind of handheld plastic crossbow and pulled the trigger. I felt something like a slapping *thwack* in my chest.

An X-ray later proved that kid had somehow shot the tube straight through the vein in my arm, up into my chest, and tipped it into my vena cava—the broad, short, stumpy vein that takes deoxygenated blood from the upper body back into the heart. I was impressed. All I could see was a bandage on my forearm.

That'll be the port, the X-ray technician told me.

I said, A port for what? I had spent four days discussing, debating, and negotiating the variety and duration of my at-home antibiotic regimen. The whole time, I thought we were talking about pills. It was the X-ray technician who first tipped me off to my mistake. According to her, I would be injecting those antibiotics and "something to flush out the system" directly into my vena cava three times a day for an indeterminate number of weeks.

During my final consultation with her before my discharge, I reminded the infectious-disease doctor that I was leaving with no clear idea about the source of my infection. She reminded me that most people carry staph on their skin and in their noses. I reminded her that I'd never had to have the stuff surgically removed until I'd visited her hospital. She reminded me that what mattered now was eradicating all traces of that nasty infection, whose origin we might never really know. I reminded her that this left me with no idea how to reduce the likelihood of acquiring another staph infection. She reminded me that my best bet for reinfection was the PICC line in that open vein on my arm. She also reminded me that this was ironic, given that I needed the PICC line to cure the first infection.

On Friday afternoon, I left the hospital with four days of at-home appointments for wound inspection and dressing changes provided by the Visiting Nurse Association; the prospect of weekly home visits from a nurse employed by the company that would supply the antibiotics, flushing fluids, and injection equipment for my PICC line; a library of tip sheets for preventing mishaps in the home and recognizing the signs of elder abuse; a slate of follow-up appointments with the surgeon, the cardiologist, and the infectious-disease doctors; and nothing to prevent my suddenly dropping dead.

It had been six months since I'd first received my genetic diagnosis. This is known as *patient making progress*.

More than fresh-brewed coffee or even my bed, what signaled a return to normal life for me was the prospect of returning to teaching. This was not a measure of my devotion. My atheism accommodates fervent praying for class-canceling weather most Mondays and Wednesdays. But I knew if I could get myself out of the house and spend a few hours not thinking about the drugs I was pumping into my body, or the infection I was trying to pump out, or whether that mutant gene was about to seize its opportunity to stop my heart's pump-pump-pumping—I knew when I returned at the end of such a day, I would really feel I was at home again, at home in the world.

So, as Peter drove me home from the hospital on Friday, I told him I was planning to teach on Monday.

Peter said, Okay. As he parked the car directly behind our back door, he asked me to wait while he unlocked the house so he could help me out of the car.

I said, Okay.

Fifteen seconds later, I heard Peter say, Where are you?

I said, I'm okay.

I was lying on the cement beside the car. As a demonstration of my fitness for life, I'd opened the car door, stood up, and collapsed. I'd felt my knees buckle and my legs go loose, and maybe I'd blacked out for a second or so. I was awake for the crash landing, I know, because I remember the *thud* of my head against the rubber tire and my neck stiffening in time to spare my skull a fracture.

Peter picked me up. After he established that I wasn't bruised or bleeding and I hadn't lost any of my attachments, he steadied me and said I had to eat something besides coffee three times a day, promise not to refuse assistance for at least a full week, and call Michelle and tell her I might be ready to teach by Wednesday, if I was lucky. Okay?

For the next four days, illness was my occupation. I had a vast and friendly staff of nurses who dropped by to change my bandages, clean my wounds, inspect my port, and check off any number of boxes on forms for my insurer, the federal government, the antibiotic-infusion-therapy company, the hospital, and Peter, who had designed and printed out a schedule for my medicine because by Sunday I was already asking him hourly if he could remember the last time I'd shot up.

It was hard work being an antibiotic junkie. Each session involved four syringes, and each session actually began half an hour before it began. I had to remember to take the eight-inch syringe of cefazolin out of the refrigerator, a step you'd think you could fudge by five or ten minutes unless you've once shot some of the cold stuff into your vena cava. And if I did remember to take the syringe out of the refrigerator, there was always the problem of where I'd put it down. After a few days in my house, those syringes behaved like my reading glasses, drifting from one unlikely surface to the next. And that meant I'd skipped step one: Establish a clean work area.

There were seventeen steps. Three times a day. And with me as the manager, the opportunities for a disaster were more than mathematical. For starters, I wasn't crazy about the quality of that catheter, which was nothing more than a cheap plastic tube anchored to my skin by a plastic cap. After a long, reckless investigation, I'd almost proved that somebody could accidentally flick off that cap, leaving the tube free to slither away. Before I did any damage, though, I recalled the *thwack* I'd felt near my heart during the installation procedure, which reminded me that my heart was precisely where that catheter would head if it went a-wandering. I left the cap alone after that. Attached to that cap was the port—a few inches of white plastic tubing I kept taped to my arm when I wasn't shooting up. This tube was outfitted with a little plastic clamp about the size of a paper clip, which allegedly prevented unauthorized access to my circulatory system. The white tube ended near my wrist in a nozzle for plugging in syringes.

Eventually, I got pretty good at establishing a skid-proof base for operations clean enough to pass as sterile—if you're willing to consider Clorox in the wash water a pasteurization process for bath towels. Three times a day, I dutifully laid out four syringes and a supply of individually wrapped alcohol pads, washed my hands and wrestled my way into a pair of latex gloves, opened several desk drawers and dug into a few piles of newspapers to locate the misplaced instruction sheet, ditched the dirty gloves, slid into a new pair, and worried that I should have washed my hands before I gloved up a second time.

The order of events after that was: Uncap the medication syringe (DO NOT TOUCH TIP!), push the plunger to get the cefazolin into the tip, recap that syringe (DO NOT TOUCH TIP!), open the catheter clamp, tear into an alcohol pad and swab the catheter valve, remove cap from first syringe of saline solution, insert and inject into system (FEEL THAT? NOW YOU REALLY KNOW HOW YOUR BLOOD SYSTEM WORKS!), tear into another alcohol pad and wipe the valve, uncap the cefazolin syringe again (PULL! DO NOT TWIST!), then twist the syringe into the nozzle (TWIST! DO NOT PUSH!) and slowly depress the plunger of the fat, eight-inch syringe for five minutes (WITH MY LEFT HAND?), tear open another alcohol pad for more swabbing, open and dock and shoot in another dose of saline, tear into another alcohol pad (INVEST IN THIS COMPANY!), prepare and inject the Heparin-flush syringe to prevent clotting in the catheter line (DO NOT TRY TO ANSWER THE PHONE!), clamp the catheter (NO! CLAMP BEFORE YOU REMOVE THE SYRINGE! HEPARIN IS AN ANTI-COAGULANT! NO! DON'T REATTACH THE EMPTY SYRINGE! YOU TOUCHED THE TIP! CLAMP THE CATHETER, YOU IDIOT!).

By Tuesday evening, Peter had conceded the obvious, I needed a new occupation.

I had become obsessed with my infusion-therapy routine and the opportunities it presented for reinfection. Plus, most of the antibiotics seemed to be bypassing my heart and doing their best work in my digestive tract. At breakfast and at dinner, illness was trumping every other topic of conversation. Even the nurses had started dropping hints like *How about those Red Sox?*

In my private thoughts, I had occasionally shoved myself aside and thought about Binny. I had met her only once, years earlier, but she'd made a deep impression, and I was always mindful of her when I saw her brother, Rob, a friend of Peter's since their Dartmouth days, who turned up often in our lives. Maybe I had sensed that Binny was for Rob what Mary Ann was for me, or maybe I had been bowled over by Binny's spirit and never really recovered. She'd had a series of astonishing adventures in medicine that seemed to culminate in a heart transplant—until she became one of the first heart-transplant survivors in the world to bear a child. Years later, her second heart began to fail her, and Rob had recently told us that her only hope was another heart and all that such a surgery might entail—all of which Binny was not likely to survive. But a new heart was her only hope.

While I was in the hospital in Boston, Binny was in a hospital in

Hanover, New Hampshire. She had chosen not to undergo a second transplantation. She'd died on Wednesday. Peter wisely told me only after I was at home.

After dinner Tuesday evening, almost a week after Binny died, Peter helped me figure out how to pack and carry my book bag without offending the weight limit for the left arm (surgery) or my right arm (catheter), without resorting to the shoulder strap (surgical site). Padding my shirt pocket with a few gauze pads for impact protection and wearing a heavy sweater over a button-down shirt made me look almost normal and meant I wouldn't do too much damage when I absentmindedly looped the strap of my book bag right over that tender pocket and surgical scar.

I was exhausted, and I still had to recalibrate my injection schedule so I wouldn't have to shoot up on campus, when I turned to Peter and said, Binny.

Peter nodded.

I said, It's hard to say if she chose to die, or if she chose her life.

Peter didn't say anything.

I said, I know I can't imagine what she endured, but I think I got a taste of something this week, a little sip of the stream she drank from every day. It's intolerable, but you can tolerate it. That's what I learned. Tolerance is a negative virtue, a failure to respond. And if you don't respond to most of what you feel, what makes you feel you are alive?

Peter didn't say anything.

I said, I'm happy for Binny. Or relieved. Does that make sense?

Peter didn't say anything.

I didn't say anything else. I could not articulate exactly what I knew at that moment, but I was certain I knew it.

On Wednesday afternoon, I picked up Michelle, drove to Tufts, and dropped her on the hill near the office we shared in East Hall, with an agreement to meet at my car when our day was done. I drove down the hill and parked in front of my classroom in the chemistry lab. Rearranging our commute so Michelle had only to walk downhill made me feel I was paying interest on classroom coverage, chicken soup, and the other favors I owed her. Avoiding my office also spared me a lot of questions from colleagues, like why I was wearing a heavy sweater on a sixty-five-degree day. I didn't want to talk about my infection or my mutation. You could call this shame. You would be right. To spare myself the insight, I called it an extension of my policy with students in my workshops, who knew I expected to see them in every class and that I was not eager to know where they were when they weren't there. I told them I trusted them as adults to respond to emergencies involving family and loved ones as they saw fit. I wanted them to know they didn't owe me explanations, and they didn't have to justify their choices, and I really didn't want to debate whether the soccer team qualified as *loved ones* if you were the goalie.

After I got out of the car, I grabbed my bag off the back seat and felt a sharp tug from the catheter in my right arm. This complicated my plan, as the bag was definitely over the weight limit for my left arm. I knelt down, looped the strap over my right shoulder where it couldn't threaten the scar, and stood up. Plausible. I bent down again and shrugged the bag onto the back seat. This worked, which meant I could shrug off the bag onto my desk in the classroom and then carry on like a normal person—except that I was now sweating like a marathoner, and I didn't think I had time to figure out how to get out of that crewneck sweater. I locked the car and looked at my wrist, where my watch wasn't.

This wasn't going so well.

I got as far as the curb and stopped short of the students streaming by on the sidewalk. Maybe it was the expectant air they gave off or maybe a new weather system was blowing in, but the breeze picked up and dried me out. The world was much cooler than the inside of my car. I looked up at the true-blue autumn sky through the smooth limbs of a midlife maple, its still-green leaves quivering like jazz hands, and I didn't think, I just said, Oh, Binny.

Maybe life is not a lesson, or maybe I am a bad student, but I knew nothing but how sweet it is to catch an unexpected breeze.

I was early to my first class. Only one young man was there to watch me shrug off my bag. I remembered he'd been early to the first two classes, too. As I unpacked, he said, I heard you had an operation.

I said, I did.

He said, You look okay.

I said, I am.

He said, I'm glad you're back.

I said, I'm happy you turned up again, too.

He smiled. I think he was wearing shorts that day, or maybe cut-off sweatpants. From somewhere above the shin, most of one of his original legs was missing. He had a handsome stainless-steel prosthetic.

I said, Is that as good as it looks?

This one is good, he said, as if he'd had a few that weren't.

I nodded. He nodded. Other students wandered in.

As I was packing up at the end of my second class, I saw a student from a previous semester's class at the door. I waved her in, and she threaded through the students who were heading out.

She waited until we were alone and then she said, Are you okay?

I smiled and said, I'm really fine.

Oh, I don't mean your operation, she said. I mean the blood on your right arm.

It was blood, all right. Sometime during class, I'd shoved the cuffs of my sweater and shirt up toward my elbows—and my PICC port with them. I saw what she had seen when I waved—a streak of dried blood that ran from my elbow and ended at my wrist. I remembered the jab of pain from that arm when I'd first grabbed my bag from the back seat of my car. I figured that's when I had done the damage. It's okay, I said. It's not bleeding now.

She nodded. She didn't look convinced.

I fished out the twisted-up end of the PICC line. I said, I have a catheter for antibiotics.

She said, Do you need a tissue or something? She seemed nervous, as if she suddenly felt responsible for my well-being and didn't know if she was up to the job.

I said, It does this all the time.

She didn't seem to find this reassuring.

I said, I really am okay.

Okay, she said, but she didn't leave.

I was sure she was going to offer to walk me back to my car.

Anyway, she said, could you write a recommendation letter for me? No rush. It's for study abroad.

Her request instantly conjured an image of a grade-school globe, the lacquered pastel surface of our round and shiny world. No rush. I don't remember where in the world she wanted to go, but I do remember how happy I was to be there.

5. *Principles of Accounting*

Ten days after the surgery to remove the hardware from the infected pocket in my chest, I returned to the hospital for my first follow-up consultations. I parked in the garage directly underneath the main lobby, which is like booking a room at the Ritz because you have to pee. Over the weekend, after a couple of painful practice attempts to put on my shoes—bending over until the pocket in my chest was pressed against my thigh and then relying on my aching arms to stuff my feet into normal loafers—I'd also sprung for my first pair of black clogs. I was feeling flush. The independent movie producer who'd long held the option on my novel *Breakfast with Scot* had almost nailed down financing, and he was threatening to write me a real check.

As I made my way to the elevator, almost every person I passed greeted me or smiled. On the elevator, medical staff and visitors alike said good morning as I stepped in, and a white-coated doctor about my age nodded his hello. I was early, so I bought a coffee in the lobby, and when I approached the milking station, a young guy in scrubs looked me over and backed away. He said, Please, and then waved me ahead.

I knew something was wrong. I checked my wrist and chest discreetly. No blood. I was wearing black slacks and a white button-down shirt, and I'd replaced my bag with a khaki blazer with patch pockets capacious enough for most of my stuff. Nothing to brag about in sartorial terms, but nothing to explain the attention I was getting. I told the guy in scrubs I was happy to wait.

He said, I'm getting mine to go. I'm outta here. Please, go ahead.

I thanked him. I added milk. I thought, *I have misjudged this place.* I credited the administration of the hospital for cultivating a genuinely friendly and humane atmosphere.

As I headed toward the surgeon's office, someone called out, Doctor! In a hospital lobby, this is like shooting fish in a barrel. A lot of heads turned. It was the guy in scrubs who'd yelled. He was rushing toward me. Your notes, he said, handing me the notebook I'd left on the counter.

Why argue? I thanked him. As he walked away, I noticed his open-back black clogs paddling across the tile. I scanned the floor. That lobby was a convention of cloggers.

You could say I passed as a doctor, or you could say I wasn't as popular as my shoes.

After a brief stint in the waiting room (not a single citizen clog), I was led into an examination room. The surgeon arrived in scrubs and clogs. He wasn't confused by my disguise. As usual, I was the one with his shirt unbuttoned. As usual, he examined my chest, rated his work "perfect," and asked how I was feeling. As usual, I said I'd feel a lot better if someone would admit that I'd been infected in the hospital. I'm sure I tossed in a couple of statistics about the rising rate of hospital-acquired infections.

I'd been squandering way too much time with my research partners at Google. As far as I could tell, there were two likely sources of my infection. One was that pimple I'd noticed on my back—an entrance opened up for infection while I was in the hospital, or perhaps the first alert my body had raised after I had been infected. The other plausible cause of the infection was the device itself. More and more infections were being traced to ICDs and pacemakers that either were contaminated during the surgery or had decayed after insertion and compromised the sterile site. I probably said something like, If that pimple wasn't the problem, I blame the surgical staff or the manufacturer—Medtronic, in my case.

I think that piqued the surgeon's interest in my pimple theory. He asked me to take off my shirt and turn around.

I took off my shirt, but before I turned around, he said, What's that? He was pointing at my right arm.

A sock, I said.

Footwear had never featured so prominently in my life. I couldn't fault the surgeon for asking. I was the one wearing three socks.

After the incident at Tufts with the blood on my arm, I'd woken up with a new blotch of dried blood near my vein and called the infusion-therapy company. The person hired to answer the phone assured me that a little bit of blood was normal. I asked how much blood was more than a little. She asked me to estimate the quantity I'd noticed. I got the sense she was not going to be impressed unless the answer was in pints. I checked this out with one of the company's nurses who dropped by later that day to change my port. She said any blood was too much blood and gave me her cell phone number. This surprised me. I hadn't pegged her as the most personable of the nurses. I did trust her because she spent more time washing her hands than I spent in the bathtub every morning trying to master the art of washing without getting almost anything wet. Before she left, the nurse asked me to find some clean white socks, and as if she didn't need anybody's permission, she cut the feet off four of them and made me cuffs to secure the port and tubing to my forearm. She said some patients were able to control their PICC lines with the adhesive tape provided by the company for this purpose, and some weren't.

The surgeon touched my back with his gloved index finger. He said he could see the lesion, but it was healed over now. He seemed to think I should be grateful he'd pointed it out.

I reminded him I had reported that lesion to at least one nurse and one doctor after my first surgery in July. He reminded me to remind the infectious-disease doctors. I was seeing them in about half an hour. Later, when he wrote to the cardiologist, the surgeon acknowledged that "the presumed source of infection was a small lesion on his back that he identifies as having first been noted during the hospitalization . . . and probably that was the portal." But he couldn't bring himself to talk to me about the origin or significance of that peculiar scar.

Apparently, the doctors had discussed it among themselves and concluded that my infection was an embarrassment, a real shame. Nobody
in the hospital was able to pinpoint the source of that embarrassing
infection, but they all knew the source of the shame.

While I put on my shirt, he said we should talk again about the
option of opening the clean pocket, the one on the right side of my
chest.

I let him know his timing was bad. Plus, this was not my favorite
topic. I was waiting to hear about a more rigorous protocol of surgical
hygiene. I didn't think *Try again somewhere else* filled the bill.

He said everyone he'd consulted thought it best to avoid the contaminated pocket. Admittedly, the right-side implant would involve more
wiring, but he said it could be worse. Some people had devices wired
up through their groins.

It is very hard to count yourself lucky while you're wearing three
socks.

I think all I said aloud was, This is not the time to talk to me about
another surgery in this hospital.

I was livid. If he was the sort of doctor who wore a stethoscope, I
would have swung him around the room a few times and felt better.
Instead, the brief flash of anger faded, and just that—a single, fleeting,
full-bodied moment of emotion—left me exhausted, which really discouraged me. I was wasting a lot of time and energy cleaning up a mess
I hadn't made. His eagerness to stick another device in somewhere—
anywhere—made me suspicious. Was he operating on commission
from Medtronic? And I still had to deal with those infectious-disease
doctors, the only adults in Boston who didn't know where most people
shopped for staph infections.

Nobody likes to wait. Nobody's mood is improved by being forced to
wait in an infectious-disease clinic, where you are greeted by the other
grim survivors like the arrival of the latest plague. One sneeze could get
you voted off that island.

I recognized the young doctor who called my name, or, at least, I
remembered her hair—a vast, untidy arrangement of pre-Raphaelite
curls and frizz so impressive that her face became a recessive trait,

eluding notice. Before I was allowed to take up billable space in an examination room, I was forced to stand on a scale in the hallway to be weighed, and then my blood pressure was taken while I was seated in a chair next to the scale in the hallway. It occurred to me that this happened every time I visited the surgeon, too. Presumably, the public setting cuts down on time-wasting questions from patients about their vital signs. Finally, the doctor led me into an examination room and asked me to remove my shirt and one of my socks. To her, my port looked "perfect."

One thing doctors learn at a Harvard teaching hospital is how to avoid mediocrity. Every mistake they make is a perfect fuckup.

I pressed for an update on the source of my infection. Someone in my network of informants had urged me to ask for a pathology report.

The doctor said all I needed to know was, it wasn't the resistant kind of staph.

I said I'd like to know more.

The doctor said that was the problem with staph. It's so common, she said.

I didn't consider this a totally satisfying response.

It *was* unusual, she added sort of wistfully, for an infected patient not to have presented with fever.

I said, By the way, the antibiotics are ruining my gut.

She said she had a drug for that, and why didn't I put on my shirt?

I said, I don't want another drug, but I do have some more questions.

She said, Fine, but you can put on your shirt. And we want to extend the course of antibiotics.

I said, Now I have even more questions.

No problem, she said. I'll be happy to answer all of your questions while you get dressed.

I said, Extended for how long?

She said, Four weeks. Maybe six. I don't think eight weeks will be needed.

I said I wanted to see another doctor.

She said, I am the doctor in the clinic today. You can put on your shirt.

I said, I want to understand what is happening to me.

She said, You have a very serious infection.

I said, I also have a very serious genetic mutation, and I would like to talk to someone who is willing to tell me which is more likely to kill me in the next three months—an arrhythmia, this infection, another infection I pick up at my port, or 150 additional doses of that antibiotic.

She left to make a call. When she returned, she said the attending doctor was busy. What were my questions?

I said I was happy to wait.

She said, He said he won't be available for at least an hour. It might be longer, but I'll call him again while you get dressed. She paused at the door. She said, You'll be more comfortable in the waiting room.

I didn't even glance at my shirt. I said, Thanks, but I'm really comfortable here.

I was absolutely willing to drop trou to prove my point. By then, even I knew the first rule of modern medicine: location, location, location. There's a reason hospitals cram dozens of chairs and sofas into their waiting rooms and toss in TVs, magazines, and free coffee. It's no time off their clock while you waste away in the reception area. But each examination room is a profit center with a single bed.

Never cause a ruckus in the waiting room or the hallway. Wait until you're somewhere it doesn't pay them to ignore you.

Five minutes later, the attending doctor turned up. He was a broad, bulky, half-bald guy, and, to his credit, he looked bemused. He sat at a desk to my right. The doctor with the memorable hair stood to my left. Several times during our conversation, he blinked or raised his eyebrows and she disappeared for a few minutes. At first, I suspected he was sending her out for reinforcements. I wouldn't have been shocked if she'd come back with a couple of muscular orderlies and four-point restraints. But nothing ever came of her coming and going.

So, the new doctor said, you have some questions.

I said, Are you going to sequence the DNA of my infection?

He said, It's not worth our time with *Staph aureus*.

I said, Is that because you infect so many people with it?

He said, There is a rising rate of infections at the hospital.

I said, Would I be better off at another hospital in Boston?

He clicked the keyboard of the computer on his desk. He pointed to a chart he'd pulled up. He said, We're doing marginally better than most of the other hospitals in town, but the differences among us aren't statistically significant. Your problem will travel with you. Once infected, you have an elevated risk.

I asked if my risk would decrease if I waited, say, a year to be re-implanted.

He said the risk was hard to read over time, and the biggest risk to me now was an infection at the PICC line.

So, I said, why do you want to keep it in me longer than two weeks?

He said, After two weeks, your pocket will look clean. It might even test clear. But we might miss some lingering intermuscular infection. If you weren't considering a new device, I'd let you quit after two weeks. But with a surgery on the horizon, the cost to your system of *not* being treated for two additional weeks is higher than the cost of being on the drug.

I said, Is it your sense I was infected here?

He said, We have seen a rising rate of infection.

I said, Could you extend that answer to a yes?

He couldn't.

I liked this guy, and I was very grateful for his time. And if he couldn't answer a simple question honestly, I didn't trust him. I'm sure he wished me no harm. But I felt he was more responsive to the opinion of the hospital's attorneys than he was to me.

He said, Are we reimplanting on the same side?

He did say *we*, and we were wearing clogs, so I said, Yes.

He said, That's another reason to extend to four weeks.

I said, Will you recommend a more rigorous antibiotic protocol for the next surgery?

He said, These are actually very interesting questions.

I admitted I was cribbing from my notes.

He said, The pre- and post-op protocol probably will not be changed.

I said that sounded risky.

He said something about the time just before surgery being our last chance to see the status of the staph. We didn't want to mask any infection, so we wouldn't want to change that routine.

I said that almost made sense.

He looked at his watch and said, Any bacteria that should be killed before the surgery will be killed.

I thought, Isn't that what the protocol didn't do for me last time?

The doctor stood up.

I don't remember if it was at the end of this conversation or after one of my visits during the next six weeks, but I asked him to call the surgeon and explain the extended course of antibiotics and repeat his endorsement of the plan to reimplant on my left side.

Initially, he seemed to take this as an affront, but he nodded his okay.

Before the doctor left the room, I asked him to make the call to the surgeon while I was in the room. This was pure improvisation.

He said, You want to listen in on our conversation?

No, I said, I just want to know you've had the conversation. This must have sounded as much like my mother to him as it did to me because he made the call. He wasn't happy, but he made the call.

The surgeon had asked me to arrange this telephone call. I remember this because the request had surprised me. I now know that the surgeon hadn't heard about the extended course of antibiotics or the implications for the implant. In his follow-up letter about my appointment earlier that morning, the surgeon had written to the cardiologist, "We are going to have to reimplant on the right [uninfected] side should he desire a second attempt at ICD therapy. Needless to say, all of this was really frustrating and disappointing for him, and I would say there is some chance he is not going to accept reimplantation."

A few weeks later, my sister Peg came to Boston to be implanted. Mary Ann had volunteered to accompany Peg, and the night before the surgery we had a little celebratory dinner, a kind of informal initiation ceremony. I'd found us a restaurant with sidewalk service so my sisters could smoke. I'd quit again, not for health reasons but because of the catheter in my arm. When I smoked, it looked a lot like an oxygen tube, which made me feel like the fat person in line at McDonald's.

It was a sunny autumn evening, breezy enough to warrant the sweaters we were all wearing and cold enough to explain why everyone who walked by was wearing a hat and coat. Fortunately, no one in my family ever feels cold, which saved my mother a fortune on heating bills during all those long Berkshire winters. When I started to shiver, I bummed a cigarette, which shut down my circulation and effectively numbed that unpleasant feeling of feeling.

I don't remember much about that dinner. I hope Peg enjoyed whatever she ate. I know she wasn't served up a lot of sympathy. She was the most like my father of the three of us, so it was obvious she shouldn't complain about getting the mutant gene, since unlike Mary Ann and me Peg had also got his genes for being well liked and easygoing. Plus, Mary Ann was living proof that it wasn't so hard to live with an ICD, and I was living proof that those doctors couldn't kill you if they tried.

When the food left on our plates had acquired a layer of frost, Mary Ann tried to attract the attention of our waitress by raising her hand. She failed. I asked her to try again. I'd noticed something familiar about her bad technique. I raised my hand. Like Mary Ann's, my hand didn't get much farther than my shoulder.

This is known as *frozen shoulder*, and it wasn't related to the weather. At home that night, I found a warning about it on the bottom of my most recent discharge papers. Naturally, I googled the condition. It was the result of not using the muscles that you were not supposed to use for several weeks after implant surgery, or after explant surgery, or while you were wearing a PICC line. I emailed Mary Ann to let her know she should probably contact a physical therapist or do a bunch of jumping jacks and push-ups.

Instead of closing the lid on my laptop, I thought about the three things I had reported to every doctor about the weeks between the implant surgery and the explosion of the infection: pimple, push-ups, and pain. I didn't think anyone could fault my follow-up on the pimple. And I now had a plan to request a prescription for physical therapy, which would alleviate the problem of risking push-ups to thaw out my frozen shoulder. But I wasn't proud of my work on behalf of that persistent pain. I wasn't certain whether that pain had been evidence of infection or if the device had been a particularly bad fit for my pocket, but I had reported it—*patient did note the generator pocket was always slightly uncomfortable*. Still, I hadn't done a damn thing about it since, as if I expected one of those doctors to pick up my slack.

I fired up my favorite search engine. I knew my first device was a dual-chamber ICD manufactured by Medtronic, vaguely rectangular, and I'd been told it was especially prominent in my chest because I was thin. That's as much as I was likely to get from the doctors. My discomfort with the pain it occasioned was being treated as a personality disorder. I limited my search terms to *ICD* and *thin* and started shopping for a new device to prevent my sudden death.

A few hours online taught me more about hypertrophic cardiomyopathy, arrhythmia, defibrillators, and medical manufacturers than I had learned in the last six months. I also found a convenient body-mass-index calculator and a promising outlet for cheap reading glasses. And I spotted a very appealing device. For a few weeks after that, I searched and searched the available outlets, but I kept coming back to the page I'd bookmarked that first night.

The model I settled on wasn't perfect, but I didn't have time to design and manufacture an ideal ICD. I was hoping to schedule my third surgery in mid-December, right after classes ended at Tufts, so I settled for an off-the-rack device. It was considerably thinner than my first defibrillator, and it was rounder—more like a stopwatch than a beeper. The sales pitch promised that this ICD would present a less prominent profile than any other device on the market. It was not a dual-chamber device. Unlike the special-offer, clinical-trial Medtronic model I'd been sold in June, which was connected to my atrium and my ventricle by two different leads, this ICD would be attached by a single lead to my ventricle only. I was pretty sure my atrium had not been identified as a suspect in the plot to kill me. As far as I understood my diagnosis, my sudden death would begin as a kind of short circuit in the ventricle, which would induce a fatal arrhythmia.

I made a note to double-check the life-or-death details with the surgeon before I put in my order.

The device of my desiring had one other distinction. It was made by a company called Guidant. Every implanted person I knew—and I knew a lot of people with the telltale bulge—was outfitted with hardware made by Medtronic, the largest of the three major device manufacturers. No one I knew had experienced any particular problems with their machines, but I had begun to suspect that the whole clinical-research project at the hospital, from DNA to ICD, was designed to guarantee a profit for Medtronic instead of, say, for me.

I figured the surgeon might balk or expect me to come up with some medical justification for ditching Medtronic. I had no reason to believe Guidant was a better bet, but it was a wild card. I had been dealt a losing hand the first time around, and the odds against me now were even worse. I wanted to mix things up. You could say I was feeling lucky, or you could say my clogs had gone to my head, but I emailed my ICD recommendation to the surgeon.

On Monday, 13 December, four days after the last class of the semester and two days before my third surgery, I had two appointments at the hospital. I met with a nurse to review my sordid history, and then I zipped upstairs for a final consultation with the surgeon. He came bearing a gift—a shrink-wrapped, vacuum-packed, single-chamber Guidant ICD. Model name: Vitality.

The surgeon let me have a good, long look, and then he said, What do you think?

I thought the photographs hadn't done it justice.

Like human beings, doctors sometimes surprise you. The surgeon was especially good at catching me off guard, which was not easy. After four weeks of antibiotic infusion therapy, I was pretty well inoculated against the charms of modern medicine. Plus, my notebooks were chock-full of details about the latest schemes and scams targeting unwary patients.

In early November, I'd basically hired myself as a private investigator to dig up dirt on medical-equipment manufacturers. It was not backbreaking work. Stick a finger into almost any portal in the World Wide Web and poke around, and you come up with something that will scare the wits out of you. The most alarming material for me involved recalls of implanted devices. None of these cautionary tales was featured in the full-color brochures or patient-information pamphlets handed out at the hospital. And yet they made for much more riveting read-ing than most of the stuff dreamed up by the PR staff at Medtronic. For more than twenty-five years, pacemakers and defibrillators from all of the major manufacturers had been behaving badly in people's bodies—wandering away from the implant site and causing trouble in a new neighborhood; leaking toxic battery fluids; getting all charged up without any provocation and shocking an unsuspecting heart; beep-ing incessantly just for the fun of it; and frequently falling asleep on the job and not responding to real emergencies.

I quit after reading three particularly grim horror stories involving Guidant devices. Plus, I'd been waylaid by newspaper accounts of the latest and greatest medical masquerade in a long time: doctors saying they were sorry.

Apparently, playing god for thousands of years and never copping to a mistake had started to take its toll. Doctors who accidentally chopped off the wrong limb or left an iPod in somebody's abdomen were pull-ing down their masks, frowning, and expressing their regret. Medical schools sponsored workshops and seminars to teach these techniques to their trainees. It was cathartic. It was humane. It was saving hospi-tals a fortune. A study conducted by the University of Michigan Health System found that encouraging doctors to apologize had reduced the fees paid to its attorneys by two-thirds and reduced malpractice suits by half. The major medical associations and insurance companies suc-cessfully lobbied dozens of state legislatures to pass *I'm sorry* laws, which sincerely encourage apologies by making everything a doctor says by way of regret or condolence inadmissible in court.

Apparently, a lot of injured patients really do feel better after a doc-tor apologizes. I hope so. Those patients will need all of their strength to comfort the other victims of their hospital ordeals—the doctors. They're victims, too. Late in November, I read a profile of an anes-thesiologist in Massachusetts who had founded Medically Induced Trauma Support Services to offer group counseling to these "other vic-tims," the medical professionals who were haunted by the traumatic patient outcomes they had perpetrated or witnessed. One week before my surgery, the *Boston Globe* published a special edition of its Sunday magazine, devoted entirely to medical issues. The cover-story headline was highlighted in bold type. "Every Surgeon's Nightmare: Leaving an Instrument Inside a Patient."

On 15 December 2004, instead of an apology, I got an extra pre-operative dose of antibiotics, which suited me just fine. They'd obviously brought in an anesthesiologist with a heavy hand, because I was asleep soon after Peter disappeared from view. For once, my services were not required. Somebody else was taking copious notes during the operation, and another somebody else was being especially careful. The account of this surgery in my medical record is encyclopedic compared with the record of the previous forays into that pocket, including several sentences detailing the hygiene standards, starting with my left side being "meticulously prepared with surgical soap, which was then allowed to air dry," and involving many iterations of the word *sterile*. After I was wired up, the anesthesiologist really stepped on the gas and drove me deep under so the surgeon could "confirm the high-voltage connections." Before he zipped it up, "the pocket was flushed with sterile antibiotic solution again."

When I awoke, Peter and Mary Ann were seated on either side of my bed in the little curtained post-op bay. Peter said, So?

I said, I did everything I could do, but he was on his own in there.

I'm sure I regaled them both with a version of my Three Ps.

1. Pimple: Despite predictions to the contrary, the antibacterial regimen was more rigorous than normal; even Peter had been impressed by the sober mood and sanitary standards in pre-op.

2. Push-ups: I had secured a promise for a prescription to physical therapy once I was allowed to use my arms again in January.

3. Pain: Although my Vitality was buried under bandages and I couldn't feel anything between my neck and my knees, I was confident that the slim new Guidant device would spare me the misery I'd experienced with that menace from Medtronic.

Mary Ann said, Time to be done with doctors.

Three and a half hours later, we were still stuck in post-op. Apparently, the hotel was overbooked and a lot of customers had requested late checkout. That's when the cardiologist turned up. I was woozy with oxycodone and apple juice, but I was happy to see her.

Peter mentioned the delay in my transfer to a new bed.

The cardiologist apologized: It *was* hard to wait.

Mary Ann suggested that the cardiologist might want to do me a favor instead of apologizing, and get me a bed.

The cardiologist apologized again: She had no influence here.

Mary Ann apologized: She needed a cigarette.

Who didn't?

The point was, the cardiologist wanted to offer me an opportunity to be part of a new clinical trial.

I said, Something else to do at the hospital?

Peter apologized: He was going to call the surgeon and tell him I needed help.

The cardiologist said several sentences I did not understand. By the time Peter returned with a promise from the surgeon that I would have a bed within minutes, the cardiologist had left. I told Peter to write down the words *nuclear imaging test* and *N hours of additional monitoring*, which was as much as I could remember.

Peter said, Another clinical trial?

I said, Yes.

Peter said, Did you agree to participate?

I said, I think so.

Peter didn't say anything.

It was a lie, I said. I was trying to butter her up in case the surgeon didn't come through with a bed.

Now I owed her an apology.

I had a great night's sleep, or else the night nurse had been warned that I was prone to problems and doubled my sedative dosage. I felt almost like myself when a friendly doctor with a notably spherical head arrived with a little laptop to test my device. He flipped open the lid and held the magnetic mouse over my pocket. He clicked a few keys on the keyboard with his left hand. He shook the mouse. He clicked a few more keys.

Finally, he said, No green light.

I said, What?

He said, I can't find the device.

I said, It better be in there somewhere.

He said, There's really no green light.

I aimed my finger at the Nurse button on my remote control.

He pulled some loose-leaf papers out of his pocket. He nodded. He said, I read the surgeon's name, and when I saw you were one of his patients, I just picked up the Medtronic. Reflex response. I see I need the Guidant system.

Later that day, when he came by to discharge me, the surgeon said he'd heard about the mix-up.

I didn't apologize.

He didn't apologize.

He said, I really hope you're happy with this one, Michael.

I said, This one's a keeper.

I think we were both pleased with ourselves and with each other.

I now know he got it exactly right in the last paragraph of his account of the surgery. "The patient tolerated the procedure well. There were no immediate complications of the procedure."

6. *Family Bonds*

Appearance isn't everything. I had inherited a propensity for sudden death from my father, but I otherwise resembled my mother. Genetically speaking, this is why I had both an ICD and serious doubts about the doctors who had given it to me.

I did not have any doubts about my Vitality. My single-chamber device from Guidant Corporation was everything I had hoped it would be: unbothersome, uninfected, and undetectable underneath a cotton shirt. It suited me just fine when I was bending backwards over the inflatable Swiss ball recommended by the superb physical therapist who had unfrozen my shoulders and unleashed my core strength. And it didn't show up on TV, though I often did in March 2005 after the publication of my book about daylight saving. The device didn't even reveal itself even when the microphone clipped to my lapel caused a blazer malfunction during a cable news interview.

The Guidant Corporation, however, was exposed a few months later.

In May 2005, a college student in Minnesota dropped dead during a bike trip. He had a genetic heart disease. He also had an ICD manufactured by Guidant. At the critical moment, his implanted device short-circuited.

It got worse. Before that young man died, Guidant had received reports of twenty-five previous failures of the same model, which it first marketed in 2000. By 2002, the company knew its Ventak Prizm 2 had a major problem, and it knew how to fix it, so Guidant had retooled the design to eliminate the problem in subsequently manufactured versions. But by mid-May 2005, Guidant had not informed any of the twenty-four-thousand people implanted with the problematic devices.

And it got worse. The first Guidant advisory to doctors was issued after that young man died—and then only because the *New York Times* informed the company it was about to break the story of the unreported design flaw. By the end of May, the number of reported short circuits was up to forty-five and two implanted people were dead. In June 2005, the company issued a voluntary recall—as opposed to a recall mandated by the Food and Drug Administration, the federal agency charged with oversight of safety issues involving medical devices.

Improbably enough, it got even worse. The FDA issued its first public-safety alert about the Guidant devices in June 2005. However, Guidant had reported its repair of the faulty design to the FDA in 2002. During the intervening three years, Guidant had also submitted reports of each device failure to the FDA. But as a matter of policy, the FDA treated such reporting from medical-device manufacturers as confidential information. As a matter of fact, the FDA had relied on Guidant's judgment that a recall was not warranted.

After the recall was announced, Guidant was outraged by the criticism it endured, not to mention how its stock price suffered. The point was, Guidant had kept quiet for the good of implanted patients. It reckoned that very few devices would actually malfunction, and the company wanted to spare people unnecessary exposure to risky replacement surgeries.

Doctors were outraged. Into my voluminous notebooks, I taped a paragraph from the 14 June *New York Times*, in which a reporter characterized the response of one indignant physician.

> . . . while the risks posed by the Guidant unit are low, they represent the type of risks that doctors need to know about. And while he said he understood a company's concerns about causing unnecessary operations, a decision about surgery was really one to be made by a doctor and patient, not a manufacturer. "You are not my father," he said. "You are not my

mother. You are just a company selling products. You have to let me make those decisions."

His outrage seemed sort of outrageous. In addition to his duties as a doctor, this guy had a gig as an "outside medical consultant" to the Guidant Corporation.

He was not alone. The device manufacturers routinely hire practicing physicians as advisors and consultants at six-figure salaries. Fees ranging from several hundred to several thousand dollars are doled out to doctors for each survey form they fill in about new ICD features, patient progress, and suggested improvements. These fees are not inducements, and neither are the all-expenses-paid symposia at tropical resorts, funding for fellowships, or private negotiation of prices with good customers—doctors who enter into nondisclosure agreements with device makers to secure discounts not available to less compliant surgeons at neighboring hospitals. "Incredibly," the *New York Times* editorialized in the late summer, "sales representatives are sometimes present in operating rooms to help surgeons select devices."

As luck would have it, I know a veteran sales representative for a medical-device manufacturer. He has a college degree. He has attended his share of seminars and workshops. His time with his surgeon clients is divided between office consultations and hours in the operating room during implant surgeries. He wants those patients to prosper. He even washes his hands and wears a mask. He does work on commission. Give me a little something to make me dozy, and I bet I couldn't tell the difference between the sales rep and the surgeon.

About two hundred thousand implanted people were affected by advisories, warnings, and recalls issued in 2005, according to the *Wall Street Journal*. The Guidant recall ultimately involved several models and almost seventy-thousand ICDs. Meanwhile, Medtronic had issued an advisory about the batteries in eighty-seven thousand of its devices. Luckily, my Vitality was unaffected. Oddly, so was my sense of well-being. I had long known that genetic inheritance was a coin toss, and in the last year I had come to think of dealing with doctors as a crap-shoot. Either way, you take your chances.

I didn't take my chance to participate in a cardiac sympathetic inner-vation study at the hospital, though I did want to know what such a proposition might involve. One of the cardiologist's colleagues in nuclear medicine called me to collect on the promise I had made while I was lying around in post-op, waiting for a proper bed. A few weeks later, the doctor sent a follow-up letter and a consent form. She was investigating the relationship between the nervous system and the heart in patients with a diagnosis of hypertrophic cardiomyopathy. Her pro-tocol didn't inspire confidence. For starters, she was demanding I not drink any caffeinated beverages for twenty-four hours before the study commenced. Coffee *is* my central nervous system.

The study involved a "blood draw," catheter placement (minor risk of bleeding, pain, inflammation, and leakage of contrast agent—a chemi-cal associated with risk of nausea, dizziness, headache, watery eyes, tin-gling sensation in the throat, itching, rash, and hives), and eight hours on an IV; an MIBG scan (nuclear imaging) after a radioactive agent (three times the average annual environmental exposure) was injected into the IV; an echocardiogram (no risk—but if you hadn't quit yet, they handed you a meal ticket and dared you to eat lunch in the hos-pital cafeteria); another MIBG scan (minor risk of radioactive iodine accumulating in thyroid and causing problems in the future); and an MRI (crossed out on my form because the radio frequency emitted dur-ing an MRI can heat up embedded ICD leads and burn tissue and skin, and the electromagnetic field can activate the ICD).

If I completed all phases, I would be paid $250. But I couldn't com-plete the MRI portion of the program without burning a hole in my chest and possibly setting off a blast of electroshock therapy, and this meant my pay would be docked by $62.50. I probably should've bar-gained with her. I bet she'd have offered me an extra $50 if I'd prom-ised to drink twice as much radioactive iodine as everybody else.

It was during the summer of 2005 that my mother admitted to me that she had become an addict. We'd logged a lot of hours on the telephone that summer. I knew she was not well. I knew this from my sister Peg, who helped my mother through those days, and Mary Ann, who called and visited the Berkshires often and forced my mother to tell her everything she wasn't telling Peg and the doctors and then reported a lot of that to me. My mother's idea of complaining was to say she hoped the annoying macular degeneration wouldn't blind her, and when things got really bad, she'd add, "I don't feel like myself." It often took half an hour to get her to admit her blood pressure was inexplicably spiking so high she often couldn't breathe, and her blood sugar was mysteriously dropping to levels so low she almost passed out while pulling a load out of the clothes dryer, and the only benefit she was enjoying from the pharmacopoeia she ingested daily was an annoying, painful, and unattractive outcropping of itchy rashes and tender lesions on her limbs and torso. Her quadruple bypass surgery, the replacement heart valve she'd had installed, and the pacemaker weren't worth mentioning because the cramping pain in her chest did not interfere with her exercise routine or daily dry-mopping when she remembered to double up on the nitroglycerine tablets.

She was the parent with the good heart.

I think it was in late July that she confessed. We were analyzing exactly what was wrong with each of her doctors—the latest installment in that summer's long-distance seminar in abnormal psychology—and she suddenly said, I am addicted to your Listerine. She had begun innocently enough—dabbing a little on problem areas—but she'd soon found herself pouring capfuls straight onto her afflicted skin, and then she'd run into the familiar problem of dealing with the distant regions of her back. She'd gotten so desperate that she recruited Peg to apply the stuff. This was serious. I knew exactly how much my mother hated other human beings touching her. Her idea of a spa treatment was when somebody else poured the coffee.

She was hospitalized twice that summer. In July, in a vain attempt to figure out what was wrong with her, she was taken in for observation. Her many doctors recalibrated medications, tested various systems, and finally released her after more than a week of intensive experimentation. As far as she could tell, it had been a bust. The one change she noticed in the weeks that followed was a deeper and deeper exhaustion that she couldn't sleep or exercise or will away.

Mary Ann forced her to allow a visiting nurse to drop by occasionally while Peg was at work, and one day in September, Peg got a call at her office from my mother. She was fine. Yes, she had a fever of about 103, and chills, and she'd sweated through several outfits that morning, and maybe she'd almost passed out a couple of times, but the real problem was the nurse, who was threatening to call an ambulance. They just won't leave me alone, she told Peg.

Peg drove my mother to the hospital, where she was whisked up to intensive care. Jack and his wife and their two eldest daughters were with Peg when I got there the next night. Mary Ann was, too. She'd been on her way to my mother's house with dinner in her car when Peg called. Joe arrived sometime that weekend.

My mother was out of intensive care when I saw her. Her johnny fit her like a ball gown. She was being bugged by an oxygen tube in her nose, which she frequently removed, and she'd also started swatting at a catheter in her arm. The first thing she said when she saw me was, I'm sorry you had to make the trip.

I spent a lot of time with her, but the next thing I really remember her saying was, No more now, right? No more. She said it to Peg. She said it to Mary Ann.

My mother would have been the first to tell you that she had given God plenty of opportunities to take her in the last five years of her life. Despite her generous offers, she hadn't died. It was an infection that occasioned her final, fevered trip to the hospital: methicillin-resistant *Staphylococcus aureus*, commonly known as MRSA, or hospital-acquired staph.

This was a grim irony, and we could have happily talked it to death had she survived. The physical peculiarities we shared tethered us till the last, and because we both treated our bodies like bothersome neighbors, we had never run out of fascinating gossip. But no matter how much work we had done on our respective hearts, it was never enough. She never revised her grim prediction that I would spend my eternal life in a blast furnace. I never revised my grim assessment of her chances of actually waking up in heaven next to my father. In our peculiar way we were true to the end, a constant source of solace and disappointment to each other and ourselves.

I wish I'd had the wit to bring her a bottle of Listerine, but all I could do for her that day was argue against the torture of toxic antibiotics.

One of Jack's daughters, a nurse, assured me that my mother's beleaguered body would soon be unable to process food and water, never mind drugs. A young doctor confirmed this and suggested dialysis, which offered no cure but would certainly prolong her misery and introduce new pain and a host of complications. When we saw my mother on Sunday night, the only people who didn't know she was trying to die were a couple of doctors and the nurse at the desk. By then, Mary Ann, Peg, and Jack were formulating a plan to have her transferred to hospice.

My mother said she was in pain. I said I could do something about that. She nodded and said she was in terrible pain. I repeated this to the nurse.

The nurse said, I know, poor thing.

I said, My mother is in terrible pain, and she needs relief right now.

The nurse said, Let me check my notes. We have her down for Extra-Strength Tylenol.

I am not making this up.

I said, She needs morphine.

The nurse said, She will have to speak to her doctor.

I said, You are confused. My mother is dying of a hospital-acquired infection—which she acquired in this hospital. You will have to speak to a doctor who can prescribe morphine immediately.

I don't think I made any threats. Maybe I mentioned the district attorney. Maybe the sheriff? I knew Jack was nearby and able to scare the shit out of most people just by exhaling through his nose.

To my surprise, the nurse agreed to make the call.

In honor of my mother, I said, While I am standing here. Make the call.

She did. The doctor delivered. My mother was moved to a hospice room. We were told it was impossible to know how many days, even weeks, she might survive. I went back to Cambridge to teach my Monday classes. I must have had a call from someone, because I headed back to the Berkshires Monday night. When my mother died, on Tuesday, Peg and Mary Ann were standing on either side of her.

I don't know where I was at that moment. I think I was at the hospital that morning, but I can't locate myself. I can't even recall where I was when someone—I can't say who—told me my mother was dead. I don't remember being anywhere.

Every death is sudden. Instead of waiting around to be taken by surprise, I rehearse mine. I lie down, I lose consciousness, my heart rhythm goes berserk without my even knowing it, and if nothing else happens, I'm dead.

This ritual is known as periodic defibrillator (shock) testing. My first invitation to this event came a little late. According to the photocopied page of instructions I received from the hospital, "we recommend that defibrillation testing be done within 3–6 months after your implant and annually thereafter." I got my first ICD in July 2004, and my chest exploded two months later, so I'd blown that invitation. However, the surgeon hooked me up with my Guidant device in December 2004, and though I saw him several times in 2005—no invitation.

I don't mean to imply he was giving me the bum's rush. Quite the contrary. Once I cleared up that infection, our briefest consultations in the examining room ran to half an hour. He'd flip open his laptop, and hand me the cord so I could hang it around my neck and comfortably settle the magnetic mouse against my chest. He'd download a bunch of data and instantly print out a running tally of my scores. I was always coming up with nothing—no new cardiovascular symptoms, no evidence of arrhythmia, no record of having received any symptomatic therapies. He'd ask me what I was writing. I'd ask him what he was reading. We had Graham Greene in common, which made us both aware we'd probably misjudged each other.

At some point, he'd warn me that he was going to test the pacing function, which was supposed to kick in if the device detected a dangerously low pulse, which was unlikely in me, given the caffeine content of my blood. Nevertheless, he'd hit a few keys on his computer and rev up my heartbeat. That was breathtaking, but much more civilized than a stationary bike or an elliptical machine. I tried several times to persuade him to open up a hardwired health club, but he thought the start-up costs were prohibitive.

I'd so often been the bearer of bad news about hospitals and doctors that I always made a point of mentioning the surgeon's generosity with his time when people asked for updates on my progress. A shrink I knew speculated that both the surgeon and I had boundary issues. I thought, *Well, that makes three of us.* A nurse I admire suspected the surgeon was acting on the advice of the hospital's attorneys. She said, You're a lot less likely to sue someone you like. But I'd never even made an idle threat or joked about litigation.

I saw the surgeon twice in 2006. Perfect scores. Better discussion than you'd get at most book clubs. And still no invitation. That's when Mary Ann said she wasn't as interested in the surgeon's bedtime reading as she was in my not dying. She urged me to invite myself. During my February 2007 appointment, I dodged a question about A. J. Liebling and asked when I should expect my overdue test. My invitation arrived in April.

The test involved anesthesia but no surgery, so instead of tying up overbooked tables downtown, the event was hosted at an affiliated hospital a few miles away. I knew the place well. The parking was cheap and plentiful, and even the inedible food in the cafeteria was affordable. The internist kept his office there, presumably because annual physical exams were loss leaders, just a way to get you into the system and identify some really expensive problems.

I knew the test was designed to prove three things: that the device could recognize a life-threatening irregularity in my heartbeat; that it still had enough voltage to correct the problem; and that the lead in my heart was intact and able to deliver the goods. I also knew I'd be knocked out for five minutes. In my life, this qualified as a party with an open bar.

Peter was my designated driver. I don't remember anything until I woke up after the procedure and looked for a clock.

An alert nurse with a broad Boston accent said, Where does the time go?

I said, That seemed like more than five minutes.

She said, It took a little longer.

I said, What took so long?

She said, He had a little trouble inducing the arrhythmia.

I said, Why was he inducing an arrhythmia?

She said, He programs your device to induce a fatal arrhythmia. That's why we have you in a hospital for the test.

I said, Just in case.

She said, Just in case.

I said, Why did it take so long to induce the fatal arrhythmia?

It didn't take so long, she said.

I didn't say anything.

The nurse was pulling the socks off someone else. She promised not to lose them. As she headed out of the room, she said, You were only in there a few minutes longer than usual. Maybe you have a stubborn heart.

I took this as a compliment. Maybe it was because her accent brought to mind my mother, who had so often bragged about the quality of her heart muscle. Maybe it was because the only other explanation was a weakness in my device.

I don't think I talked to the surgeon. I had the impression from someone—maybe the nurse, maybe the guy on the gurney next to mine—that he typically invited a lot of implanted patients to these parties and went right down the line, simulating and staving off death all morning. I know the surgeon had taken a few minutes to find Peter in the waiting room after the procedure, because when I saw Peter he passed on the news that my results were perfect. And I know I never got another invitation to put my Vitality to the test.

I was, however, invited to the 2007 Toronto International Film Festival. That persistent producer had made a movie of my novel *Breakfast with Scot*. It occasioned a lot of fun for me, but the most memorable moment, the most momentous, was a moment of darkness.

Eight years after the novel had been published, almost three years after I got my Guidant ICD, and two days after the first classes of the fall semester at Tufts, I was seated next to Peter. We were dead center in a jam-packed theater with stadium seating—and the women in the seats in front of ours were short. We each had a cup of coffee, conveniently at hand courtesy of the built-in beverage holders. The lights faded. The companionable crowd quieted and disappeared. Peter leaned into me. And nothing. Darkness. Nothing. Darkness until the electric crackle of suddenly spinning film jolted us both, and that spark lit up the screen.

Just about a month later, on a Monday morning in mid-October, I was bent over our dining room table, groggily separating the sections of the morning newspapers. We get three newspapers, so this counts as Pilates. If the *Boston Globe* is particularly thick and the *New York Times* is particularly dense, this shuffling of sections also counts as reading the *Wall Street Journal*.

Medtronic.

Medtronic?

I flipped back in the *Journal* pile. It was in a headline on the front page of an inner section. "Medtronic Pulls Defibrillator Wires Off Market." The subhead text began "After 5 Patients Die," and I immediately skipped to the body of the article and scanned the first few paragraphs. "Medtronic . . . 235,000 patients . . . prone to fracturing within blood vessels . . . massive electrical jolt . . . Medtronic . . . Sprint Fidelis defibrillator leads . . . risk of surgery to remove . . . could prove significantly larger in scope than the problems that arose in 2005 . . . Guidant Corp . . . "

Guidant's problems were in the past. I had a handy file of news clippings to prove it. In the last year, Guidant had been sold to the local biotech giant Boston Scientific. It was not Guidant but Medtronic that had agreed to shell out $40 million to satisfy a couple of whistleblowers who'd complained about payoffs to doctors in the spinal-device implant business. And though a scary Canadian study had recently turned up a 6 percent rate of major complications during ICD-replacement surgery, I'd survived unscathed. My problems were in the past.

So what was bugging me?

The problem was Sprint Fidelis. It was an absurd brand name that seemed instantly familiar. I double-checked. I read the *Journal* story until I found a sentence that definitively and singularly linked the faulty leads with the manufacturer that had not made my device. "When a Medtronic Sprint Fidelis lead fractures . . . "

I was safe.

Sprint Fidelis. It sounded like a fundraising run for the Marines. *Semper Fidelis*. That's why it was familiar. *Semper Fidelis*. What did it mean? Always Faithful. Sprint Faithful. Spring Forward.

It was easy enough to grab my wallet and check my airport-security travel card. GUIDANT VITALITY DS/VR T135.

If I knew anything, I knew I had a Guidant device. I'd seen it in the shrink-wrapped package before I was implanted. Everything on it, all the information I'd received about it, everything printed anywhere within my immediate reach, identified it as a Guidant, not a Medtronic. And yet I knew I was about thirty seconds away from dumping my entire medical record on the dining room table.

I peeled back the lapels of my bathrobe and peered inside, as if I might find a brand-name tag dangling down there. Barely a bulge. I headed into the bathroom, faced the mirror, and turned on the examination lights. It looked nothing like my first device, nothing like any Medtronic I'd ever seen. But appearance isn't everything.

7. Second Verse, Same as the First

By eight o'clock on 15 October 2007, the fanned-out sections of three morning newspapers were buried on the dining room table beneath my medical record—a splay of photocopied observation forms, cardiology reports, nursing notes, discharge summaries, heart-healthy recipes, and drug-interaction warnings. I shuffled that deck about a dozen times before I found the narrative record of my most recent surgery and an inventory.

Implanted Hardware

Pulse Generator
Implant Date	12/15/04
Position	PECTORAL, SUBCUT
Manufacturer	GUIDANT/CPI
Model No	T135
Model Name	Vitality VR

Pace-Sense Leads	PS1	PS2
Implant Date	12/15/04	
Position	RV APEX	
Manufacturer	MEDTRONIC	
Model No	6949	
Model Name	SPRINT FIDELIS	

A normal person might have zeroed in on that final entry, which proved that the electrical wire (PS1) threaded through one of the veins in my chest and anchored into the wall of my heart at the apex of my right ventricle (RV APEX) was prone to fracturing and fraying. The Sprint Fidelis lead had already been identified as the cause of hundreds of malfunctions in similarly outfitted people, and as a suspect in at least five deaths.

But old habits die hard. I was counting myself lucky, the secular version of counting your blessings.

The blank space under the heading PS2 on my surgical inventory meant I had only one bad lead. If I hadn't shopped for a single-chamber device on Google, I might have ended up with another ICD like the first one I'd been given—the super-special, clinical-trial Medtronic with dual-chamber pacing, which would have left me with two of the bad leads. Luckily, the staph infection had exploded only a couple of months after implantation of the lead I needed and the one I didn't, and that was barely enough time for scar tissue to form and complicate the lead extraction. Scar tissue often forced a doctor to accidentally snap the lead and lose some of it in there or puncture the vein while tugging, an injury that sometimes went unnoticed until the patient had bled to death.

I'd had the bad lead for almost three years. I decided to call the surgeon. It was early, but with almost a quarter of a million people waking up to learn they might be implanted with faulty leads, I figured his dance card would fill up fast.

Not that there was a shortage of device doctors; it was experience that was in short supply. These days, anybody can stick a defibrillator into you. After the surgeon and his colleagues persuaded Congress to extend Medicare coverage for implants—expanding their potential client base by about five hundred thousand—demand for devices exploded. Manufacturers and professional associations responded by offering weekend courses for doctors who didn't want to waste time training like old-fashioned electrophysiologists. Naturally, rigorous new professional standards were established. These didn't interfere with the supply side of the business. All of the guidelines and qualification criteria were strictly voluntary.

I surely knew that eminently credentialed electrophysiologists with years of experience at a Harvard teaching hospital made mistakes. But I also had a photocopy of an article in my 2006 file, from the *New York Times*, about a bunch of doctors in South Carolina who'd been trained in ICD implantation at a local bistro and hotel. In the same file was a clipping from the *Wall Street Journal,* in which a Medtronic spokesperson warned against explant surgery, estimating that "the lifetime risk of dying from medical/surgical complications is 33 times greater than from having a [defibrillator] malfunction."

I wasn't going to be scared into living with a faulty wire, but I didn't want a doctor doing the extraction while he was ordering lunch. Plus, I'd had pretty good luck with the surgeon so far. I wasn't dead.

The surgeon wasn't taking calls that morning. When I explained why I was calling, the receptionist said, You'll want to speak with the coordinator of the device clinic.

I disagreed, but she transferred me anyway. I began the conversation by referring to the story in the morning newspaper about the problem with Medtronic's Sprint Fidelis leads.

The coordinator said, I haven't read any story like that.

I said, It's about the ICD leads being recalled.

She said, It's not technically a recall.

Okay, so maybe technically she hadn't *read* the newspaper story, but she had heard about it.

This wasn't going so well. I wasn't sure whether she worked for the surgeon, the hospital, or the device manufacturers. I also wasn't sure whether I was involved in medical treatment, industrial research, or a scientific experiment.

I said, I have the bad lead.

She said, I'm afraid I don't know what you're talking about.

I said, I'd like to talk to the surgeon.

She said, I'm going to have to call you back. She hung up.

I scooped up my medical record and put the surgical-inventory sheet on top of that pile. I called the nurse practitioner who worked with the surgeon. She wasn't answering her telephone, or maybe she was screening her calls. I left her a message and decided to give the coordinator fifteen minutes to call me back. I paged through the scattered newspapers, trying to find the section of the *Wall Street Journal* where I'd spotted the Medtronic story. After a few frantic passes through the whole pile, I found nothing. I really thought I might have made the whole thing up.

I stepped away from the table. My hands were inky. My bathrobe was at half-mast. I hadn't yet had a cup of coffee.

I rectified all three problems, and when I returned to the table, I saw the headline on the front page of the *New York Times* for the first time. "Patients Warned as Maker Halts Sale of Heart Implant Part."

The telephone rang. It was the coordinator. Oh, Michael, she said in a sweet, jokingly reproachful voice, I am really happy to tell you I have good news. You totally overreacted.

I said, Not yet.

She said, I checked.

I didn't say anything. I was zipping through the *Times* story. "Medtronic estimated that about 2.3 percent . . . 4,000 to 5,000 people, would experience a lead fracture . . . jolts can be extremely painful . . . $6 billion global defibrillator market . . . Medtronic $12.3 billion in sales last year . . . will not pay for procedures to replace functioning leads that patients want take out to head off possible problems."

The coordinator said, Anyway, there is no need to worry yourself. You have the Medtronic Quattro lead. The potential for problems is only associated with Medtronic Sprint Fidelis leads.

I could tell she wanted me to thank her and hang up. I wanted to hang up, but I couldn't bring myself to thank her. So I told her I was sure I had one of the bad leads.

She said they weren't bad, and I had the Quattro lead, anyway. She told me she had spoken to the nurse practitioner, and then she added, I am reading directly from your record, Michael. And she made it clear that this was even more tedious than the morning's *New York Times*.

She was reading my medical record, and so was I. The coordinator of the device clinic was right. I had once had the Quattro leads. They were screwed into the wall of my heart in July 2004—before all the fun began.

I told her to scroll through my medical record to December 2004.

After a few minutes, she said, Well, I think you might have one Sprint Fidelis lead.

I said, One bad lead.

She said, Your doctor will be in touch with you.

I said I wanted to see him.

She said his first open appointment was in November.

November was two weeks away. I said I wanted to see him sooner.

She said, Okay, so I've put you down for November first at 8 AM.

An hour later, the nurse practitioner called. I asked her why I had been implanted with a Guidant device but hadn't been given a matching Guidant lead.

She said, You have a Medtronic lead, Michael.

I said I hadn't known the devices and leads were mix-and-match out-fits when I was shopping on the Internet. Was there a reason I hadn't been given a Guidant lead?

She said, Your lead is subject to a patient advisory at this point.

I said that advice might have been more useful before I got the bad lead.

She said, We're going to follow up on the advisory by using your home monitor to do a little higher surveillance on the lead. The nurse practitioner didn't waste time answering questions when she was try-ing to get her point across.

Since the spring, in lieu of actually seeing and talking to the sur-geon while my data was downloaded quarterly, I had been using a telephone-size, at-home transmitter with a magnetic mouse. Essentially, the mouse flipped a magnetic switch in my ICD, which activated the transmission of stored data—monitoring records, evidence of any pac-ing problems, and delivery dates for pacing and shock therapy required in the last three months. These data dumps took five minutes, tops. The transmitter was plugged into my telephone line, and the information was sent to a website maintained by the device manufacturer, where it was accessible to the surgeon and his staff.

The appeal of this arrangement was immediately recognizable to anyone who had ever carved out time in a workday for an office appointment, traveled to a hospital, paid for parking, and sat for an hour or two in a waiting room. At-home monitoring also reduced the cost of these mandatory sessions to an insurance co-payment for the patient and a transmission fee of approximately $30 for the physician, who could make more than that per minute just from rent on each of his overbooked examination rooms. Of course, remote monitoring was a compromise. It had killed the book club and eliminated my reporting on minor discomforts and weird, onetime symptoms I'd experienced and forgotten to log in my notebook.

The nurse practitioner told me she'd activated a weekly-checkup program on my transmitter, which was distinct from the quarterly interrogations I had been performing.

I said, I have to transmit data fifty-two times a year for the rest of my life?

She said, The monthly interrogation is different from the new weekly scans for device alerts.

I said, So I have to transmit data sixty-four times a year?

She said I wouldn't be charged for the weeklies.

I said, I want to get rid of the bad lead.

She said, When you see the surgeon in two weeks, he will reprogram your device to reduce the impedance.

I said, I want to get rid of the bad lead.

She said, You might have to remind the surgeon you have the Guidant device but a Medtronic lead, which needs to be reconfigured.

I said, Reconfigured?

She said, He'll reconfigure lead alerts down by about 1,000 ohms, so we can pick up any issue quickly.

I said, How many ohms is normal?

She said, Everyone is different.

I said, Does *impedance* basically mean *resistance*?

She said, We're getting deluged with calls. This has caught everyone by surprise. You should write down any questions you have before your appointment with the surgeon.

The next day, the *Wall Street Journal* reported that the risk posed by ICD leads "has long been an open secret among doctors."

One week later, I received a certified letter from the hospital. It was unsigned, as if maybe it had originated as a fax from Medtronic or the FDA. The letter assured me that "the chance of malfunction affecting your lead appears to be low." It was a form letter, so this optimistic prognosis lacked the personal touch. It arrived along with two press releases from the FDA and a letter from Medtronic assuring me that "the chance there is a problem with your lead is small. You are more likely to experience complications from removal."

But by then the story was more complicated. If you googled *lead* and *Medtronic,* you knew that at least one death apparently associated with Sprint Fidelis leads had been reported to the FDA in 2006. In the medical press, it was widely considered a safe bet that the failure rate for those leads was not going to remain at Medtronic's estimate of 2.3 percent. One poor woman was becoming famous on the blogs for having received dozens of unwarranted shocks thanks to the bad leads, each shock like a kick in the chest from a horse. Congress was threatening to investigate. The FDA responded by threatening to swallow its own tail—promising to investigate its regulatory standards to figure out if tougher testing standards for implantable devices ought to be considered sometime in the future.

Meanwhile, Medtronic was congratulating itself for having erred on the side of caution. This was certainly true of its compensation offer. If you were lucky and could prove your lead had fractured but hadn't killed you yet, Medtronic was offering to send you a new lead and $800 toward the cost of surgical replacement. Estimates for that procedure from bloggers around the country began at $12,000 and climbed to twice that amount.

I wondered which hotels their electrophysiologists patronized. I'd yet to get in and out of the hospital for anything less than $30,000, not including parking.

When I saw the surgeon, he flipped open his laptop programmer and reconfigured my ventricular-pacing impedance from 2,500 to 1,800—ohms, I think, but I really am not certain about that. I don't blame the surgeon. He was very forthcoming during our long discussion—sometimes alarmingly so, which I appreciated. I was tired of scaring myself silly, and he had a lot of hair-raising stuff that hadn't turned up yet on the web.

I asked him what he thought about Medtronic's estimate of the failure rate.

He said 2.3 percent was not good.

I asked if he had a sense that it would go higher.

He said anything too much higher would put it in the intolerable range.

I offered to let him pluck the lead out with tweezers right there in his office.

He said, I know you are discouraged.

I said I found dealing with the device coordinator especially discouraging.

He gave me his email address and the number for a telephone he actually answered and told me not to talk to anyone but him from now on.

To thank him, I said, Why did you give me the Sprint Fidelis lead?

He said he'd wanted me to have the best lead available. The Sprint Fidelis was thinner than any other lead on the market, and since he'd already been in and out my veins, he'd wanted to minimize the risk of insult to my body.

I asked if the leads frayed because they were so thin.

He thought so. He guessed that the demand for innovation had gotten ahead of the materials science. He said the problem was a little worse for me, as I was so young and so healthy.

In the good old days, those had been my assets.

He said there was some evidence that the leads were more likely to fray in young, active patients.

I told him I'd sworn off push-ups and was absolutely willing to give up all physical exercise.

He said, The problem is, I can't predict the risk of that lead over thirty or forty years in you—thirty or forty years during which you probably won't ever require a shock.

I don't know what I said next. He had put his finger on the paradox of my genetic diagnosis.

He didn't say anything.

I had a mutant gene. But unlike my father, I wasn't overweight, and unlike my too-soon-dead brother, I had no symptoms that warranted pharmaceutical or even dietary intervention. And now I had the Sprint Fidelis lead—which was really redundant. That lead was as unpredictable as the mutant gene. Both increased the risk of a short circuit in the electrical system of my heart.

At some point, I complained that the precipitous decline in my health had began with a geneticist who had identified a mutation that now seemed to be the least of my problems. Genetics had gotten ahead of physiology. I had been hospitalized three times since my diagnosis. As far as the internist and cardiologist and surgeon really knew, I might well have been safe until I developed classical cardiovascular illness or profound hypertrophic cardiomyopathy.

The surgeon said, If you ever do.

I said, So why was every doctor at this hospital certain I was at risk?

The surgeon said, Family history.

My family also had an unbroken history of not requesting autopsies. How had one mutant gene with uncertain bearing on the physical well-being of my body convinced every doctor at the hospital that I needed a prophylactic ICD?

The surgeon said, If the only tool you have is a hammer, everything is a nail.

Interrogating my device with a magnet once a week was easy and painless, so I took the opportunity to torment myself with the futility of the exercise. At-home technology had reduced the burdens associated with reporting, but it had not reduced the need for expert analysis. At the end of a long week, did I really expect the surgeon to download my latest data dump instead of an episode of *Lost*? Plus, the pressure on physicians to prescribe remote monitoring as a substitute for clinical care exponentially increased with every advisory, warning, and recall from the device manufacturers, who regularly recommended more monitoring instead of risky replacement surgeries. And that meant more data in the bank.

I hardly needed an assistant to make matters worse, but the device coordinator did what she could. Two weeks after my appointment with the surgeon, she inexplicably canceled the series of appointments I had made with him and wrote me a letter to confirm that my next transmission was scheduled for March 2008. When I called to tell her I was transmitting weekly, she said, Let me check.

Wherever she went, she didn't rush back.

I checked, she said. She added, I have no record of weekly transmissions in my file, so I have not been forwarding any information to the surgeon about those readings you say you've been doing.

I said, *You* check my transmitted data?

She said she *was* the device-clinic coordinator.

I transcribed my notes from this conversation, minus the italics, and faxed a summary and a copy of the letter canceling my appointments to both the surgeon and the nurse practitioner. In response, I received an email from the surgeon assuring me everything had been straightened out. He also reminded me to email him directly from now on—maybe as a favor to me, maybe so the device-clinic coordinator wouldn't quit her job.

Every week, I sent my data out and the bad news poured in. A study of very young implanted people—most of them under twenty-one—turned up a Sprint Fidelis failure rate of 4.9 percent. Among the speculative reasons cited were the additional stress on hardware caused by faster heart rates (characteristic of young hearts), physical activity, and the physical strain on the lead caused by increased thickening and stiffening of the heart muscle—the classic symptom of hypertrophic cardiomyopathy, the diagnosis that occasioned most device implantations in children and young adults, as it had mine.

The disease caused the lead more stress? This was like having a neurotic bodyguard. The more you needed his protection, the more likely he was to freak out and kill you by mistake.

Before Thanksgiving, the third-largest device maker—after Medtronic and Guidant—made headlines. Four of its leads had reportedly perforated the hearts of implanted people. The company did not issue a recall, though one of those leads had migrated from the heart to within a few centimeters of a patient's skin. Luckily, I'd never considered dealing with this company, based on its name alone—St. Jude Medical. In my neighborhood as a kid, St. Jude was known as the patron saint of lost causes.

In January 2008, Medtronic CEO Bill Hawkins told the *Wall Street Journal* that the company did not yet understand the elevated failure rates for the leads. He did guess that some "failures may be due to a surgeon's implant technique, or simply due to complications in patients with chronic medical conditions." If he was attempting to fend off the individual and class-action lawsuits being filed by the dozens, he needn't have bothered. In February, the U.S. Supreme Court handed the device manufacturers an all-purpose shield against those pesky personal-injury lawyers. The court asserted that federal law trumped state liability laws in litigation concerning devices that had undergone the FDA approval process. Justice Antonin Scalia, writing for the eight-to-one majority, argued that liability litigation would stymie innovation. Medtronic spokesman Rob Clark told the company's hometown paper, the Minneapolis–St. Paul *Star Tribune*, the court's ruling was "an important decision for the medical device industry and our continued ability to innovate and bring lifesaving technology to patients."

The only reliable antidote to the news was a regular dose of William H. Maisel, a doctor who headed up the Medical Device Safety Unit at another of Boston's Harvard-afilliated teaching hospitals. From the moment the bad-leads story broke, Maisel had repeatedly asserted that Medtronic had known long before October 2007 about the potential for problems. In March 2008, he published a brief history of the Medtronic lead failure in the *New England Journal of Medicine*. Seven months before the recall, according to Maisel, Medtronic had alerted physicians around the country to incidents of elevated failure rates with the company's leads. While it assured physicians the reports were not statistically significant, in May 2007 the company applied for approval of a new lead design, which was granted by the FDA in July. Medtronic continued to sell the old leads until mid-October 2007, when at least five deaths were being investigated.

I don't know about the device manufacturers, but I found Maisel's work heartening even when it gave me the heebie-jeebies. For instance, Maisel and eight colleagues with a sense of irony had stuffed a tiny circuit board and an audible electronic buzzer into a plastic bag filled with bacon and ground beef. Why they chose bacon and ground beef to mimic the skin and soft tissue in which an ICD is typically embedded is open to speculation. They did specify the hamburger was 85 percent lean. This experiment was designed to identify vulnerabilities in wireless implanted devices. The results were published in the proceedings of the 2008 Institute of Electrical and Electronic Engineers' Symposium on Security and Privacy.

Using available software radio technology to attack (their term) the ICD, they were able to flip the magnetic switch and download data—which typically is accompanied by confidential personal and medical records. They could also alter the therapeutic settings or turn off the device from a discreet distance. The buzzer they'd put in that bag of meat was a crude model of their proposed innovation—an ICD-based alarm to warn the wearer of a wireless invasion.

In a loose-fitting shirt or a sweater, my ICD was not immediately apparent. Still, it was alarming to consider how often I was identifiable by setting or segregation as a person ripe for hacking or attack —in the waiting room of the device clinic, or during a pat-down at an airport. If this seems an arcane concern, try this experiment: For one day, wear a sandwich board that promises, *If you ask, I will tell you my Social Security number, insurance data, and details of my medical history.*

But what really set off bells in my head was another story from the *Star Tribune*. It was published on 6 March 2008. I ran into it while trolling the World Wide Web, looking for trouble.

The Minneapolis Heart Institute Foundation had tracked the effectiveness of the lower-impedance, stepped-up interrogation and transmission regime I was observing weekly. The data showed that "the monitoring technique for determining when a Sprint Fidelis lead is going to fail is relatively ineffective in preventing adverse clinical events." In fact, it had failed in at least 70 percent of the patients whose Sprint Fidelis leads failed during the study. They were first alerted by unwarranted shocks.

Medtronic issued a press release claiming that the study "provides no new information that would alter our patient-management recommendations."

In early April 2008, I saw the surgeon and asked him about the Minnesota study.

He urged me not to quit my weekly routine.

I asked him about a few other discouraging studies.

He asked me if I'd read anything by A. J. Liebling yet.

I told him I didn't love living with a prophylactic device that might suddenly attack me.

He asked me if I was going to spend the summer in Ipswich. He'd remembered Peter and I had a very little house—sixteen feet wide—thirty miles north of Boston. It was very old, so it made you feel young. It was beset by structural peculiarities, so it made you feel sturdy. And it was near a tidal river with stinky flats you could smell when it was low tide, which is when you wanted to go the broad barrier beach a few miles away. The surgeon reminded me to bring my transmitter to Ipswich and plug it in. He claimed he needed the data.

In October 2008, the surgeon investigated my device. He confirmed what he had observed in my transmitted data (somebody had been doing his reading): There was evidence of deterioration of the lead. This may or may not have been responsible for the accelerated depletion of the battery in my Guidant device. He wanted to pull out the lead and the device and insert a new Medtronic Maximo II ICD (as thin as my Guidant, but shaped like a shield) and a Sprint Quattro lead—the model he'd inserted the first time he got into my pocket. I requested a date for surgery in early December, right after the end of the Tufts semester.

I knew this surgery was a gamble, and every bookie I consulted had an idiosyncratic method of calculating the odds. On any given day, 250 Americans died as the result of a hospital-acquired infection. The last time I'd checked, the infection rate for implant surgeries had topped out at 5.5 percent. The published risk of serious injury associated with lead extraction—including death—ranged from 1-point-something to 7 percent. And I had been repeatedly reminded that every intrusion into that pocket doubled my risk of complications.

In early November, Medtronic released the results of two long-term studies of the Sprint Fidelis lead. One reported a 3.8 percent failure

rate; the other reported a 6.3 percent failure rate. The highest average rate of failure I'd read for all other leads was 0.06 percent. A lot
of bloggers claimed Medtronic was still lowballing. I just wanted that
bad lead out.

I didn't do the math. I had decided to go all in with the surgeon. You
could call this earned trust, or you could call it blind faith.

One week before the surgery, I was in an unfamiliar little examination room in a new building at the hospital. While someone stuck me
all over with electrodes that she wasn't always able to make stick and
eventually administered an EKG, a sweet but skittish nurse detailed the
pre- and post-op antibiotics the surgeon had in store for me. Before she
was finished, she interrupted herself and recounted a trip to somewhere
she'd given herself for her birthday, which ultimately left us both looking a little lost. She recovered well. She handed me a plastic bottle full
of anti-everything body wash, and she told me to use it to clean the
pocket area for three days before surgery. I was grateful for this innovation in hospital hygiene. It would save me a ton of Listerine.

The nurse sent me down a flight of stairs for a blood draw, and as I
was preparing to leave the hospital, a receptionist told me I had to go
back upstairs. I asked her why. She said the nurse wanted to see me.

After a few minutes in the upstairs waiting room, I saw the nurse. She
looked really jumpy. She whispered, I don't want to upset you.

I said I would bear that in mind.

She said, It's probably nothing.

I said, It rarely is.

She said, I just want someone else to have a look at your EKG.

I said, Why?

She said, It's probably nothing. It's probably your device.

I said, Call the surgeon.

She said, I'm sure it's the device that threw things off.

I said, Call the surgeon and the cardiologist.

She said she'd already called somebody. As she walked away, she
said, Don't worry.

I might have called the surgeon, or maybe Peter, if I hadn't left my cell phone in the car. I was really more astonished than worried, though ten minutes went a long way toward righting that balance.

Finally, I saw the nurse returning. I'm sure she didn't really walk sideways, but that's the impression I have. When she was near me, she whispered, It's nothing.

I said, What is?

The nurse said, Your EKG.

I said, Something about it was worrisome.

She said, It was nothing. I wasn't worried. I thought your device had probably just interfered. Not interfered, inter . . . I just wanted to be sure. The doctor said it's absolutely fine. It's nothing to worry about.

That was as far as we got before she slipped away. I don't know why I didn't tackle her and demand a better explanation. I'm surprised I didn't walk directly across the street to the old, familiar building and track down the cardiologist. Instead, I remember thinking I would bring it up with the surgeon.

Apparently, I just couldn't put enough eggs in that one basket.

I taught my last classes of the semester on Monday afternoon, and first thing Wednesday morning, 10 December 2008, I was in a johnny on a gurney. Peter was standing beside me. The whole gang was running around with those crazy matching hats and tie-on gowns, masks at half-mast, spirits high. Whatever the many nurses were up to, they weren't causing any pain. The surgeon came by a couple of times, always with the other surgeon—a compact and straightforward guy who'd been around a lot during the infection and explant episode. We all behaved as if that was a happy memory we shared.

After I'd signed away my rights the requisite number of times, the other surgeon zipped into view and said, We're going to have somebody put in a line from your groin. You won't feel a thing.

I didn't know if not feeling was good news or bad news down there. I said, Up to my heart?

The other surgeon said, If the lead cracks or snaps during the extraction, we want to have another approach.

I said, You're worried that the scar tissue in my vein is profound.

He said, Your problem is you know too much.

I said, I do now.

He said, The line we're inserting is a precaution. If we did need access, we wouldn't want to stop and put the line in.

A dark-haired guy, maybe thirty-five, appeared. One of the surgeons introduced him as the anesthesiologist.

I thought, *About time.*

For a few seconds, he just stood there, shifting his gaze from Peter to me. When he finally spoke, he led with an apologetic tone about the prescription for full anesthesia. Some people, he said, experienced nausea or headache.

I said, There's always somebody who doesn't like something, no matter how good it is.

The anesthesiologist looked at Peter and smiled—sympathetically? My angle was bad. Finally, he bent over my arm to ready my intake valve. He said, I loved that movie *Milk*. Have you guys seen it?

Really.

Way too quickly, the anesthesiologist added, With my wife. I saw it with my wife. But we loved it. Both of us. We cried. Both of us.

Peter said we hoped to see it soon.

I might have said something else, but the other surgeon turned up again, which got my attention. He hadn't been bearing a lot of good news. I think the surgeon arrived in his wake, but I couldn't see his face.

The other surgeon said, We have one more thing to ask you.

I said, Okay. I didn't mean it, but I did say it.

The other surgeon said, I'm doing the lead extraction as it is, so would you mind if I also did the implant?

This was the first I'd heard about the other surgeon extracting the lead. This is known as informed consent.

The other surgeon said, The surgeon will be right there the whole time, but I'll already be—I'll be in there already. Is that okay?

The surgeon wasn't the surgeon. The lead was not able to lead. The Guidant was half-Medtronic. Everything was mutating.

I felt Peter's hand on my shoulder. I looked up. Peter widened his gaze.

I said, Okay. I meant, *I ordered that anesthesia ages ago. Who's running this bistro?*

When I woke up in post-op, a pasty young doctor was standing at the foot of my bed. He picked up my chart, flipped through, pulled out one page, shoved it back in, closed the chart—and then he did a double-take. He opened the chart again and pulled out one page.

I said, What's so interesting?

He said, You know.

I didn't say anything. I knew the page he was holding was an EKG.

He said, You know that you had a heart attack, is all.

I said, I've never had a heart attack.

He said, Uh-huh. He put the EKG back in the chart. He walked away.

8. The Other Lazarus

After the fourth surgery, I was wheeled out of post-op and installed in a big, new room in the hospital's big, new building devoted to cardiovascular care. I hadn't packed my tape measure, but I'd guess the bedroom was twelve by twenty-five feet. This made for a lot of long walks from the solitary bed, along the wall of floor-to-ceiling windows, past the full-size sofa, and finally left into a bathroom so vast that you always ended up feeling you hadn't done enough in there. The roundtrip was not without its rewards. The view over the red brake lights of backed-up traffic on Huntington Avenue and out to Mission Hill—a little height of land stacked up with triple-deckers—was a sweet reminder of where you weren't. The long walk back to bed also brought to mind the line in the vein near my groin that had been rather recently removed.

I had a lot of visitors that night. Every doctor who dropped by greeted me with the same two words—*Great room!*—and walked right past my bed to the wall of windows to check out the view. I didn't mind. My new device was wireless, so it was actually possible for them to hack into it and do whatever needed doing from a distance. Plus, postoperative examinations seemed sort of superfluous by then, what with my perfect record of perfect results.

As long as he was in the room, Peter was besieged by invitations to spend the night. The couch, we were told a dozen times, pulled out. I'm crazy about Peter, but I wasn't crazy about people issuing invitations to overnight guests on my behalf. Of course, Peter wisely took a pass on the sleepover. He knew as well as I did that an upholstered sofa was a staph party waiting to happen.

My least favorite of the many big, new features of my big, new room was room service. Instead of just bringing you a tray of inedible food like they do in normal prisons, the management forced you to order up your own punishment. Availing myself of room service meant I had to locate my migratory eyeglasses to read the menu; retrieve the menu without disturbing the cranky patch of stitched-up skin above my heart; understand what was printed on the menu while high on oxycodone; retrieve and dial a telephone with catheters in my arms; and then hope I'd remember what I'd intended to order, which I already knew I didn't want to eat.

The hospital charged almost $80,000 for my surgery and overnight accommodations. However, after reviewing the itemized bill, my insurance company shelled out only $60,000. The room-service menu didn't include prices for each selection, but that chicken dinner and breakfast omelet I didn't order apparently saved somebody a fortune.

It was a cold day in early December 2008 when I checked out of the hospital. I was mindful of my brother Gerard, who had died on a cold December morning five years earlier. This wasn't mordant sentimentality. It was a sense of place.

The last time I saw Gerard alive, we were standing outside that hospital. My mother was in a room high above us in intensive care, sleeping off her double-header cancer and bypass surgeries. Mary Ann and Peg were with her. Jack would be there first thing the next morning. I owed Joe a call. I can't remember if he was trying to time his visit or if I was meant to report on mine.

Long before my genetic diagnosis, the hospital had replaced the family home. Since my mother's illness had forced her to seek advice and care in Boston, the old world was a-tilt. The center of gravity had shifted from the moral to the medical. Holidays of yore were replaced by diagnostic tests and consultations and operations. Instead of olive oil and stinky cheese, I turned up with a notebook and a willingness to ask too many questions. Each hospital reunion occasioned a lot of contact with the siblings who were still in contact with my mother—advance planning and schedule coordination, divvying up of duties, and exhaustive post-game analysis with Mary Ann.

For my future, it was good practice. In my relationship to the past, it was a reorientation, but not a transformation.

It was late evening, early fall, and way too cold to be standing around in shirtsleeves, as both Gerard and I were. Probably I had a cup of coffee and Gerard had a bag of something from the café in the hospital. He had a weakness for its oatmeal-raisin cookies. He had been wearing a suit jacket, but out of loyalty he'd taken it off, folded it, and placed it on a low concrete bench behind us.

There was a lot behind us—everything we hadn't said, time we had not spent together. We had never harmed each other, and neither of us was holding a grudge or owed a debt. We were happy to be together. I think our infrequent encounters and companionable conversations always left us pleasantly surprised and a little disappointed in advance, as if we both anticipated what the other wouldn't do to follow up or cultivate the opportunity. We pretty reliably proved each other right.

We never talked about our hearts. I mean, we never once inquired about the status of the muscles in each other's chests, even with a father felled by his at forty-four and a mother eight floors up above us in a coronary-care unit. The topic never came up, just as it didn't with my brother Jack or even with my brother Joe, with whom I've spent endless days and nights discussing and dissecting every other organ, organization, and organizing physical, psychological, political, and philosophical principle for the last fifty years.

This willful inattention to our most obvious vulnerability was consistent across periods of alienation and intimacy, moments of personal triumph and trauma. The point was, comparing your fate to your father's was false pride. The point was, it was hubris to think you might be at risk.

The last time I saw Gerard, he looked very tired. I said he was welcome to spend the night with Peter and me in Cambridge. He knew that I knew this was an offer he would refuse. He was famous for wanting to get back to his family.

He thanked me, but he said he wanted to go home. He added, You should come up to the Berkshires for a weekend. He meant if I visited my mother and Peg, then he and Pam would happily stop over for dinner.

A few months later, I drove to the Berkshires for his wake and funeral.

In the years following his death, I often wondered what Gerard hadn't said that he might have said that night. Even I knew that he knew he had cardiovascular complications. When his son was diagnosed with hypertrophic cardiomyopathy and outfitted with an adolescent ICD in the early 1990s, the geneticist entered the story through a colleague who worked with children's hearts. That was when many of my siblings sent blood samples to the geneticist's lab. At the time, the purpose of that project—the search for a hereditary link—was clear to some and not to all. The specific idea of identifying individual genes, stereotypical mutations, and custom-tailored therapies was well beyond our ken.

As far as I knew, no one who had submitted a sample had heard about the fate of that investigation. It's protocol, of course, to force donors to sign away the right to benefit in any way from material profits or medical therapies that might result from such research.

A few weeks after Gerard died, Mary Ann tracked down the geneticist. She urged Mary Ann to consider ICD implantation. This conversation led to the genetic testing of Mary Ann and me and our siblings in early 2004. In the midst of that conversation with Mary Ann, the geneticist mentioned that she had spoken to Gerard about the identification of the inheritable genetic mutation he'd passed on to his son.

None of the people who knew Gerard best can say exactly what my brother knew before he died. His son was the only family member with an identified manifestation of the characteristic disease. Maybe Gerard believed he alone had inherited something from the father he so closely resembled. Maybe being alive at fifty-two was enough to persuade my brother that the mutation originated with him and not my father. Maybe Gerard was waiting, trying to figure out how he was going to tell the rest of us that we had to learn to live with sudden death again.

I don't know what the geneticist told Gerard or when. I contacted her again in early 2008, before my fourth surgery. I had just learned that the weekly at-home monitoring I was doing was unlikely to prevent a problem with the Sprint Fidelis lead. I was pressing the surgeon to take the bad lead out, which meant I was headed once more back to the beginning—and I figured I might as well go all the way back.

When I emailed the geneticist, I reintroduced myself, reviewed my recent adventures, and told her I was writing a book.

> The project is an attempt to examine how a person can identify a reliable source authority for the story of his life. I am hoping you will be willing to talk to me. My questions presently are of two kinds.
>
> First, I want to better understand the research that led to the identification of my condition. I am reading and trying to bridge the gap between conventional sources for non-scientists and results published in refereed journals. . . . Second, I want to better understand the sequence by which my status was identified . . . [which] bears on my reading of the (vast) literature emerging on the development of practical, ethical guidelines to govern the intersection of research, diagnosis, and privacy.

Three weeks later, the geneticist emailed with apologies for the delay and urged me to call her laboratory to set up a telephone date. A week later, we spoke for forty-five minutes. She gave me a good talking-to—a jam-packed lecture that began with her work to identify families with cardiomyopathy and sped through the process of tracing the source from chromosomes—"a zip code, but not a street address or identity"—to the delicate string of amino acids in a specific protein. I got the sense that the myosin binding protein C was not especially well understood—it was subtle—and that the effect of the mutation I'd inherited was further complicated by the participation of many other proteins in the contracting and relaxing of my heart. My mutation was predictive of hypertrophy, but the disease could be quiet for a long time, and other genes and behaviors influenced its development in unpredictable ways.

And that was the easy stuff. I have eight pages of notes, which I have often consulted. Some of them are still encrypted in a shorthand I apparently invented and forgot. I was left with a few open questions. For instance, I think I may have a peptide or two that is not as long as it should be—or else I am incorrectly decoding *poppy beads = lost truncations*.

I asked the geneticist three times when she had identified an inheritable mutation in my family, but I didn't get an answer. The first time, I interrupted her midsentence and she let me know she wasn't taking questions yet. The second time, she invited me to a half-day conference that she and the cardiologist were putting together for patients like me and their families. The third time I asked about her conversation with my brother, she gave me the conference date and the name of the person to call for a reservation.

Every time I asked anyone about this information, I got exactly what I got by not having talked to my brother when I'd had the chance. I got nothing.

The geneticist called me a few weeks later and asked if I'd be willing to speak to a reporter from the *Boston Globe* who wanted to interview someone whose heart-disease management had benefited by genetic diagnosis. I frankly considered this better PR for my book than for her lab, but even so, I hesitated. She'd hit a nerve.

You are about to go to confession in public. I sounded just like my mother to myself. There was a cure for that. *You don't have a nerve there.* Any doctor could tell you so. I agreed to be interviewed.

Early in May 2008, I attended the half-day conference led by the geneticist and the cardiologist, which was not nearly as rigorous as my private lecture. I asked the geneticist if I could email her a few questions, and she encouraged me to spell out exactly what I wanted to know.

In June, I spoke to the *Globe* reporter. She promised to show me every draft of the story, and she was true to her word. The photographer sent by the newspaper asked if he could take a picture of me with the device showing. I felt sorry for the guy. He'd beat around the bush before asking, as if he didn't want to offend me. He was a veteran photographer, but he was a rookie when it came to shame. I'd anticipated this question when the geneticist first mentioned the article. As planned, I told the photographer I hadn't worked topless since I'd stopped doing push-ups. He settled for a head shot.

I emailed the geneticist a sterling report on the reporter along with specific questions about the chronology of her identification of the mutation I'd inherited, her conversation with my brother, and the results of the tests her lab had run on all that blood my family had donated in the early 1990s. She didn't respond.

In August 2008, I emailed the geneticist again. I was not hoping to unveil a secret. I figured the geneticist had expected Gerard to pass on news of the identified mutation to his siblings. She had encouraged Mary Ann to spread the news to her siblings. I made it clear again to the geneticist that I had no axe to grind with her or with my brother. I wanted to understand the limits and the limitations of clinical-research protocols. I was also trying to make sense of my own delayed response. After my genetic diagnosis, I'd arranged to let three months pass before I had the first implant surgery.

I assumed my behavior had been a little peculiar. It often was. But was it pathological? I was also trying to illuminate the relevant family history and identify any mutations that had interfered with standard research and clinical procedures so I could accurately account for my life with sudden death.

That assay was inconclusive. The geneticist did not respond. You could say I had hit a nerve, or you could say I had not hit a nerve. I concluded nothing. I was right back at the beginning, not really knowing where I stood.

Two weeks after the fourth surgery, on 29 December 2008, I saw the surgeon—another holiday at the hospital. The bandage was off, the scar was sealed up, and my bottle of post-operative antibiotics was as empty as my gut. We were in an examination room. He'd brought along a companionable young woman—maybe a resident, maybe a newly hired electrophysiologist, maybe police backup.

He didn't need any protection from me. At last report, thirteen deaths had been associated with the Sprint Fidelis, so I was genuinely grateful to be rid of that bad lead. I didn't even ask why he hadn't performed the surgery. What was the point? I knew what I needed to know for my own peace of mind. I knew enough to ask the next time.

He gave my scar and the surrounding site high marks, but the other surgeon's work did not earn a *perfect*. I told him the Medtronic felt a little bigger, a little heavier, and a little more prone to tipping off to the side of my chest than the Guidant. He said my pocket needed a rest. He also said the device he'd selected had a proven record of long battery life, so with any luck I wouldn't have to be unzipped for seven or eight years.

I said, Thank you.

He said, You deserve a break.

I said, That bad lead almost did me in.

He said, It's the first one I regret, the infection. That one could have been prevented.

I should have said, Apology accepted. Instead, I brought up the heart attack.

He said, You told me about that already.

I remembered that he had assured me in post-op that I had never had a heart attack. Still, I wanted to know what to say if the mistake occurred again.

He said it was a stupid mistake, but not uncommon. The thickening of the muscle in hypertrophic hearts can be misread as the healed aftermath of injury sustained during a heart attack. He said it was the kind of trick question they give you on your boards—and he added that any qualified doctor should know better.

You have to hope the doctors are learning as much as the patients at this teaching hospital.

Early in January 2009, I emailed the cardiologist. I wanted to talk through the history of my diagnosis and treatment. I was cashing in a favor she didn't owe me, as I had refused to participate in her colleague's nuclear-imaging study when asked. The cardiologist almost instantly wrote back and offered me a choice of times to talk.

Anything I understand about the past and future of my heart is based on that conversation. Plus, she corrected my false impression of genetic research as a process of refinement and narrowing; instead, every advance in precision—clearer vision or better aim—yields a vast new array of potentially significant targets. The initial focus on the genome gave way to the study of ten or so sarcomere genes, which opened up a field of more than eight hundred mutations and the prospect of thousands more. The cardiologist confirmed my sense that no clear link had been established between each mutation and its physiological consequences. My mutation has no characteristic clinical signature.

We have your DNA and your family history and you, she said, but we don't have a piece of your heart to look at under a microscope.

After a few silent seconds, this struck us both as funny.

I admit there was a panicky moment when I'd thought she might be angling for a sample.

Before she hung up, the cardiologist urged me to make an appointment for a clinical exam and asked how I was feeling. I told her I was fine since I'd found out I hadn't had a heart attack. She asked me which EKG had caused confusion. I gave her the date of the pre-surgical consult. I explained that the nurse had been thrown off by the effect of my device, and the doctor in post-op had misread the evidence of cardiomyopathy.

I could tell she wasn't buying either of those excuses. She let me know she had pulled up my record with the EKG in question. Then she giggled.

I said, What's so funny?

She said, No one could mistake this for a heart attack.

I didn't say anything.

She said, No one could mistake this for your EKG.

It wasn't hilarious yet to me, but she did have an infectious laugh. I said, What's wrong with it?

That really made her laugh. She said, This is crazy. It's like somebody mixed up the electrodes for your arms and legs. It's irrelevant. No doctor could mistake this for your EKG.

I first met the cardiologist late in June 2004. By then, I'd known for three months that I had inherited the genetic mutation that put me at risk of sudden death. I chose the date of our first meeting. You could say I delayed it so it wouldn't interfere with my teaching that semester. You could say I delayed it so I could complete the manuscript for *Spring Forward* before my deadline. You could say I didn't want to screw up the trip to London and Florence that Peter and I had planned for late May.

I'd say I could believe I had inherited a stray paternal gene. But sudden death? I couldn't quite believe I was that much like my father.

So off to London, where Peter had a couple of days of business to conduct at the National Gallery, and then to the business of vacation. After several solo trips to Italy over the years, Peter and I finally made it to Florence together. If you are about to die, I have a hotel to recommend with wrought-iron balconies hanging above the Arno and coffee service from friendly guys in tuxedos. Compared with the hospital, they're giving the rooms away. And if the view and local treasures of the Renaissance aren't enough to keep your mind off your problems, you can take a short train trip to Padua to see the frescoes painted by Giotto on the barrel-vaulted ceiling of the Scrovegni Chapel.

I'd wanted to see Giotto's painted story of salvation for twenty-five years, and I'd chosen not to go to Padua every time I was in Italy. I was waiting for the right moment. This one qualified because Peter was with me and I was still alive.

My long delay was rewarded. A painstaking restoration of the seven-hundred-year-old frescoes had been completed in 2002. But there was a price to pay for waiting. Giotto's masterpiece had been outfitted with an iron lung, a complicated air lock-and-filter system designed to extend its life. My time with Giotto was limited. No more than twenty-five people could be inside the chapel at once. It got worse. After fifteen minutes in a dehumidifying chamber, each batch of bone-dry visitors was allowed to spend exactly fifteen minutes with the frescoes. There are thirty-eight painted scenes from the lives of Jesus and his mother, not to mention the Last Judgment and angels galore. Just to secure a place in line, you have to book a time-specific ticket in advance. I booked a dozen.

The Scrovegni Chapel is the only spot on Earth with a vista that rivals the night sky. Don't trust anyone's description. If you have only one day in your life to spend in Italy, google the Sistine Chapel on the train to Padua.

I wasn't looking for him, but during my second or third pass through, I looked up and saw my old friend Lazarus—the real one, the Lazarus who was dead until Jesus decided to bring him back to life. Whatever that operation had involved, you could tell it had been completed recently. Two guys were still dealing with the marble slab they'd pulled away from a hole in the side of the hill where Lazarus had been interred.

Lazarus was surrounded by well-wishers. He was standing at the threshold of his tomb. He was wrapped in linen bandages from head to toe. His face was exposed. His skin was the color of the bandages. With his arms bound to his belly and his knees slightly bent from the pressure of his wrappings, he didn't look too steady on his feet.

Jesus was waving from the other side of the panel, surrounded by another bunch of people. He couldn't move without stepping on Lazarus's sisters, Martha and Mary, who were bowing down before him with gratitude and awe. The next time through, I saw that Jesus wasn't waving. He was holding up two fingers, giving Lazarus the peace sign. A few other people had their hands up in the air. You got the sense that everybody was impressed.

On my last pass-through, I sat down in a pew and stared at Lazarus. He wasn't smiling. If he still had his teeth, I'd say he was gritting them. I think he was concentrating on staying upright. I'm sure he was grateful. I know he was bewildered.

Acknowledgments

Before I could see a path through these events, Jeanne Heifetz saw the possibility of this book. I leaned on her encouragement and insights from start to finish. Mary Ann Matthews credited and considered every thought that occurred to me, read every draft, and helped me to see what I meant every time. Michelle Blake reliably provided incisive critical readings, genuinely useful suggestions, and her sustaining spirit. And at a critical juncture, Phil Bennett gave me just what I needed—a measured view of the wider world and unmeasured enthusiasm.

I am especially grateful to Jack Shoemaker, who made me feel like a writer even when I was flat on my back and unable to feel anything else, and to Trish Hoard, whose astute editing and wit improved the final manuscript and my mood.

I am happy to acknowledge publicly my personal debts to the many friends and relatives, and the nurses and doctors who cared for me over the years, many of whom answered many questions as I tried to make sense of those years. I'm in the hole for everything—from the superb soup Dennis McFarland made and delivered every time I needed it to the nuts in the sublime *mandelbrodt* and brownies Alexandra Zapruder baked and boxed up when calories were called for.

Peter Bryant was, as ever, the ideal first reader, and the writer's true heart.